FEMA

THE STOREFRONT FOR DISASTER RELIEF

A BACK ROOM OF HIDDEN AGENDAS

BY CHAD BECKWITH SMITH

www.femasbest.com

Copyright © 2017 Chad Beckwith Smith (Library of Congress catalogue # in progress)

COVER ART BY: MIDDLEMEN GENERIC GRAPHICS

This is a work of nonfiction, but incorporates two specific chapters of fictional events. In chapters seventeen and twenty-six, characters, places and incidents are either products of the author's imagination or are used fictitiously. Any similarity to actual people or events is purely coincidental.

All rights reserved. No part of this book may be reproduced, stored in a retrieval system, or transmitted in any form or by any means, electronic, mechanical, photocopying, recording or otherwise, without the prior permission of this book's author.

www.femasbest.com

Printed in the United States of America

DEDICATIONS

My gratitude to all current members of PAFI for their insights when writing this book.

To my mother, thank you for teaching me to persevere.

To my Uncles, Harry Elting, and Edson Emerson Beckwith, former CEO of Braniff Airlines, and his wife, Aunt Jane, you are all fondly remembered.

To my good friends Bryan O'Brien and George Kindermann.

And to the American public, I hope, that through my efforts to prompt questions never fully answered, this work will result in positive changes long-overdue.

Contents
Introduction

1	FEMA'S ROOTS	1
2	EXECUTIVE ORDERS	7
3	FEMA'S DIRECTORS	11
4	FEMA'S REGIONS	17
5	TYPES OF DISASTERS	20
6	HOW A DISASTER GETS DECLARED	30
7	FEMA'S PRIME CONTRACTORS	36
8	OPERATION BLUE ROOF	42
9	DEBRIS REMOVAL	50
10	FEMA Trailers	56
11	HOUSING INSPECTION PRIME CONTRACTORS	70
12	HOUSING INSPECTORS	80
13	HOW ONE BECOMES A HOUSING INSPECTOR	82
14	HOW AN INSPECTION WORKS	93
15	THE INSPECTION/THE INSPECTOR	99
16	THE PRATFALLS OF HOMEOWNERS INSURANCE	120
17	TWO DAYS AND NIGHTS IN THE LIVES OF TWO INSPECTORS	124

18	THE SUPERVISORS	155
19	SCAMMING THE INSPECTOR?	162
20	DEATHS AND ILLNESSES IN THE FIELD	170
21	AMUSING ANECDOTES/INANE QUOTES	175
22	HOW THE SYSTEM IS WORKED	187
23	PAFI	202
24	ANDREW, KATRINA, AND LESSONS LEARNED	209
25	THE DARK SIDE OF FEMA	221
26	HURRICANE OTTO 9/24/2032	262
27	SOLUTIONS TO THE QUANDRY?	278
28	CLOSING THOUGHTS	301

www.femasbest.com

INTRODUCTION

"History is a set of lies agreed upon."

Napoleon Bonaparte 1769-1821

In 1989 I became a FEMA contracted housing inspector, proud of the stature and relishing the opportunity to assist victims of natural disasters such as hurricanes and floods. But as time passed, from disaster to disaster, my original intent was inadvertently intersected by factions of greed, cynicism, ambivalence and nefarious behavioral predilections by those who dictated policies I'd never fully understood. I wondered why some people received assistance while others equally as needy did not. In many ways I was disillusioned.

After performing several thousand FEMA housing inspections encompassing many declared disasters, I decided to embark on a research project in 2006 in order to facilitate some semblance of rationality within a complex system equivalent to a mathematical equation seemingly only understood by those who possess an Einstein brain. But in the end, a high IQ wasn't necessary to delineate what I'd become a part of; this supposed paternal entity which successfully purveyed itself in falsified fashion.

In 2007 I terminated my association with Parsons Brinkerhoff, one of two disaster housing inspection contractors at that time. In that same year I filed suit against Parsons Brinkerhoff and Dewberry Davis, the two prime contractors for inspection services, in an effort to force them to recognize and recertify all of their contracted inspectors as actual employees. Later in this book I'll be providing information on these firms.

In the end, I'd finally realized that ethics are non sequitur in the disaster housing inspection program, and that is why I decided to throw caution to the wind within this effort to relay the truth. Although I've generally focused on events up to and including hurricane Katrina, the system remains basically the same. As opposed to active years of multiple disasters, such as the 2004 Florida hurricanes, and Katrina, Rita and Wilma

www.femasbest.com

from 2005 — all designated as "Catastrophic" events — subsequent years have spawned less powerful storms. In 2008, hurricanes Gustov and Ike were the major events, and in 2009 forward there was little activity. In 2010 Hurricane Alex made landfall, in 2011 there was Irene, and then 2012's Isaac and Sandy. In 2016, hurricane Matthew, albeit not a catastrophic event, made landfall and is added to that list.

So as to not be redundant, particular disaster information presented for Katrina, Rita and Wilma is but a mirror image for all those above-captioned major declarations. At the time of this writing it's too early to present full information on hurricane Matthew, but some will be included.

Regardless of the negative aspects of FEMA, it nevertheless remains the only hope for salvation for American citizens experiencing any natural disaster. However, little known facts about FEMA have yet to be disclosed to the American public in this particular form. The intent of this book is to not only serve anyone who has applied for FEMA disaster assistance in the past, but is also designed to enlighten future applicants about the actual process that brings a federally contracted housing inspector to your storm-damaged or destroyed home.

Succinctly, it was also written in an effort to share with you about the birth of an artificially created federal agency whose roots are clouded in mystery and misinformation, and about its failures in coming or not coming to your aid in times of national disasters. There are some who refer to FEMA as "The Federal Mismanagement Agency" or "The Federal Enablement Management Agency." Others refer to it as "The Secret Government" or "The Shadow Government." In truth, all may be applicable, for it seems that there are virtually no safeguards in place to prevent rampant fraud when FEMA comes to town, no viable entity to finitely discover its peripheral agendas. Until now, that is.

Within these chapters, efforts were taken to dispel some conspiracy theorists' notions, but others will be addressed in a chapter entitled *The*

Dark Side of FEMA, for they could be based on truth. As well, every effort was taken to present to the reader a forthright view of a federal agency that has somehow evolved into a charitable organization for some all-too-willing to take whatever the government will allow. Conversely, and unbeknownst to most, disaster relief is just a small part of the agency's mantra.

Encompassing multi-national prime contractors and the many layers of subcontractors within a seemingly successful pyramid or Ponzi scheme, if you will, most everyone makes money from FEMA. Somehow, disaster relief has transposed to disaster capitalism. In the end, one might surmise that the agency only exists to support well-paying jobs for those ensconced in it.

From the advent of an idea originating within the Harry S. Truman administration, FEMA has systematically evolved to its present form, seemingly impervious from any overseer governmental department to quell its apparently bottomless coffers and innocuous directives. From catastrophic hurricane Andrew to hurricane Katrina, the intricacies of the agency will not only be explored, but also the processes' involved that culminate in payment for disaster related damages that oftentimes more resemble a shopping list for anyone who chooses to fill out a simple application.

Yes, the Federal Emergency Management Agency *is* the first line of defense in protecting its citizens when disasters strike. However, within the ever-rapid evolution of this somewhat nebulous entity, no one can accurately predict how they'll respond to future disasters, or even if they will be there in the future to offer relief when hurricanes, floods or earthquakes will inevitably strike. In truth, no one can accurately say what directives may eventually affect us all. Certainly, only FEMA's/DHS's top echelons know that truth.

Although there are definitive explanations as to where FEMA's mammoth

www.femasbest.com

funding for disaster relief actually originates, there remains the possibility that their peripheral funding emanates from sources that may sound more conspiracy-based than rational. Regardless, some disaster assistance applicants choose to believe that it's simply their tax dollars coming back to them. Others may say that it doesn't really matter, as long as it's there. In effect, that mindset equates to either entitlement or enablement. Maybe it's just a product of desperation. Your home is destroyed or badly damaged. You have no insurance. There's only one place to turn. You call FEMA. Unfortunately, there's only about a 35% chance you'll receive significant financial assistance.

Stemming from massive losses of life in both Andrew and Katrina, the nefarious behaviors of FEMA remain mired deep in media conjecture and denials by federal and state officials. To date, many people are still unaccounted for in both hurricanes' aftermath, and one can only wonder if Andrew was but a precursor for things to come. Within that, those two hurricanes will also be examined, as both are similar via a dysfunctional response by the very agency directed to provide disaster relief.

It is my hope that you'll attain a better understanding of the inner-workings of a federal agency out of control, of its oftentimes complex nature, and about FEMA's housing inspectors. It is also hoped that the American public will somehow find a way to not further depend on FEMA, but rather find a way to survive when the agency may no longer be willing or able to assist. After these chapters are read and absorbed, you'll have a complete view of how the system works from this handbook of sorts. When starting this project I found that I could easily fill 800 pages on this subject, but deferred to instead write a concise book that wouldn't bore the reader. Regardless, by the time you finish reading it you will know more about FEMA than that housing inspector who may arrive at your door. This has been an amazing journey for me. I hope you enjoy the trek.

FEMA

CHAPTER ONE

FEMA'S ROOTS

"The journey of a thousand miles begins with one step."

Lao Tsze: 604-504 BC Chinese philosopher and founder of Taoism

The actual beginnings of FEMA can be traced back to The Congressional Act of 1803. This was the first legislation dealing with disaster relief. The recipient of this early form of federal aid was the town of Portsmouth, New Hampshire; a fire destroyed extensive areas of that city. I can't help but surmise that whatever assistance was doled-out, it was probably virtually devoid of bureaucratic red tape and everything else that, today, inevitably culminates in a disaster within a disaster.

In modern times — though many people only realized the existence of FEMA after Hurricane Andrew in 1992 and the Northridge, California earthquake of 1994 — its roots began in 1951 to 1953. In the beginning, the basic concept of emergency management originated during the Cold War era, when the threat of a nuclear attack seemed imminent and was sometimes discussed over that night's TV dinner. But different flavors come in many forms. In this case it's a succession of governments and presidents that have taken its first giant leaps for the betterments of mankind, or supposedly so.

Whether it may be a matter of debate if President Harry S. Truman is now turning over in his grave, it was he who started the series of events that led to what FEMA has become, or not become. The first step on the ladder of lineage with their three and four letter acronyms was the creation of the Federal Civil Defense Administration (FCDA), an agency responsible for monitoring disasters within the United States. This entity was mandated to report to the president in the event of these occurrences, but it did not offer any forms of assistance to either local or state governments. That may seem like a nebulous enterprise, but for anyone who understands the inane inner-workings of government this would be deemed as apropos.

The Office of Defense Mobilization (ODM) was then created, coordinating the federal response during an attack, and formed within the Department of Defense (DOD). Additionally, the ODM evolved into an agency that was also responsible for coordination of relief efforts in the aftermath of a disaster. Then, the ODM and FCDA merged to form the Office of Defense and Civilian Mobilization (ODCM). Based in the president's executive office, this entity was allowed to distribute funds to both local and state governments per the Federal Civil Defense Act. These funds were solely used for civil defense preparedness activities, but it nonetheless jumpstarted the concept that federal, state and local governments all shared in the responsibility of emergency management.

In 1961, a newly created office within the DOD was formed. Called the Office of Civil Defense (OCD), this creation oversaw all emergency management activities via its in-house liaison, named the Office of Emergency Planning, but was renamed later to the Office of Emergency Preparedness (OEP). By the turn of the decade, emergency management responsibilities were attended to by over one-hundred various federal departments, such as the Department of Housing and Urban Development (HUD), which coordinated actual relief assistance to disaster victims and then ferreted through the system via the Federal Disaster Assistance Administration. Finally, we've just about reached that top rung, confusing as the journey may have so far seemed.

In 1979 FEMA truly arrived. In lieu of several significant and destructive storms in the 1960's to 1970's, such as Hurricanes Betsy, Camille and Carla, and the southern California earthquake of 1971, governors from various disaster-prone states urged President Jimmy Carter to streamline existing emergency management systems. He acceded, duly creating the Federal Emergency Management Agency—or FEMA, an all-inclusive entity that would incorporate all key sub-agencies under one roof and into one consummate agency. At last, response and recovery programs, combined with mitigation and preparedness mantras, could flow easily to those affected by hurricanes, floods, earthquakes, fires and so on.

Unlike now, wherein contracted inspectors perform their tasks utilizing handheld computers, disasters in the United States and its territories, such as Guam, Puerto Rico and the Federated States of Micronesia, actual FEMA and HUD personnel conducted rudimentary inspections using a simple paper form format. Unfortunately, they were also enjoying a nice salary, long lunches and short workdays, thusly accumulating a backlog of people awaiting much needed assistance that caused many obvious problems. The solution was to "bid-out" this and other tasks, such as debris removal, to various private contractors, and which is the system still used today. However, this may also be due to change, but more about that in a later chapter.

For now, we'll continue onto FEMA's lineage, and the last rung on the ladder.

FEMA's upper-echelons include a director, deputy directors of varied departments, and a chief of staff, all politically appointed. With ten regions covering the entire United States and its territories, each demographic is governed by its own region, such as Arkansas, Louisiana, New Mexico, Oklahoma and Texas in Region VI (six), or Region IX(nine), which encompasses Arizona, California, Hawaii, Nevada and the pacific islands. Roman numerals are used for some unknown reason. However, I did ask that question a couple of times and never received an intelligent answer. Maybe it's simply a space-saving technique.

FEMA's partners traditionally include all local and state emergency management agencies, twenty-three federal agencies, and the American Red Cross. With seven distinct departments, such as Regional Operations, US Fire Administration, Federal Insurance and Mitigation and Information Technology Services, FEMA's mission to "Lead America to prepare for, prevent, respond to and recover from disasters" was a directive that held much promise. However, all things change, sometimes for the worse.

When 9/11 altered our lives, so did it adversely affect a fairly smooth disaster relief machine honed to near perfection by Director James Lee Witt. On September 20, 2001, President G.W. Bush created the Office of Homeland Security (OHS), effectively ending FEMA's singularity and viability, but not glaringly so until the 2004 and 2005 hurricane seasons that were pockmarked with fraud, inspectors with criminal records, payments to disaster applicants who in fact weren't even affected, et cetera. Those particular concerns will be addressed in later chapters.

With former Pennsylvania Governor Tom Ridge named by George W. Bush to head OHS, and directed to report directly to the president on all national security issues, FEMA took a giant step backward, victim to yet another drastic---but this time fatal change. Instead of placing national disasters to the forefront, OHS's mission was "To develop and coordinate the implementation of a national comprehensive national strategy to secure the United States from terrorist threats or attacks." Essentially, FEMA became a lame-duck agency of sorts, absorbed into the labyrinth within one of the largest-ever restructuring efforts of the US Government. Regardless, the shift of focus from national disasters to terrorist related issues cannot be overlooked, and it remains a forbearer of things to come in the near future should this shift continue.

On November 25th, 2002, President Bush signed the Homeland Security Act, once again instigating yet another major restructuring process while creating the Department of Homeland Security (DHS). With an initial budget of just under 37 billion dollars, 22 sub-Agencies, and just under 200,000 employees, the second largest government department was created in the blink of an eye., At its inception, four subsectors were brought under the wings of a giant bird in flight: Border and Transportation Security, Information Analysis and Infrastructure Protection, Emergency Preparedness and Response, and Science and Technology. Unfortunately for FEMA, it was shifted to be included within Border and Transportation Security instead of remaining as a division of Emergency Preparedness and Response, thus effectively removing the teeth from a once formidable disaster relief machine.

As it may seem, the last rung on the ladder has been reached with the absorption of FEMA by DHS, basically functioning as a clearing house within the complexities of government anomalies. Additionally---and in deference to the much aligned FEMA, this poignant departure from a once independent agency to a dependency of DHS harbors little hope that it can once again be what it was at its pinnacle. Certainly, that possible eventuality may affect us all when the next Katrina or Andrew strikes, when the next earthquake rocks your world, or the next major flood drowns you in misery.

As each particular elected president leans toward certain predilections, FEMA's lineage also changed within those leanings. With Carter in office, the agency was at its highest productive level within the president's dictum of successfully incorporating all prerequisite sub-agencies in order to create the perfect entity for the perfect storm; a complete and sensible guideline for emergency management. With Reagan and George Bush and onto to his son's presidency, disaster relief took a definitive and poignant backseat, those presidents opting for more attention to civil defense in the shadow of Russia's breakup. Conversely, President Clinton's intent was to reverse the trend back to focusing on national disasters, and appointed James Lee Witt as the agency's director, the only one at that juncture in FEMA's history to have a background in emergency management.

Some researchers have approximated that FEMA normally employs about 2500 personnel and had about 5000 reservists, but its current number of employees is about 6,654 and includes a number of full-time staffers. Its 2008 budget was 8.2 billion, and together with budget cuts every year since becoming part of DHS, it appears there's no predilection to divert funds earmarked for terrorist threats to disaster-relief. In 2003, many of

www.femasbest.com

FEMA employees qualified for retirement. Though many decided to do so, some transferred to other agencies, while others were simply herded into DHS like cattle to another pen.

Yes, FEMA's roots are complex. Its once formidable limbs are now a shadow of what they once were. As 2006 and 2007 were virtually hurricane-free pertaining to major U.S. landfalls, our luck can only last so long. It may be next year or the year after or several more after that when we experience another season like 2004 and 05, but it's only a question of *when* and not *if*. The question we may ask ourselves, is what would befall us should FEMA not be there to aid us in our time of despair and need? Katrina showed us the probabilities of a nightmare magnified. As history teaches that change is the only constant, we all may learn that lesson the hard way.

2

EXECUTIVE ORDERS

INSTANT LAWS/DISTANT RAMIFICATIONS

"Only Presidents, editors and people with tapeworms

have the right to use the editorial "we": Mark Twain 1835-1910

Essentially, FEMA was created in a uniquely artificial fashion, albeit sanctioned by many presidents past and present. Congress or the Senate weren't involved in passing it, nor was any other governmental entity. Rather, it was born from what's called an "Executive Order" (EO). These executive orders, signed by the president whenever the need arises to enact one, need only be published in the "Federal Register" to become law. Simply, The Register is a daily publication listing rules, proposed rules, executive orders and presidential documents. As unconstitutional as this may sound, it's all perfectly legal, though maybe not in the moral sense. It's in this way that many laws are passed, and it explains why all of a sudden our lives change in varying degrees.

It was via Executive Order # 12127 on March 31, 1979 that FEMA was essentially born, and further augmented by Order # 12148. Soon thereafter, Order # 12656 was set in motion, its main ingredient being that the National Security Council was the primary office that would enable any emergency power. Additionally, this particular order would grant the government the right to isolate groups of civilians of their choosing, thereby "Federalizing" the National Guard to take control of all ports of entry, borders, and domestic airspace. Further, and even more alarming, it also affords the U.S. Government increased surveillance and intelligence gathering of citizens, and constricts freedom-of-movement within domestic borders. Subsequently, many other orders were published in the Registry, most of which are contrary to FEMA's primary responsibility of responding to national disasters. But contrarily, these addendum orders, in fact, appear to be vehicles to supplant a nefarious purpose, for there can be no other explanation as to their existence. I'll list some of these orders associated with FEMA, all of which are contrary to democracy, and essentially suspend the Constitution and Bill of Rights.

Executive Order # 11000: Allows the government to mobilize civilians into work brigades under Government supervision.

Executive Order # 10995: Allows the government to seize and control all facets of the media, meaning *all* radio and television stations.

Executive Order # 10999: Permits the government to take-over all farms and food supplies.

Executive order # 11004: Allows the finance and housing authority to relocate communities, build new housing with public funds, assign specified areas to be abandoned, and establish alternate locations for designated populations.

Executive Order # 10998: Gives the Government the inalienable right to seize transportation of any type, including private automobiles and trucks, all commercial vehicles, and exercise complete and total control for seaports, highways and waterways.

Orders # 11000 to 11005 were revoked by Executive Order 11490---and then, that order was revoked by Executive Order 12656. Confusing, yes---I agree. However, the original language remains intact, no matter the labyrinth of ascension. Some more of these Orders will be listed in a later chapter, but for now, you may get the general idea. Although we may try to make sense of these, there seems no plausible reason for their existence except to excise total control over a population at the time of FEMA's choosing. Regardless---and as stated in the introduction, some conspiracy theorists notions will be dispelled, while others may harbor some truth.

Executive Orders are not a modern-day facilitation, as they were invoked back to the days of Abraham Lincoln's presidency, who'd signed the first Order; # 1. However, while some presidents rarely used this vehicle, others appeared rampant within their utilization of it. George W. Bush signed 263 Orders, Clinton 363, and Reagan 380. The record-holder seems to be Franklin D. Roosevelt, who'd signed an astronomical 3,466 from 1933-to 1945.

And so, within this particular avenue with which to supplant whatever desired result via a president's predilection, Executive Orders, although not being passed through the normal channels such as Congress or the Senate, are still legal and will continue to be enacted with no recourse from either American citizens or peripheral government entities. So much for democracy, one may correctly surmise.

On July 6, 1989, President Bush signed EO # 12681, which essentially gave FEMA the right to spy on any American of their choosing. Within the verbiage of the order, its National Preparedness Directorate would also include primary functions pertaining to Intelligence, counter-intelligence, investigative or national security tasks. On May 9, 2007, President Bush again reasserted the role of the Federal Government by issuing Directive NSPD-51/HSPD-20. That presidential directive states that in the event of a "catastrophic emergency," all essential national functions may be taken-over by the Executive Branch and the Department of Homeland Security, which of course, means FEMA. To explain the difference between an EO and a Directive, the latter lapses upon a change of administration, whereas an EO remains in force unless revoked by another president. Otherwise they are identical in scope. Preceding Bush's EO, President Clinton's order # 12919, which amended or revoked thirteen other EO's, dictated that additional presidential powers could be delegated to the director of FEMA.

www.femasbest.com

Within the context of "Continuity of Government," and which we'll be addressing in a later chapter, this would, in effect, give that director full executive powers should he be the highest-ranking survivor in a nuclear war or other catastrophic event that claimed the lives of the president, vice president and speaker of the house, which is the modern day lineage of ascension. Under that scenario, FEMA would be running the country.

Unfortunately, the greater number of Executive Orders pertaining to FEMA results in a suspension of the Constitution, and effectually eradicates Americans' liberties under the Bill of Rights. Reasons could be massive civil unrest, nuclear attack, or an act of terrorism such as 9/11. All the pieces are on the presidential jigsaw table, to be put together when it becomes necessary for whatever reasons deemed suitable for the appropriate occasion. This is the reality we live with. Hopefully, these "reasons" will never become reality.

3

FEMA'S DIRECTORS
"Politics doesn't make strange bedfellows, marriage does"

Grouch Marx: 1895-1977

Beginning from the time that President Jimmy Carter created FEMA, the agency has had fifteen directors. Some served as "acting" directors for one month or so, while only eight of them survived for multiple years. The longest tenure was that of James Lee Witt, from April 1993 to January 2001. Mr. Witt was the only one of two FEMA Directors with previous experience in disaster management to date; that being his tenure as the director of Arkansas' emergency management agency. The current director, Craig Fugate, was Florida's director of emergency management from 2001 to 2009. Otherwise, the following list is pockmarked with inadequate resumes and political favoritism at the expense of taxpayers who expected something better than what they'd received.

1: John Macy. This first "Senate-confirmed" Director of FEMA served from 6/79 to 1/81.

2: Bernard Gallagher (acting) from 1/81 to 4/81.

3: John McConnell (acting) from 4/81 to 11/85

4: Louis Giuffrida from 5/81 to 9/85

5: Robert Morris (acting) from 9/85 to 11/85

6: Julius Becton from 11/85 to 6/89

7: Jerry Jennings (acting) from 5/90 to 8/90

8: Wallace Stickney from 8/90 to 1/93

9: William Tidball (acting) from 1/93 to 4/93

10: James Lee Witt from 4/93 to 1/2001

11: John Magaw (acting) from 1/01 to 2/2001

12: Joe Allbaugh from 2/0101 to 3/2003

13: Michael Brown from 3/2003 to 9/2005

14: Thad Allen (inter-acting/lame-duck) 9/2005 to1/2006

15: R. David Paulison (acting) from 1//2006 to 5/2006

16: R. David Paulison: 5/2006 to 1/2009

17: Craig Fugate: 5/2009 to current.

Many of the names on this list may have excellent credentials within their ascribed fields, but the only ones truly capable of being a FEMA director are those with previous disaster-related experience. It would seem that it shouldn't be difficult to appoint that person from the ranks of State emergency management agencies, but it nevertheless appears to be a conundrum on FEMA's part to provide due diligence in that regard. As an example, no sane person would hire a swimming pool technician whose only experience was swimming in one, or hiring a wannabe financial advisor who'd previously only advised his friends or family in matters of money. Apparently, however, this basic safeguard doesn't matter to FEMA. Another mystery yet unsolved.

For a moment, let's imagine that in your own workplace or office, a friend of your boss got that promotion that many others were more qualified to receive. Upsetting it would be, I would think. In lieu, it's truly amazing that such an important position as director of FEMA would be handed to someone who possesses absolutely knowledge of how to coordinate any aspect of disaster relief, but that rather, their claim to that seat was awarded for past favors or other inane reasons. As the saying goes; "It's not what you know but who you know." Maybe this is yet another example of that adage.

As a political dumping ground for political appointees, FEMA has other directors and deputy directors than are too numerous to list in entirety. For example, there's a Director and a Deputy of External Affairs, of Public Affairs, a Chief of Staff and Deputy Chief of Staff, and on-and-on it goes. Although they don't get any publicity to speak of, sometimes, albeit rarely, their names may be mentioned in a media report. But for them, their positions don't warrant any real attention. However, two of these folks *did* receive media scrutiny when faking a news conference during the October 2007 California wildfires.

Asking the questions were Deputy Director of External Affairs Cindy Taylor and Deputy Director of Public Affairs Michael Widomski. Soon thereafter they were "disciplined," but in a nature not quite fully explained and would probably amount to a slap on the wrist. In yet another example of FEMA's oftentimes irrational powers of decision-making, Taylor was promoted to be the Director of the Private Sector Office, and Widomski assumed her previous Deputy Director post. I hope they regret their fifteen minutes of fame, but have my doubts.

The most recognizable name from our list of directors would probably be that of Michael Brown, the director at the time of hurricane Katrina. While his White House biography stated that he had emergency management experience within his position as "Administrative Assistant" in the city of Edmond, Oklahoma, the head of public relations for that city denied that Brown had any oversight duties whatsoever, further explaining that the position was more akin to an internship. In following years he studied law and practiced in Enid, Oklahoma, suffered a failed attempt to win a Congressional seat in 1998, and enjoyed a stint as Chairman of the Board of the Oklahoma Municipal Power Authority. The hydroelectric plant at Kaw Reservoir was named in his honor, and I sometimes wonder if Mr. Brown wishes he ended his quest for fame at that point. As in the adage, "any publicity is good publicity," I'm reasonably certain that his performance during Katrina proves converse to those words.

About two years before being appointed FEMA's Director, Mr. Brown was the "Judges and Stewards Commissioner" for the International Arabian Horse Association for two years. After lawsuits were filed against the organization pertaining to disciplinary issues, he was forced to resign in 2001. In deference to Mr. Brown, it's plausible that he'd bit off more than he could chew when accepting the directorship of FEMA. And pardon the pun.

In a later chapter covering hurricane Katrina, Mr. Brown's tenure as Director of FEMA will be more closely examined. For now, we'll continue-on to Louis Giuffrida, the fourth FEMA Director and also with a very interesting history. A close associate of Ronald Reagan, Mr. Giuffrida was Deputy Attorney General of California, whom also organized the California Specialized Training Institute and trained state employees in emergency management and police counter-terrorism activities. Additionally, he attained the rank of General in the California National Guard, was president of the Specialized Management Services Company, and was director of The California Specialized Training Institute. During his tenure with FEMA, Mr. Giuffrida developed many of the agency's civil defense programs and oversaw many disasters. However, he was forced out of office in 1985 after it was revealed that he'd spent government funds to build a private residence in Emmitsburg, Maryland. Mr. Giufridda's name will appear again in the later chapter, *The Dark Side of FEMA*.

Apparently, it's not the hallmark of FEMA for its directors to enjoy longevity. For whatever reasons, it only stands to reason that fifteen directors within twenty-nine years should be far less. And this could be the core issue of why the agency seems to always be in flux. Using the example once again about your office or workplace, imagine how it would be if a new superior or boss appeared once every two years. Certainly, aspects of the business would suffer due to that, and I surmise that same malady would infect FEMA, much as it would the CIA, DEA, FBI, ATF, and so on.

James Lee Witt, the tenth director of the agency, stands out as the model for what directors should be. When I was deployed to declared disasters during his tenure as a FEMA housing inspector, every relief effort was executed with professionalism and exacting guidelines as opposed to the current debacle. Witt's system retained an aura of national prominence and when in the field we all felt pride within the work we were doing. Yes, there were still instances of fraud, but nothing like its present and rampant form.

In 1996, an editorial from the Atlanta Journal-Constitution stated that "FEMA has developed a sterling reputation for delivering disaster related services, a far cry from its abysmal standing before James Lee Witt took its helm in 1993." So, how is it that he turned-around a dismal and dysfunctional Agency to a prototypical disaster relief machine? Simple: He ended the staffing of the agency previously inundated with recipients of political patronage, eradicated layers of bureaucracy, but most importantly, he instilled a finite spirit of preparedness and service to the customer, while also astutely listening to the ideas of local and State officials to make the system work even better.

Mr. Witt's tenure oversaw 348 Presidential declared disasters, encompassing over 6500 counties within the 50 states and U.S. territories. Included was the 1997 Red River flood, the costliest to-date earthquake and a dozen major hurricanes. Although eight years may not be a long time for anyone to exist in the same job capacity, I can only imagine his stress endured during his directorship. Every housing inspector I know still remembers the spirit he instilled in us when working those 16-hour days, seven days a week, for oftentimes months on end. To this day he is missed by those veteran inspectors who still try their best to do a good job. And their numbers are, as the years pass, rapidly diminishing.

Every beginning has an end and every end has a new beginning, I'm not quite sure if FEMA can ever retrieve that new beginning left to us when Mr. Witt always called the right shots. The current director may want to emulate his predecessor, but unfortunately, he's saddled with the

www.femasbest.com

bureaucracy that the Department of Homeland Security has now suffocated the FEMA that was, but could be again if not for innocuous dictums and senseless complexities.

4

FEMA'S REGIONS

In the ongoing effort to keep this book simple, you can somewhat compare the regions of FEMA to satellite offices, setup to support the main offices in Washington D.C. The agency's ten Federal Region Centers (FRC's) splice the map of stateside USA and its territories within a supportive system that augments assistance wherever a disaster is declared. Each region is aligned in the same basic fashion, though some cover more geographical territory than others. For instance, Region IV—or four to those who forget their Roman numerals — covers the largest area of all. Each region has a headquarters; In Region IX — or nine, it's located in Oakland, California; In Region IV it's in Atlanta, Georgia. It is an amazing place.

Housed in a 37,734 square foot subterranean facility on a thirty-eight acre site in Thomasville, Georgia, and built to withstand catastrophic storms or a national security event, Region IV employs about one-hundred full-time personnel. This facility—or "asset" as FEMA refers to all of their headquarters, has its own water and power sources and a full range of telecommunications systems to support virtually any operation. So when the next federally declared disaster occurs in Alabama, Florida, Georgia, Mississippi, North and South Carolina or Tennessee, the states that Region IV covers, try to envision a large bunker far below the earth where the beginnings of the process take root. It's a "war-room" of sorts, wherein it's man against nature. However, these facilities are also designed to coordinate a different type of war: that being man against man.

Every office has a Defense Coordinating Officer (DCO), who acts as a liaison to enhance communications between FEMA and the DOD. The designation of a DCO is fairly new, created by Congress after hurricane Katrina. No real surprise there, for communication breakdowns were rampant within that disaster, and bad press is something that FEMA *does not* like. We can only hope that the addition of this new officer will prevent any more of the same maladies.

Aside from their multi-faceted tasks, these regions also maintain close relationships with state and local partners, such as the Red Cross, and support relief efforts pertaining to water and food supplies, etcetera. Development of emergency management capabilities and providing technical assistance regarding response and recovery planning are also part of every region's mandate. Additionally, and typically, each region can draw from a cadre of approximately 500 disaster assistance employees (DAE), basically "reservists," who are all experienced in areas ranging from the delivery of disaster assistance to dispersal of public information. Included in that 500 is the Disaster Survivors Assistance cadre (DSA), sometimes referred to as "door-knockers" because they are the ones who canvass neighborhoods to try and convince disaster victims to apply to FEMA for assistance. Members of this cadre typically make about $15 per hour, and are generally very nice people, but the problem is that many of them have to sometimes cajole homeowners and renters to register for assistance while not having *any* damages to their residence, but who'd only had food loss or motel expenses that a subcontracted housing inspector can't help with. In the end, it's all about FEMA garnering as many applicants as possible in their penchant to fortify their purpose to the American public.

In virtually every FRC is a lineage of officers. There's a Director, Deputy Director, a special assistant to that Director, an External Affairs Director, and an Emergency Analyst. Additionally, there's a Flood and Mitigation Division with its own separate Director. The National Flood Insurance Program (NFIP) is administered by FEMA, and when you apply for disaster relief and obtain an inspection by a housing inspector, the form you sign at that inspection will have verbiage pertaining to that program. For mitigation, applicants under the Individual Assistance program (IA) are no longer entitled to funds in the effort to prevent future damage to a home. There will be more on that in later chapter.

You now have an overview of what the FRC's functions are during a declared disaster. Without them, the system couldn't subsist. In actuality, and should a major disaster occur that threatens major portions of the United States, all ten regions will combine to assist. Some FRC's are above ground and some are not, but each is a mirror image of the next in regard to their directives. Fortunately, the scenario has not yet occurred where their combined efforts would not prevent a massive loss of life and property. If multiple climatological anomalies such as a major earthquake and a major hurricane such as Katrina or Andrew were to strike at the same time, I suspect that even the most diehard optimist could not expect FEMA to address such a catastrophe in capable fashion.

As in yet another adage, "only time will tell," I believe that it's also a question of when and not if in regard to most major disasters. A new hurricane season is approaching. Let's all hope that multiple disasters of magnitude do not strike at the same time.

… www.femasbest.com

5

TYPES OF DISASTERS

"Here's to the pilot that weathered the storm"

George Canning: 1770-1827 British Statesman and Prime Minister

For most of us, a disaster is a disaster. However, FEMA designates their particular types and assigns them a disaster number, such as DR (Disaster Relief) #4250, the designation given to the 2016 Missouri floods. Emergency declarations and major disaster declarations are the two main entities, and throughout the history of FEMA — and before its advent when administered by preceding offices — there have been many of each category. Virtually every single state and US possession/territory has been declared, which proves that no location is immune to a disaster. Texas leads the pack for declarations, with a total of 343, followed by California with 255, and Florida at 139. The least number---only one declaration — is for Typhoon Mike in November of 1990 and which struck Palau, a beautiful Island group in the Federated States of Micronesia, a USA trust territory. To clarify, a Typhoon or Cyclone is simply a hurricane under another name, specifically because of hemispheric nomenclature. When a storm emanates in the northwest pacific it's called a Typhoon. When a storm is borne in the Indian Ocean or southwest pacific, it's called a Cyclone. They share the same storm-related specifics, but simply utilize a different moniker. However, most typhoons and cyclones tend to be more powerful than Atlantic hurricanes, mostly due to much warmer and greater area water environments.

The interpretation of an emergency is defined as "any occasion or incident that the President of the United States determines federal assistance is required to augment state and local relief efforts." Since emergency declarations often tend to be of smaller magnitude than major declarations, they cannot exceed the federally mandated dollar amount limit of five-million-dollars, unless the President deems that additional funding is necessary in order to achieve the desired results of re-building infrastructure. While most of us are only familiar with storms such as floods, hurricanes, winter storms, tornados and earthquakes, there are many other anomalies that will also trigger a federal response, whether in the form of an emergency or a major declaration.

For instance, there have been emergency declarations for West Nile Virus, the Space Shuttle disaster, the 9/11 terrorist attacks, and even two events for drought. Emergency declarations differ in the type of assistance FEMA administers in a major disaster declaration, as relief is focused on damage to utilities, roads, bridges and the like. Typically, this is fostered on a cost-sharing basis, wherein FEMA and the local governments each take financial responsibility to repair particular infrastructures damaged by a storm. Typically, this is 75% FEMA funded and 25% state funded. Also, the Small Business Administration (SBA) will offer assistance to business owners damaged by the event.

There are sixteen basic designations for disasters. Most are self-explanatory while others are not. For those, a brief explanation is provided.

1. Biological Threat: Biological incidents either man-made or otherwise, which can kill or disable a populace. Biological terrorism is also included in this category, specifically threats emanating from peripheral entities which are deemed hazardous to the population or agricultural infrastructure.
2. Chemical Threat: Terrorist attacks, industrial or transportation accidents (such as chemical spills) that can affect the general populace.
3. Earthquake.
4. Fire.
5. Flood.

6. Heat: Extreme heat periods wherein a segment of the populace is adversely affected by weather anomalies, or when agriculture is also affected. Drought is a byproduct of this.
7. Hurricane.
8. Landslide/Mudslide
9. Radiation + Nuclear/Radiation: Emergencies from either terrorist attacks or nuclear power plant disasters, such as the Three Mile Island event of March 28, 1979, which cost one billion dollars to clean up within a three year period.
10. Tornado
11. Tsunami.
12. Volcano.
13. Wildfires.
14. Winter Storm.
15. Severe Storm.
16. Space Weather: This refers to the variable conditions on the sun, which can influence the performance of technology used daily, such as the Internet and all other forms of communication. These conditions are usually described as an event of volatile solar flares.

Converse to an emergency declaration, a major declaration (such as a strong tropical storm, a hurricane with wide-ranging damage, or a massive flooding event) will trigger a much wider response in the form of Individual Assistance for home owners and renters. Once again, the affected state must pick-up the tab for 25% of all costs relating to relief efforts. For a catastrophic event such as hurricane Katrina or Andrew, the federal response becomes immense. For example, when Katrina struck the gulf coast, virtually every regional office became involved and 43 separate declarations were enacted within that massive effort to deal with the mayhem.

Notwithstanding, and also pertaining to a major declaration, business-owners can apply for SBA assistance, which extends low interest loans to help stricken individuals get their livelihoods restarted. Many applicants had told me they'd received a "packet" from SBA upon being denied for individual assistance. The reason for this is to entice homeowners to apply for a loan in order to rebuild their domicile, as they didn't qualify for a grant. This grant is never to be repaid, but from my experience, most had deferred from applying for the loan.

No matter what type of disaster FEMA designates it to be, all are governed by the Robert T. Stafford Relief and Emergency Assistance Act. Passed in 1988 and named after Robert Theodore Stafford, a former governor of Vermont. As a Congressman and Senator, he helped pass the law that still dictates current parameters of disaster-relief. This act specifies how disasters are declared, the types of assistance provided, and the cost-sharing guidelines between local, state and the federal government. The Stafford Act also establishes two levels of incidences, that being Emergency and Major disasters.

Simply defined, emergencies are "any occasion or incident that in the determination of the President of the United States is needed to supplement state and local relief efforts. As said before, emergency declarations typically tend to be smaller events, and total federal assistance cannot exceed 5 million dollars under the guidelines of the Stafford Act, unless the president determines that additional assistance is essential to recovery. Following is a list of those aspects of recovery:

1: Utilize all resources, facilities and personnel to assist and augment state and local relief efforts.

2: Coordinate disaster relief assistance.

3: Provide any and all applicable assistance via federal agencies.

4: Remove debris that poses health and safety hazards to the public infrastructure.

5: Assist to distribute medicine, food and other necessary disaster relief supplies.

6: Provide technical advisory assistance to state and local governments.

Item # 1 dictates that FEMA personnel will be in the field to assist local officials, and coordinate the inclusion of the Red Cross and other relief entities to assist those who require help should their homes or other issues be affected. However, we must keep in mind that homeowners or renters will not be offered individual assistance from FEMA under this form of declaration. Simply, those needs cannot be addressed via any other avenue other than within a disaster that warrants individual assistance. .

Item # 2 is basically the same as # 1, but with specifics to address infrastructure repairs and rebuilding. These may include washed-out roads, bridges failing, or telephone and electrical systems that require extensive repairs that are far-above what local or state budgets can reasonably afford.

Item # 3 is somewhat inclusive of the others, but allows some leeway for local and state governments to apply for further monetary aid as the effects of damage become more severe than first determined, usually by virtue of ongoing damage assessments.

Item #4 refers to debris, such as tree limbs leaning on telephone poles, or trees or other debris blocking roads or entrances to public offices or buildings. Again, I must stress that if your home has fallen trees blocking its entrance — say on your front or back lawn — FEMA will not remove them because it's an Emergency declaration and not a Major.

Item # 5 is linked to item # 1, and redundantly so.

Item # 6 simply means that FEMA personnel will be available to offer specialized assistance when required. This may be anything from advising how to prevent future infrastructure damage from storm-related anomalies to the proper way to set a telephone pole so it doesn't lean at a ten degree angle shortly after the work-crew leaves the site. And yes, that has happened.

As opposed to an emergency declaration, and as said before, a major disaster invokes the types of assistance we're all familiar with when FEMA comes to town. Essentially, if a disaster causes damage of sufficient severity and scope to warrant major disaster assistance, the president has the sole authority to declare it as such. Within that event, this particular declaration empowers FEMA to bring any and all of its resources to the stricken area.

On television and radio you will hear that federal funds are available to storm-affected homeowners and renters alike. An inspector, such as I was, will come to your home and survey the damage to your home. Much like the game of roulette, one's lucky number may appear via the silver ball of FEMA's determination of your particular needs. Your neighbor with less damage then yourself may get a nice fat check that requires no repayment, while you, with more damage, may get nothing but an application for an SBA loan. Yes, FEMA money is apparently not meant for everyone with gaping holes in their roofs or those with flooded basements spawning a new generation of mosquitoes, but it sometimes appears to be a God-given right for those who know the system and how to work it. Again, this aspect of the disaster relief mechanism will be addressed in a later chapter. For now, we'll get back to the basics of a major disaster.

FEMA's interpretation of this category, and per the dictums of the Stafford Act, specifies that "damage of sufficient magnitude will warrant major disaster assistance." To that, many options are then available to affected residents. Among these are:

1: Utilize, donate or lend federal resources, facilities and personnel to state and local governments.

2: Distribute medicine, food and other necessary supplies.

3: Remove debris, clear roads, and construct temporary bridges.

4: Make available search and rescue teams.

5: Provide emergency medical care, shelters, and other temporary facilities.

6: Provide information and technical advice.

7: Utilize the resources of the Department of Defense.

8: Provide unemployment assistance, food coupons/other assistance to affected individuals, and authorize loans of up to $5 million for local governments to recover lost tax-base funds as a result of the disaster.

9: Pay up-to 75% of state and local infrastructure repair/replacement costs.

10: Provide financial assistance to both private and non-profit utility companies.

11: Provide eligible households up to $32,000 in assistance.

Some of these major disaster relief mechanisms are self-explanatory, but item # 11 may be the most important one on the list, as it affects every homeowner in the affected area who applies for FEMA disaster relief. Under the provisions of the Stafford Act, this is the "cap-amount" any applicant homeowner can receive. Included are funds for temporary relocation and medical/ special needs. This is the highest dollar figure allowed, whether you lived in a mansion or a trailer. Additionally, renters are also afforded financial assistance, though not in the same manner. Later in the book we'll focus on the inspection process, delving deeper into those complexities. For now, let's continue with this chapter.

Under the guidelines of the Stafford Act, a major declaration is qualified as: *"Any natural catastrophe, including Hurricanes, Tornadoes, High-water, severe storms, wind-driven rain/water, tidal waves, Tsunami, earthquake, mudslide/landslide, volcanic eruption, snowstorm, and drought."* Additionally, any fire, flood or explosion is included, regardless of the cause and of sufficient magnitude to qualify as a major disaster. Other types of catastrophes, such as riots, civil disturbances and evacuee situations have been excluded from this list by FEMA, but should be included, and hopefully so. These three particular disaster types, somewhat redundant in nature, are not currently covered under the Stafford Act, and it seems logical in our ever-changing world and general social unrest that civil disturbances have a distinct possibility of occurring.

Outside of the Stafford Act, other agencies also provide additional disaster-recovery assistance for affected individuals of hurricanes, floods, and the like. The Department of Housing and Urban Development (HUD) is a good example, providing Community Development Block Grants to affect rebuilding efforts, and the aforementioned SBA.

We've now become acquainted with virtually every type of disaster, and we're also aware that their numbers are far greater than most people would have imagined. We know about Katrina and Andrew, but there are many other disasters which also changed the lives of many in the negative sense. Hurricane Rita, which struck the gulf coast on the heels of Katrina, was a very devastating event, but had struck within a smaller demographic; many rural areas were only affected. Hurricane Wilma, striking within a close time-frame to Rita, hit central Florida's heavily populated cities and towns with category 3 wind-speeds and left a swath of destruction in its wake. Having worked in the field as a FEMA subcontracted housing inspector for both Katrina and Rita, I can attest to the fact that any hurricane is a disaster within a disaster, no matter what its name. The worst part is a storms aftermath. Everything changes forever, life is never quite the same: Oftentimes, for the inspector as well.

During the very active hurricane season of 2004 — several hit Florida — some folks are still recovering. Those storms, named Charlie, Francis, Ivan and Jeanne, remain important as to those affected individuals who'd

www.femasbest.com

endured Katrina; all of those storms left an everlasting mark for those affected folks. In astounding numbers, since the advent of FEMA in 1979 via Executive order # 12147, well over 1200 Emergency/Major disasters have been declared as of 2016, both stateside and for its territories. In the years before FEMA, when disaster relief was administered by its precursors starting in 1953 and up to 2016, a grand total of 3841 declarations have been enacted. Once again, it would be wise for all of us to remember that it's usually not a question of if, but when. Virtually none of us are safe no matter where we may reside. Many times I've heard applicants express their belief that since they endured a major hurricane "they've already had theirs." I'd heard some folks say the same thing after the 2004 Florida hurricanes. Wilma proved them wrong. Hopefully, they won't one day be proven dead-wrong.

The 2006 to 2007 hurricane seasons were prognosticated to very active, but no significant landfalls occurred. Some attribute this to the "misinformation" of actual effects of global warming, while others simply defer to the unlikely scenario of catastrophic storms continually wreaking havoc upon us. Hurricanes Dean and Felix of 2007 diverted from their Caribbean basin track that's usually the precursor to USA landfall, and instead struck Mexico and Nicaragua/Honduras. Luckily, one of them didn't strike the US east coast or gulf-coast mainland, but will that luck last? One can only await the outcome of this coming season.

For some, that hope is converse with that of others; FEMA money is the key to survival for those with nothing to lose but everything to gain. Much like an annuity, grants to applicants have become a right. Although most are honest and forthright, there still remains a faction that works the system to their own advantage. After completing thousands of inspections, I can well-attest to that malady, as many of my fellow housing inspectors will also concur. Sadly but true, an approaching hurricane is the equivalent of Santa Claus coming to town for some, while for others it's a death knell; the life they'd built with hard-earned money disappears in hellishly howling winds that can never be perfectly described.

We've now reached the stage of this book where you know about FEMA's history; how the initial system works, and who does what during a disaster. As we proceed to the next chapters we will explore the actual process of how a disaster gets declared, why some get money while others don't, and most importantly, learn about the flaws in a system that *should* work but usually don't.

www.femasbest.com

6

HOW A DISASTER GETS DECLARED

"Time heals what reason cannot".

Lucius Annaeus Seneca: 3 B.C-65 A.D. Roman Philosopher

You know the hurricane is coming and you're preparing your home as best possible, keeping one eye on the television and one ear to the radio while nailing plywood over windows that are no match for the winds to come. A placebo, as it may turn out to be, but at least you've done everything humanly possible.

Important documents such as home insurance and credit card information, vehicle titles and health insurance cards, are safely enclosed in three tiers of plastic Ziploc bags that will ensure their survival should the hurricane's track follow you wherever you go and when the inevitable onslaught arrives. Your wife filled the car's gas tank and the four five-gallon containers you purchased after you learned your lesson of the hurricane sixteen years previous---and the one you were certain would be the last you'd ever experience. But as you watch the track on the television and hear the voice on the radio devoid of any levity, the culmination of your worst fears comes to bear.

"Oh-no, not again," you quietly say, desperately hoping that the hurricane will stray off-track and head towards Newfoundland or anywhere else but here. But this is southern Florida, an appendage that sticks out like a sore thumb on the hand of the continental USA. Although always an opportune target for horrendous winds and rain, a feeling of imperviousness had engulfed the states' population as opposed to memories of what happened in the past. The last nail in driven onto the last piece of plywood to cover the remaining bare window, and you gather your wife and three children into the car for the long drive to northern Georgia, where you've booked a hotel room at twice the price because everyone's doing the same thing as you.

Remembering FEMA's response many years ago that was inadequate at best, you hope that things have changed for the better, but somehow know the same dysfunctional efforts will occur once again. The stories of Katrina fill your mind as you drive away from the life you knew, hoping and praying that the hurricane will divert from track, but rationalize that Newfoundland has a scant population and are hearty people that can deal with wind and rain more than you. In the backseat, the kids are crying and they don't understand what's happening no matter how you try to explain. You offer solace, even though you doubt it yourself.

"FEMA's going to help us rebuild our house if the storm takes it, guys."

"What's FEMA, daddy?"

"Our government: The President of the United States is going to make sure we'll be ok."

You say those words but know that you're lying, for the memories of Hurricane Andrew are still etched on the faces of you and your wife while now driving an unfamiliar road. For sixteen years, a feeling of safety enveloped you both like a warm blanket on a cold winter night because you'd thought that could never happen again, that lightning couldn't strike twice. Two years of rebuilding the home destroyed on Cutler Ridge, and you wonder if the decision was correct to take-on that effort. The ten-thousand dollars from FEMA and another sixty-thousand from your insurance company, whose only concern was collecting monthly premiums rather than abiding by their contract, is recalled. You remember the double shifts at work and when cashing in the IRA and loans from family to once again make a house a home.

www.femasbest.com

"Is FEMA going to make my bedroom okay again?" your three-year old daughter asks.

"Better than before," you say.

This hypothetical scenario could take place anywhere on the gulf-coast, eastern seaboard or anywhere a disaster could strike, but this particular example would not apply to an earthquake, as effective warning systems are not currently available. But the fact remains that the captioned family could be your own at any given time. As we know, many disasters have affected the United States, but how many applicants have there been? How many millions through the years? How many have felt the same emotions as that family on the unfamiliar road to Georgia or beyond? So what is the lineage for a disaster to actually get declared? And who ultimately makes that decision? In answer, it's the President of the United States, authorizing FEMA to provide disaster relief under the articles of the Stafford Act. With a stroke of a pen, the system starts its engine that oftentimes desperately needs oil.

Virtually impossible to completely research, we could safely say that hundreds of millions of disaster victims have applied for assistance over the years. Of that number, roughly 35% received what they'd construed as "adequate" assistance. Of these, more renters than homeowners received checks, and this seems to be the predilection of FEMA: to assist the lower income bracket of the population. Yes, I realize this statement may be interpreted as unbelievable, but the fact remains that renters represent the mainstream of FEMA applicants. If not for the renter-applicants, the treasury of funding that the agency has traditionally enjoyed would fall victim to budget-cuts. I also offer the fact that homeowners are more than likely to make a higher income than those who simply rents a space in which to domicile. Within one of the clauses of the Stafford Act, it places a "cap amount" of roughly $32,000 for any homeowner, no matter the magnitude of their damage. This cap doesn't include ancillary assistance, such as special needs.

Aside from these issues, which will be further explored, we first have to understand how a disaster gets declared in the first place. What does happen when a hurricane or flood strikes? How *does* the federal assistance work? This is how:

Every disaster is obviously different within its scope and type. Typically, floods, tropical storms and hurricanes offer some advance warning as opposed to sudden events such as earthquakes. As an example, when a storm or hurricane of magnitude seems an inevitable reality, a series of steps are taken to prepare for the onslaught. Primarily, evacuation orders are given, though these are not always mandatory. Secondly, and based on the calculations of the National Hurricane Center and the National Oceanographic and Atmospheric Administration (NOAA), then all available state and local emergency management entities gear-up. FEMA does also.

When a storm of sufficient scope makes it obvious that Preliminary Damage Assessments (PDA's) will reveal the widespread damage prognosticated by NHC or NOAA, the governor of the affected state, or states, will request that the President of the United States issue a Major Disaster Declaration. Upon that information, the President will usually abide by that request, making all components of the Stafford Act available to residents of the soon-to-be affected area.

PDA'S are an integral part of the declaration process. They must be done in order to offer a full view of damage, thusly allowing the exact type of federal assistance that should be warranted. For instance, if a Tropical Storm or Hurricane is declared a major disaster *before* landfall because of its prognosticated heavy winds and rain, but proves to be far less destructive due to a sudden decrease in winds and/or rain---or simply because the storm had an evil sense of humor, then the ensuing PDA's may show that its damage was mainly centered on public utilities, roads, bridges and the like, prompting a shift to an emergency declaration.

www.femasbest.com

PDA's are conducted via ground level observations and sometimes through airborne teams of federal, state and local emergency management officials who survey affected areas to correctly ascertain the storm's scope and the type of assistance required. All relief efforts are directed through the Federal Coordinating Officer (FCO) who is appointed by FEMA. In turn, this FCO works closely with other federal agencies, charities, state and local governments, police and firefighters. As converse as it may be, an FCO--- an employee who has received specialized training for this particular post — is not the actual director of FEMA at this juncture. I just wanted to clear that up. Remember, I'm trying to keep this simple. It's not easy at times.

Within our hypothetical scenario of major hurricane's landfall, the governor's request to the President has been approved for declaration. Evacuees have been clogging interstates in a quest to get out of harm's way, but many have elected to stay with their homes, whether out of personal predilections or without the financial means to make their way to safety. During the hours of an approaching hurricane Katrina, this was exactly the case for many thousands of New Orleans' residents. For all of us, we might think about how frustrating that would be; the lack of a car or money to purchase fuel turns out to be the death-knell for you and your family. Sometimes, I wonder if forced evacuations should be the norm in situations such as our imagined hurricane. Transportation provided by the government, of course.

To continue, peripheral organizations such as Red Cross have been mobilized, local and state emergency management agencies are preparing for the worst, the National Guard is on alert and mobilizing, and every wheel in the disaster relief machine is turning in the direction of a catastrophe being tracked on television screens in many-many different rooms and headquarters. FEMA's regions have also been on high-alert, ready to assist the affected regional office, just as they did during Katrina. In Washington, FEMA is closely monitoring the progress of the storm, for it is they who must be the major coordinator of whatever transpires. The hurricane's track is as NOAA and NHC have predicted. No miracle is in sight. Memories of any hurricane endured come back, but you still hope for the best. After all, FEMA will help. Won't they?

Contractors for such necessities as food, water, temporary shelters, debris removal and the like are also all gearing-up for the impending carnage. Other contractors, such as Vanguard Emergency Management and PB Disaster Services, are already placing housing inspectors on "Standby." Though there are many contractors who have a specific place within a disaster, Vanguard and PB will be the most important to your fortunes or your misfortune. It is they who subcontract the inspector who comes to your door.

In the following chapters we'll examine each and every one of these contractors, with the hopeful result of understanding what they actually do. And in those segments, we'll also discover who makes the most money, and how and why the FEMA subcontracted housing inspector benefits the least.

7

FEMA'S PRIME CONTRACTORS

"There was a time when a fool and his money were soon parted, but now it happens to everybody".

Adlai Stevenson: 1900-1965/ American Statesman

The greatest money to be made, in relation to draining FEMA's coffers, is undoubtedly enjoyed by its prime contractors. From debris removal to roof-tarp installations, trailers to food supplies, massive profits are being made to an unsuspecting public that doesn't understand the actual inner-workings of the program. As said, housing inspectors are subcontractors, and that will be addressed in the following chapters when we discover who actually hires those inspectors who call you in the evening and arrive at your door the next day. For now, we'll focus on the types of FEMA contractors, including those associated with the housing inspection services.

Remember, the following captioned firms are all contractors and *not* actual FEMA employees. The men/women actually *removing* that debris on the roads and in your front yard are the lowest and final tier of subcontractors, just like the FEMA housing inspector who comes to your storm-ravaged home.

Most "bid" contracts are of a five-year duration, such as the current housing inspection firms of Parsons Brinckerhoff' and Vanguard, and Dewberry Davis in the past, but it's often business as usual. Beyond comprehension, some contracts are simply awarded to firms via either political connections or that they were in the right place at the right time, possibly because of time restraints and lack of foresight on FEMA's part. This comportment seems to be the product of successful business practices, wherein certain firms are continually awarded multi-million-dollar contracts, and which every tax-payer subsidizes. We must also understand that these contracts are physically awarded by the United States Army Corps of Engineers (ACE) via an interagency agreement signed in April of 2005. It is they who manage the contractual process for FEMA, who by statute, is in charge of the program but whose resources are stretched too thin to manage it themselves.

In a New York Times report in September 2005, it was stated that two of the major contractors for FEMA, Kellogg, Brown + Root and the Shaw Group, have been represented in the past by the lobbyist and past FEMA director, Joe Allbaugh. Additionally, he was President Bush's campaign manager. To further complicate/implicate this particular convenience, he was also a fellow classmate of Michael Brown at Oklahoma State University. Yes, it may seem to some that this could be a mere coincidence, but then again, I'm not of the volition to believe in coincidences. Kellogg-Brown and Root is a subsidiary of Halliburton, formerly headed by Vice-President Dick Cheney. Maybe the adage "it's not what you know but who you know" is exact. Kellogg isn't a major player in Operation Blue Roof or debris removal, but The Shaw Group was, and it is they and their fellow prime contractors who we'll be exploring in this chapter.

AshBritt, Inc, another firm, is a long-term debris-removal prime contractor and was represented by a lobbying firm named Welch Resources and headed by Mike Parker, a former head of the Army Corps of Engineers. According to AshBritt spokeswoman Carol Sanders, and quoted in an article from "The Hill publication in October 2005, she said: "Lobbyists don't have anything to do with who gets a contract. Who you know does not matter." Included in the Hill report, AshBritt *also* hired Adams and Reese in 2003, a New Orleans lobbying firm, and also procured the services of former Louisiana representative James Hayes, a Democrat who later became a Republican. Personally, I'd like to know why they hired lobbying firms in the first place if it "doesn't matter." There will be more on AshBritt in this chapter.

Acting Director David Paulison (remember him being hastily inserted into the directorship of FEMA after Michael Brown was jettisoned), was quoted as saying in a FEMA press release during the latter stages of Katrina's relief efforts for residents of New Orleans: "In the immediate response phase for hurricane Katrina, our priority was to get relief quickly to those in need. The oversight safeguards are in place for those emergency contracts so critically needed when disaster struck, and we will now use competitive strategies everywhere possible, placing priority on the use of local and small disadvantaged businesses as we move into the long-term recovery phase."

As the press release further stated, emergency contracts were issued for technical assistance and critically needed services, such as setting-up disaster recovery centers, the hauling and installing of temporary housing (FEMA trailers), and other logistics needed in the wake of hurricane Katrina in early September. Further, it was stated that technical assistance needs would continue in the long-term recovery process, as installation of facilities also continued to require ongoing maintenance. According to a FEMA press release on November 7, 2005, fifty-eight contracts were awarded to twenty-one small business for a total dollar-amount of $81,677,821, and thirty-four contracts were awarded to large business for a total of $26,476,495. These figures may seem astronomical, but we must also keep in mind that these dollars are split among ninety-two companies. Compare that to the sums awarded to the few we'll soon be examining, and it's a drop-in-the bucket.

When reading the previous FEMA press release, it beggars a palatable translation sorely needed. The verbiage is designed to sound sensible but refrains from fully explaining what is actually transpiring — much like plausible deniability — and we'll dissect those words. As anything government is always complicated and complex, I'll do my best to simplify.

To sign contracts with firms [approved] by FEMA when they first apply to be a purveyor of disaster-relief services, it certainly wouldn't make sense to sign those contracts with a debris- removal company in Wyoming, where only seven major disaster declarations have emanated from. Conversely, it *would* make sense to have those particular companies firmly held to contracts in historically affected geographical areas such as the Gulf Coast, Florida, and the lower eastern seaboard. Sense to them means senseless to us. Basically, what Director Paulison offered was an open-ended contracting auction without benefit of proper bidding guidelines, but *possibly* designed to aid certain companies that were of a higher stature within the framework of eligible contractors. How else could we misinterpret his words when contractors won tasks with higher bids than those with lower figures? Certainly, something's amiss, and as the following dollar amounts will testify.

In various newspaper reports, including articles in the New York Times, Louisiana Times Picayune and the Seattle Times, it was widely reported that the emergency contract for debris- removal alone during the aftermath of hurricane Katrina totaled more than $500 million. One of the recipients of that particular contract was "won" by the Pompano Beach, Florida-based company named AshBritt, with purported ties to [then] Mississippi Governor Haley, and was a client of Governor Barbour's lobbying firm. Other firms with lower bids were passed-by, and some local companies were mysteriously excluded. According to these reports, AshBritt had "worked" other hurricanes for FEMA, and is purportedly politically well-connected.

AshBritt became a prime contractor of record for this particular task, and in deference to them, they had to supply logistics, housing for out-of-state workers and other essential elements to insure the completion of their contract. But local labor was and always is a core ingredient of recovery. In lieu, how many in a declared disaster area would prefer to have local firms tasked with removing debris from your home or neighborhood?

www.femasbest.com

What seems to be missing from virtually every FEMA contract is the aggressive predilection of including home-grown efforts to assist disaster victims in dire need, and at the most stressful time one could imagine. In lieu, Section #307, Item #1 in the Stafford Act states that: *In general, in the expenditure of federal funds for debris clearance, distribution of supplies, reconstruction, and other major disaster or emergency assistance activities which may be carried out by contract or agreement with private organizations, firms or individuals, preference shall be given, to the extent feasible and practical, to these organizations, firms and individuals residing or doing business in the area affected by each major disaster or emergency.*

When in the field, I'd sometimes spoken with local subcontractors working for a nebulous entity awarded fat contracts, and a few times I'd even inspected their homes. For some, it worked out well in the financial sense. For most it didn't. I remember conversations with local debris-removal workers who'd lamented about their almost 20 hour days/seven days a week work schedules, but were nevertheless happy for the opportunity to make money. On various blog sites, I read entries from workers who didn't get paid and had sought assistance from any agency available. Most were under the false assumption that FEMA *itself* would be responsible for paying them, and this is one of many reasons why FEMA is the agency some love to hate. It may be wise to remember that the ones who removed those tree limbs or trees that blocked the entrance to your home were simply a cog in the complicated and oftentimes unfair wheel of disaster-relief that is, in fact, disaster capitalism. Always, there are winners and losers. In truth, everyone loses, whether in loss of morality via greed or in tangible forms, such as your damaged home that will never be quite the same even after you've rebuilt it, should you have been fortunate to have done so.

No one but AshBritt knows their exact net profit derived from that particular $500+ million contract, but it must have afforded many millions on the plus-side of their ledger. Unfortunately, no one can exactly calculate the savings to the American taxpayer should the bidding process have been forthright and fair. AshBritt was paid $23 per cubic yard (envision a pickup truck filled to the max and piled high, roughly 1+ yard) of debris removed, including its processing and disposal in public landfills. Alternatively, the local government of several Mississippi towns found contractors who *would* perform the same task for roughly $10 to $12 a cubic yard — *including* processing and disposal. Keeping this task as community-based endeavor so as to subsidize the local work-force is all-important, but apparently tends to fall victim to the greed and apathy of others who are devoid of a sense of community. This same comportment may also be compared to Operation Blue Roof and the FEMA trailers.

Additional information will be discussed in another chapter, pertaining to what FEMA allocates via dollar-value for trees fallen or cubic yards of debris when a housing inspector visits your home, but for now we'll focus on the roof tarps that most are familiar with, whether up-close and personal or from a distance. On a personal note, I never could understand why some subcontractors made more holes in roofs from putting them on than existed previously. Believe it or not, I've seen an entire roof sheeted with that infamous blue, even though the actual storm damage was less than ten-square feet.

www.femasbest.com

8

OPERATION BLUE ROOF

"There is sufficiency in the world for man's need, but not for man's greed".

Mohanda K. "Mahatma" Gandhi: 1869-1948/ Indian political and spiritual leader

Kinda' like pitching a tent in the woods, but with the benefit of an existing substructure, installing a tarp on a roof is not an exercise in quantum physics. However, the price that FEMA paid the winner of this particular contract must have been laughing all the way to the proverbial bank. Should you call any local building supply outlet, a 60' x 40' (2400 square feet) medium-grade blue tarpaulin will cost anywhere from $100-130. Should you contact Copper-State Roofing Supply in Phoenix, Arizona, they'll quote you $101.95 for that same expanse of tarp. In September of 2005, FEMA paid 6.6 million dollars for incalculable amounts of this product from All American Poly, located in Piscataway, New Jersey, sans competitive bidding.

Before fully exploring the basics of installing one of these tarps and its actual cost, we'll find out about the firm who actually won the contract for supplying them. After that, the sub-contractors will be examined in this many-tiered enterprise.

Under the clause of the Stafford Act that we've read, the preference was to utilize contractors living or residing in affected disaster area. But this malady, that FEMA hasn't yet corrected, continues unabated. In a 1993 Government Accounting Office (GAO) report that focused on federal disaster management, it was found that federal agencies consistently failed to mobilize local companies to undertake certain tasks and failed to administer advance preparations because they were unsure or doubtful about the Stafford Act's statutory guidelines. In an examination of federal responses to hurricane Katrina, the House Select Committee, that investigated the preparation for and the response to Katrina, found that the Stafford Act's ambiguous statutory guidance regarding local contractor's participation resulted in very few local firms receiving contracts for debris-removal and other necessary services.

From the above captioned statements and from my own research and knowledge of contractor/FEMA relationships, I was still prompted to augment those truths, and found them in many newspaper articles about rampant instances of price gouging and favoritism. Although my belief is that FEMA could do a better job of appeasing public opinion in regard to awarding such lucrative contracts, local entities should *always* hold first preference in obtaining them. The fact may be that some enterprises are ill-equipped to definitively and efficiently task-out large contracts, whether debris removal, roof-tarp installation, or supplication of alternative housing needs, but my opinion holds firm that local firms *have* to be an integral part of the disaster-relief process, At the least, their inclusion would aid a local economy in desperate need of funds injected to suffering coffers.

All American Poly, who was awarded that 6.6 million dollar contract for supplying roof tarps for hurricane Katrina, has enjoyed previous contracts with FEMA. According to its President and CEO, Jack Klein, within in a corporate profile, he'd stated that "the company has an excellent relationship with FEMA, and they responded to our needs as we did theirs." He'd also said that "There were some misconceptions about our being awarded some work without a bid…..that this firm was working under a continuous bid. We had always remained competitive." In summation, Mr. Klein stated that FEMA doesn't deserve the media-bashing and he hopes to continue working with FEMA in the coming years.

From my previously expressed opinion regarding the inclusion of local firms to be involved in disaster declaration relief efforts, I can well understand their plight and frustration. The American taxpayer is also victimized by this apparent and successful exercise on the part of large corporations obtaining maximum profits for minimal effort, whether being in that right place-at that right time or not. As concisely as possible, the cold-hard-monetary facts pertaining to the profits derived from Operation Blue Roof are to follow.

Please keep-in-mind that "furring-strips" (wooden 1x2's---the lowest grade that hold the tarp in place) and nails/screws are usually supplied by the prime contractors — and are very cheap in price. All costs are approximated, and mostly represented in "squares." A square is 10 foot x 10 foot, or 100 sf. For our purposes, All American Poly's projected manufacturing cost is profiled in actual square footage. Since we can only project the actual cost, we can still somewhat ascertain an approximate figure based upon Copper-State Roofing Supplies' retail (per sf) cost of a 40' x 60' tarp. The actual blue-tarp material is arbitrary at best in the monetary sense, when compared with the peripheral charges that prime contractor and certain subcontractors enjoy.

    1: Copper-State's (retail) cost per sf of a 40' x 60' (2400 SF) tarp = .5 per sf.

    2: All American Poly's manufacturing cost of a 2400 square-foot roof-tarp = 1.2 cents. This approximation is based on the guidelines of 100% profit from purveyor-to-purveyor. It could be a bit less or a bit more. Either way, it matters not, as we'll soon know how many roofs got tarps.

    3: Cost of 2400 sf of roof tarp that prime contractors (such as the Shaw Group) are paid via FEMA contract = $160-175 per square.

    4: $65-75 per sf to *next-tier* subcontractors such as A-1 Construction + Roofing ($95-100 profit per square for # 3).

    5: $25-30 per sf to *further* subcontractors such as Wescon Construction ($70-75 profit per square to # 4).

6: $2-4 per sf to the ones that actually put the blue on your roof = $23-26 profit per square to #5.

7: The *actual* installers, figuring a crew of four men, would earn each of them about $30 for less than 2 hours labor. A crew of two would obviously make about $60 each. Depending on the distance from house-to-house — oftentimes entire stretches of block-after-block are decimated — a four-man crew could easily tarp seven to eight homes from six o'clock in the morning to eight in the evening, specifically during the long daylight hours of summer when hurricanes usually strike. Each member of this four-man crew could make $240 per day, a two-man crew about $300 per day, as their speed would be inhibited by less manpower. A very speedy crew could tarp ten to twelve homes a day, thereby maximizing profits.

In this multi-tiered system, All American Poly supplies the bulk material per their contract, the prime contractors hire the next-tiered contractors, and it regresses to the layer of the actual process of the workers installing the tarps.

Aside from All American Poly, seven FEMA prime contractors with fingers in the pie for roof-tarps are listed below, including their Katrina-era contract amounts:

1: The Shaw Group, of Baton Rouge, Louisiana: Contract amount = $63.8 million.

2: LJC Construction, of Alabama: Contract amount = $50.3 million.

3: Simon Roofing, of Ohio: Contract amount = $45.3 million.

4: Ystueta INC of Alabama: Contract amount = $4.1 million.

5: Carothers/Aduddell of Oklahoma/Lousiana: Contract amount = $60 million.

6: Ceres Environmental Services, INC of Louisiana: = $60 million.

www.femasbest.com

7: S +M and Associates, INC of Mississippi: Contract amount = $12.2 million.

As you've noticed, both Ystueta and S+M have a lower contract amount than the other five contractors. This is because they are both categorized by FEMA to be "disadvantaged businesses" and they were added to the list as "add-ons" to both reflect the "concern" of expediently addressing the need to install all of those roof-tarps and to abide by the mandate of the Stafford Act.

Many of these firms have had ongoing contractual associations with FEMA, such as The Shaw Group and Ceres Environmental, the latter being also awarded a separate contract for hurricane Katrina's debris removal. Additionally, and much akin to its counterparts, Ceres has been the recipient of numerous and varied contracts for many years. Carothers/Aduddell was a joint-venture awarded contract. For that firm, FEMA awarded $1.65 per square foot, or $165 per square. Additionally, they also had other tasks associated with their contract such as minor roof repairs and the like. I'd always thought that Christmas only comes once a year, but I guess that for some of these firms that rule does not apply when a major hurricane makes landfall.

Now, we'll focus on the first tier of the contracting process: that being the manufacturer of the infamous tarps loved or hated depending, of course, on your particular association with them. While allowing a bit of leeway either in the plus or negative, All American Poly seemingly made approximately $5.9 million for simply supplying the roof-trap material for 52,000 homes in Louisiana impacted by hurricane Katrina, 18,000 adversely affected by hurricane Rita, and 47,000 homes in Mississippi for Rita, for a grand total of 127,000 structures that required tarps. We know that All American Poly received $6.6 million from FEMA for supplying the raw tarp material for hurricanes Katrina and Rita in 2005, but how do we figure out how much they actually made? Again, we can approximate the profit, give-or-take a few dollars.

1: American Poly's cost for 2400 SF of tarp = $28 (at 1.2 cents per square-foot)

2: 247,000 (2400 SF) homes tarped = $690,000

3: American Poly's contract with FEMA to supply tarps = $6.6 million

4: American Poly's cost for 247,000 (2400 SF} tarps = $690,000

5: American Poly's profit = approximately $5.9 million.

We must keep in mind that a 2000 SF home will require additional square-footage of tarp, as a pitched roof will add to the area. Additionally, many homes would be less in square-footage but some would be more, making the 2400 square-foot approximation reasonable.

After gleaning all this information about the Blue Roof program, some of you may think that a solution to the high costs and enormous profits made by out-of-state prime contractors could be alleviated by simple and logical measures taken by local and state governments. Since the actual tarp material is so cheap, then why don't hurricane-prone areas keep a supply on hand? And if so, wouldn't that take one step out of the myriad red tape and confusion? Why couldn't these local and state governments maintain a database of qualified contractors to do the work in liaison with other local subcontractors who would have a moral interest in assisting their community's disaster relief efforts, rather than those who don't share that emotion?

The simple answer is that the system is set-up to *make* it complicated, and unfortunately, it doesn't have to be. If it was a simple process, than all the firms captioned above wouldn't be privy to all those huge profits, and that appears to be the prime directive of both FEMA and the Army Corps in the contractual realms of politics and profit. Funny, I'd always thought that disaster relief was all about rapidly assisting disaster victims and not about adding to their misery via wasted tax dollars and corporate bottom-lines. Welcome to the world of disaster capitalism.

At this point, you now have a basic understanding of the infamous Operation Blue-Roof, and the knowledge of costs that go with it. Probably, you'll never look at one of them again in the same way, and maybe even imagine dollar signs embossed on them. And we may also wonder what happens to those tarps after getting damaged via the elements and sunlight. Who takes them off? Are they ever used again?

Usually, once you've had one on your roof you own it and are responsible for its disposal or removal. But if lucky, your contractor will have included its removal or disposal within his estimate. If not, then that equates to yet another expense. Regardless, you'll pay out-of-pocket should your insurance company or contractor not bear the cost and FEMA also denies your claim. However, *should* you be lucky enough to have one still in good shape after its use, then you have a free tarp to cover the boat, car, motorcycle, or possibly hire some seamstresses and start a custom raincoat company. Within those choices everyone's a winner, just like the debris removal contractors that we'll now study.

To end our exploration of Operation Blue Roof, I couldn't resist including a very unique letter, that an applicant gave a copy to an inspector friend of mine when inspecting their home for hurricane Wilma in 2005. I hope you enjoy it. It's priceless.

    Dear FEMA,

    We have toxic trailers and now we have toxic houses. I received a blue tarp for my roof when it was damaged by hurricane Charlie in 2004 and now I'm getting another one for my roof again damaged by hurricane Wilma. Seems to me it's like getting a cut and putting a bandage on it. Well, it surely protects the wound for a bit as it was designed to do but if you never take it off the skin starts to die and infection begins. Same for your roof tarp. The tarp keeps the rain out of the house for a short while but with the Florida sun being what it is, the tarp begins to deteriorate and the rain comes gushing in and traps the moisture in the house and infection and mold begins.

So now we have FEMA housing people in toxic trailers and toxic houses. The poor that had no insurance start to get sick and they miss work and they become poorer and can't fix their roof and are forced to sell a mold infested house for pennies on the dollar but with a great view of the ocean. Smart businessmen move in and pick up the house for a song. The poor homeowner gets to say thank you FEMA for all your help.

Meanwhile, people with insurance don't pay for the tarp removal or for all the holes that need to be filled, but those without insurance are stuck. We're all not all carpenters here you know. And how much does it cost for dump fees at landfills for these tarps? How big of a mountain does millions of crumpled up tarps look like? How many flat tires do all these loose nails produce?

Heck of a job FEMA, just like your former director Brownie did. You don't know what you're doing.

9

DEBRIS REMOVAL

"Money doesn't change men, it merely unmasks them. If a man is naturally selfish or greedy, the money brings that out, that's all". Henry Ford" 1863-1947, Founder of Ford Motor Company

We know about AshBritt previously profiled, but there are other corporations also awarded debris-removal contracts from FEMA. Since we already possess the basic knowledge of how these contracts work and the multi-tiered subcontractor venues and so-on, we don't have to cover all those bases again. For now, let's delve into these prime contractors and their profits.

The four prime-awarded debris-removal contracts for hurricanes Katrina and Rita in 2005 were:

1: AshBritt, of Pompano Beach, Florida.

2 : Ceres Environmental Services, INC. (remember them?), of Brooklyn Park, Minnesota.

3: Environmental Chemical Corporation, of Burlingame, California.

4: Phillips and Jordan, INC., of Zephyrhills, Florida.

AshBritt was paid approximately $23 per cubic yard for work in Mississippi (remember the pickup truck filled with debris?), and they subcontracted their next-tier firm to actually remove it for about $9 per to a company named C+B Enterprises. Within this subcontract system, the "built-ins" explained below may have been separately negotiated, possibly a 50-50 split. Within these contracts were those aforementioned built-ins that stipulated certain items to be added to the initial contract figure. Some of these items are as follows:

1: $79 for a "hanger," which is a limb two-inches in diameter or larger that requires removal because it poses a safety hazard.

2: $100-700 for a "leaner," which is a tree leaning at more than thirty degrees.

3: Up to $ 395 for removal of stumps and additional payments should the hole need fill.

The total value of the contract was $500 million with an additional $500 million option, and AshBritt doesn't even own any trucks! The second $500 million was an "option" that apparently was tapped into, thereby increasing Ashbritt's actual contract amount to almost $600 million. Ceres Environmental was paid approximately $16.36 per yard for work in Louisiana, as well as the remaining two contractors also in Louisiana. Ceres' first-tier subcontractor was Loupe Construction from Louisiana, and they in turn subcontracted to another firm for roughly $10 per yard. So-on-and-so-forth, we know how it goes. Confused yet?

According to a report issued by the Army Corps of Engineers on September 15, 2005, each prime contractor's duties under their contracts included debris removal, debris disposal, demolition, and other recovery work. These "awarded" contracts---and according the Corps — were based on criteria such as, past performances, technical capability, ability to provide sub-contracting goals for small and disadvantaged businesses, ability to respond, and price.

The Corps is incorrect about past performances, per the information at the end of this paragraph, but their ability to provide subcontracting goals and their ability to respond are the two things they're correct about; they were already assured when Katrina made landfall and were immune to the open bidding process, in its truest sense. For past performances, an AshBritt contract was terminated by the city of Biloxi, Mississippi in December 2005 for "Failure to make required progress." It may also be noted that according to an Associated Press (AP) news report in March 2005, AshBritt has contributed $224,824 to federal candidates and parties and political action committees since 1999, the bulk of which went to the Republican Party. So much for coincidences and fair play, we may presume.

According to a May 2008 report by The Project on Government Oversight (POGO), it was ascertained that 80% of dollars spent on Government contracts---which is approximately $1.5 billion — had been awarded without full and open competition. Additionally, the Government Accountability Office (GAO) estimated that 58.8% of the hurricane Katrina contracts awarded to long-term prime contractors before November 30, 2005 was of non-competitive varieties. The justification for allowing no-bid contracts was based upon "The urgent need for rapid emergency response." Other government reports have found that 50.5% of those contracts have continued to be awarded noncompetitively, despite the fact that an emergency action is no longer required and, therefore, no longer justifies no-bid contracts.

Further, the report goes-on to say that "The most glaring example of the negative impacts of non-competitive contracting was the four no-bid contracts awarded to Fluor, CH2m Hill, Bechtel, and the Shaw Group, all awarded after Katrina hit. FEMA awarded each company a contract with a ceiling price of $500 million. On October 6, 2005, FEMA Director Paulison testified before the Senate Homeland Security and Government Affairs Committee that he has "Never been a fan of no-bid contracts, and that FEMA would rebid all of those no-bid contracts." Rebidding did occur, however, until August 2006. In fact, FEMA actually *raised* the ceilings on those contracts, authorizing more than $3.3 billion to the four companies. To offset public criticism, FEMA awarded up to $3.6 billion in temporary victim-housing contracts to small and minority-owned firms. Or so they said......

Even though we may think that $23 per yard of debris doesn't compare with the approximated blue-roof cost of $2500-$3500 per 2000 square-foot home, the amount of debris a hurricane or tropical storm can unleash on roads, houses and their access-points is truly staggering. I mention access-points because this is part of the criteria with which FEMA allocates money to homeowners who've been affected, and when they get issued an inspection. This will soon be addressed in the chapter dealing with the actual process of housing inspections, but for now, we'll ascertain how much money the prime contractors could have made. Using the same formula utilized for Operation Blue Roof, the profits for all four debris removal contractors can be fairly approximated.

We know that about 187,000 homes had roof damage that warranted a tarp, but many more houses were also adversely affected and didn't require those tarps. From my experience when performing housing inspections during hurricane Katrina, I can say that virtually every home I'd inspected had some debris removal issue. Some had three yards while others had six, and still others had ten to twelve cubic yards, either on their roofs or blocking the access to their home (remember the criteria). Additionally, we need to include all the debris and fallen trees on streets, roads and highways.

According to the Army Corps' estimations, a total of 100 million cubic yards of debris was removed, disposed of and processed by the four captioned prime contractors. According to the Army Corps, approximately 20,000,000 cubic yards of debris were removed, and 19,000 tons of spoiled food (supermarkets and such) were disposed of by August, 2006 by AshBritt alone. Yes, they also have a contract for *that*, and totaling $5.7 million. Since AshBritt's debris removal contract in Mississippi was for $23 per yard (including those built-ins), and they pay the first-tier contractor $12-14 per yard, we can safely assume that they make $9-11 per yard. 20 million yards multiplied by 9 comes to $180,000,000, and that was only estimated on the

August 2006 figures. Not bad for a firm that doesn't even own its own trucks.

Even though AshBritt has to manage the on-sight work of removing debris, house and feed out-of-state personnel and so-forth, the figures are still beyond comprehension. Certainly, it seems that FEMA could do a much better job to placate the public regarding where their tax-dollars should go, rather than constantly award these lucrative contracts to those with political connections and thusly enjoying undeserving preferential treatment. Again, I stress the importance of hiring local firms to be the vanguard for debris removal programs, both for preserving the local economies and because it's the correct thing to do. In lieu, the Stafford Act actually mandates this, In Section #307, Item #1, which we've read in a preceding chapter.

Essentially, FEMA is violating that clause of the Stafford Act by doing business as usual with their corporate friends. It *is* practical and feasible for local firms to be the vanguard of debris removal. In a later chapter titled *Solutions to the Quandary*, I'll be expanding further on this.

Down-the-line in this apparent and elaborate pyramid scheme, AshBritt and the other prime debris-removal contractors paid their next-tier subcontractors to actually perform the work. From $12.00 to $14.00 per-yard, these subcontractors paid yet other subcontractors, and the beat-goes-on. For example, the lowest tier contractor was making about $2.50 per yard. Obviously, there's no need to beat a dead horse about the enormous profits AshBritt and the other three prime contractors made, so we'll end this chapter.

Within the hidden agendas we'll be reading about later, the contracts constantly awarded to repetitive firms beg for erstwhile review and monumental change. In itself, the debris-removal program seems an agenda of sorts, though hidden no longer. There have been Government oversight committees investigating all these companies and their fat contracts, but the sad truth is that the system is too embedded with politics and favoritism to allow any change in the near-future. And in that near future, hurricanes such as Katrina will spawn the same excuses that "experienced and proven firms" are the ones to depend on, and not enough time was available to open-bid the contracts. For this season we can expect the same: A waste of money and massive profits for those that just happen to be in the right place at the right time.

In the next chapter, we'll briefly look at the infamous FEMA Trailers. Yes, there are many other types of prime contractors for FEMA, but to address them all would make this book very large and boring, and I'm trying my best not to make it so. Bear with me. The best is yet to come. Soon, you'll know exactly how a home inspection works, how the system is fraught with errors, and how disaster-relief applicants are awarded all that money.

/ www.femasbest.com

10

FEMA TRAILERS

"Every beginning comes from some other beginnings end"

Lucius Annaeus Seneca

They're really nice for a family vacation, but certainly are not for extended living. And as such, this is the case for the tens of thousands of Katrina refugees who'd experienced the cramped quarters of a travel trailer — or in some cases a cheap modular home — and the approximately 25,162 folks in Louisiana *and* the 10,362 in Mississippi who were still occupying them five years later. Although FEMA has been in the process of closing down the "temporary" trailer parks, many had occupied them on the land where their houses once stood, a grim and constant reminder of what life used to be like. Having a roof over your head may seem like a blessing for a while, but after months and months of this lifestyle it feels like a curse. And then there's that persistent issue about formaldehyde that folks were breathing in.

The formaldehyde debate is still raging and lawsuits have been filed by applicants suffering the effects of that poison; a cottage industry of sorts has been created from this particular FEMA debacle. No one has yet won such a lawsuit, to my knowledge, but I wouldn't be surprised if some are successful. Since this aspect of the trailers is very important to explore, we'll take a little time to get to the true crux of it. Once again, I'll try to keep it simple.

Formaldehyde, a chemical compound also known as methanol, is a gas with a very pungent smell and has been associated with modular homes and trailers for decades. It's a carcinogen, an invisible vapor that slowly and methodically literally sucks the life out of the ones who live with it. Since the modern advent of recreational trailers and modular homes, this chemical has been omnipresent in their construction materials, such as the plywood of the pressed-wood variety, (commonly called "chipboard") which requires specific glues to bind them, and resins that also contain levels of formaldehyde, which are employed as adhesives for carpeting, walls, floors and cabinets. Again, this is nothing new, but the core reason that this well-known fact has become an issue is simply because the trailers were never meant to be lived in for long periods of time, and as we know, they have.

Manufactured under the assumption that they'd be utilized for weekend trips or a few months on the road, the knowledge that the chemical may be harmful was always known, and sometimes even to purchasers of them. The acceptable level of the toxic substance was not fully explored by most buyers, possibly because they'd mistakenly and blindly trusted the manufacturer. As opposed to trailers, modular homes *are* designed to be occupied for sustained periods of time, much like any standard form of housing construction. Their toxic levels are usually lower than trailers.

In a report from the Environmental News Network in September 2007, it was reported that The Agency for Toxic Substances and Disease Registry, a sister agency to the Center for Disease Control (CDC), set minimum risk-levels of exposure to formaldehyde *below* which a person would be unlikely to experience any ill effects. In that particular report, that minimum risk-factor is roughly 0.04 parts per million (ppm) for one to fourteen days of continuous exposure, 0.03 for up to one year of continuous exposure, and 0.008 for exposure exceeding one year. Per those figures, it was found that levels of formaldehyde levels in some FEMA trailers measured at twenty-five times the acceptable risk-levels. In independent testing conducted by the Sierra Club of forty-four FEMA trailers, it was found that concentration levels as high as 0.34 parts per million existed in all tested units. As an example of those levels, it was equal to what a professional embalmer would be exposed to while on-the-job. Exposure to formaldehyde in doses of 0/1 ppm may cause watery eyes, a burning sensation in the eyes and nose and throat, headaches, difficulty in breathing and skin-rashes.

In retort, FEMA sent-out press releases in an effort to convince the public that their concerns were being expediently addressed. In response to an MSNBC.com article of July 23, 2006, Homeland Secretary Michael Chertoff ordered air quality testing of FEMA trailers in an effort to determine whether or not formaldehyde gas was present in concentrations that could be toxic to occupants. Consequently, FEMA transferred that testing order to the Environmental Protection Agency (EPA). Prior to that, FEMA's scope of testing consisted of measuring toxic levels in a trailer occupied by a pregnant mother and her infant child in April of 2006. That test showed Formaldehyde levels that were *seventy-five* times higher than the exposure levels recommended by the National Institute for Occupational Safety and Health.

In July 2006, EPA and CDC officials consulted with FEMA, warning them that trailers were likely to have high levels of formaldehyde. In a July 11, 2006 email, EPA told FEMA that "The levels we find after testing may well be more than one-hundred times higher than the health-base level." In consultation with EPA, FEMA developed an alternate plan to test trailers to determine formaldehyde concentrations emanating from the trailer during living conditions. As it was, this plan was ultimately rejected and FEMA instead opted to test unoccupied trailers with windows open, ventilations fans running, and air-conditioning units running. By this form of testing, those results became the basis for their claim that the risks of formaldehyde exposure were minimal.

It will remain to be seen what FEMA will do in order to supply alternative housing for disaster victims when the next major storm of flood occurs. But *will* they repeat the same irrational system of obtaining them? Will they fight the lawsuits with the fortitude deserving of an apathetic agency that has so-far proven that the hidden agenda of feeding the ravenous mouths of corporate prime contractors eclipses its original purpose?

FEMA spoke of seeking solutions to alternative disaster housing needs in response to the trailer fiasco, but a formative program is still not in place. As of 2016, FEMA had offered an alternative plan to supply disaster victims with actual mobile homes — as opposed to travel trailers — but that offering nevertheless involves additional logistics that will result in yet another frail attempt to correct it. Connecting utilities and site-work for those MH's requires more manpower than setting up travel trailers, for instance. Further, the cost per unit is greater than a trailer, and it just doesn't make sense. The issue of apathy seemingly exhibited by the preeminent agency responsible for assisting disaster victims *has* to absolutely adhere to total responsibility. If not, then FEMA has no moral right to profess any intent of that nature. Nevertheless, others, not relegated to FEMA's version of palatable information, still exist.

A floor supervisor named Terry Green, who worked at Gulf Stream Coach factory (manufacturing travel trailers) in Etna Green, Indiana, was quoted as saying that his crew worked at breakneck pace for months, which forced the company to use cheaper wood products. Additionally, he stated that "Quality suffered dramatically because of the drive and pressure to put these trailers out." In a statement on FEMA's website at that time, nothing pertinent was addressed and no blame admitted. As it seems, FEMA's predilection for saving face at all costs apparently supersedes its duty to preserve the health and well-being of the occupants of trailers supplied by its prime contractors at enormous profits. Within that alone, we should, in the future, carefully consider where any salvation during times of crises originates from, and tread softly when accepting it.

Hidden agendas are oftentimes cloaked within a shadow of substance, enough to cause doubt among the few, but instill belief in the many. Always, there will be those that pose questions, but usually the lemming-factor supersedes the immediate need for the truth.

www.femasbest.com

For most disaster victims who rely on FEMA to come to the rescue, we might ask ourselves *why* they continue to align themselves with multi-national corporations that care not about the suffering of the individual, but care only to adhere to the bottom-line of profit. And now, we will explore those profits. For readers of this book, their own truths will be readily apparent or not.

Four contractors were initially installed as primes to supply trailers, modular homes and logistics. All of them are very familiar to the Department of Defense and FEMA, and to us.

    1: The Shaw Group, in Louisiana. (Don't you hate these guys already?)

    2: The Fluor Group, in California.

    3: Bechtel National INC, in California.

    4: CH2M Hill, in Colorado.

All of the above contractors are multi-nationals, are long-term clients of FEMA, *and* are under contract for other various federal services. No real surprise there. They specialize in construction, project management and everything in between. One-stop shopping, as it may be. But let's not make the mistake of affording them any sense of decency or responsibility to their fellow man. Their objective is to always adhere to the bottom-line and to hell with anyone else, for within the corporate world of fat contracts, and suffering no consequences for their greed, the human element does not exist.

In the immortal words of Thomas Jefferson, "A government big enough to give you everything you want is strong enough to take everything you have." And that statement should ring soundly to us all. Shady deals consummated in Washington DC's dark and thickly paneled offices are hopefully vestiges of the past. Accountability must be justly administered, should any poignant changes become visible on the horizon of sanity and morality. I hope you read this book, President Trump.

And now, we'll continue to study the corporations previously captioned.

Bechtel National is the same outfit that won the joint-venture contract in Boston, Massachusetts for the "Big Dig" project that went over-budget from $2.6 billion to 14.6 billion, took fifteen years to complete instead of the seven per the original contract estimation, and was subsequently sued for infractions pertaining to improper construction techniques. At one time, George Shultz, the former Secretary of State in the Reagan administration, represented Bechtel when he was with the investment bank of Dillon Read and Company. Bechtel's influence was also expanded via former Defense Secretary Caspar Weinberger, who acted as General Council for that firm in the late 1970's. In a New Yorker magazine article in May of 2003, it was revealed that members of the Bin Laden family invested several million dollars in the Freemont Group, a private equity fund, and which was owned by the Bechtel family.

The largest engineering company in the United States and the ninth largest privately held via its family ownership, Bechtel's past awarded contracts are immense in scope. In Saudi Arabia, they'd built the "Jubial Industrial City in 1976, present population over 70,000, and it's one of the most modern small metropolises in that country. In Iraq, their construction and other contracts were worth a staggering $685 billion, which would make one pause for thought. One was a contract to build a chemical plant, transpiring not long after Saddam Hussein faced international condemnation for using poison gas against the Kurdish people. In England, Bechtel participated in the building of the "Chunnel," the undersea highway that links England to France. In 1930, they helped build the Hoover Dam. And the list goes on. As said at the beginning of this book, I could write well over 800 pages on the subject of FEMA.

Fluor has had many government contracts, including one in 2007 that was awarded by the U.S. Army to feed, fuel and house American troops in Iraq and Afghanistan, and this corporation has been involved in roughly eighty domestic natural disasters. They are also a Fortune 500 company with over $9 billion in revenue every year since 2002, and they are the largest traded construction firm in the world. In South Korea, Fluor constructed that country's first oil refinery in the 1960's, and had accumulated $3 billion for contracts in Iraq. In Afghanistan, they were awarded a $500 million contract for rebuilding a dam, roads and a bridge. In Iraq, they won two contracts, one worth $500 million and the other for $600 million, both for construction of water treatment plants, sewage collection and solid waste management. Additionally, another contract was worth $155 million, that being for electric power generation. Fluor's former chairman, Phillip J. Caroll, spent thirty-seven years with Shell Oil Company, and was chairman of the board, advising Thamir Ghadhban, the head of Iraq's oil ministry. As all the above information can testify, Fluor is powerful and very well-connected, just as every prime contractor is.

The Shaw Group was represented by the lobbying firm of New Bridge Strategies, headed by former Director of FEMA Joe Allbaugh, and got its first large contract from Halliburton, whom Vice President Dick Cheney was formerly CEO of. Since then, Shaw has risen from its humble beginnings in 1987 to a stature equal to the other prime contractors. From 1994 to 2003, they'd acquired sixteen firms, thusly elevating them to a publicly traded entity and a Fortune 500 company. Within its scope of services, such as energy and chemicals, environmental /infrastructure, maintenance and construction, Shaw garnered over $1 billion in contracts from the Department of Defense from 1998 to 2003, one of which was a $75 million award for renovations at Al Kasik military base in Iraq. Another Mideast contract was a joint venture with Centcom in 2004, thusly called Shaw/Centcom Services LLC, for construction work in Kuwait, Saudi Arabia and Iraq.

Domestically, Shaw acquired approximately $338 million within seven contracts for hurricane Katrina, which, in post-Katrina, were being investigated by the Department of Homeland Security's Inspector General, Richard Skinner. Those investigations are of the norm: Improprieties and cost over-runs and everyone gathering as much government money in the shortest possible time. Still very much active in obtaining stateside contracts, Shaw won one in March 2008 with the US Air Force Center for Engineering (AFCEE), and for whom they've done business with for fifteen years. It's who you know.

Politically, they're firmly planted and supported, just as all the other corporations are. While also being represented by New Bridge, Shaw's president and CEO, Jim Bernhard, was the head of Louisiana's Democratic Party until stepping down post-Katrina. Edward Badolato, Shaw's executive vice-president, has served with the Department of Energy and served on the President's Commission of Critical Infrastructure. Alphonso E. Lenhardt, a senior vice-president at Shaw, was the Sergeant at Arms in the United States Senate, and no doubt, a perfect place to fasciculate many connections and friendships.

On February 13, 2013, The Shaw Group was acquired by Chicago Bridge and Iron Company (CB&I) for three-billion dollars. CB&I is a multinational Netherlands-based engineering and construction provider with approximately 40,000 employees worldwide. During the Obama administration, Jim Bernhard was being considered for the post of Energy Secretary. Much like Parsons Brinkerhoff, we now have two multinational corporations privy to FEMA no-bid contracts, and both are based outside of the U.S. There's something wrong with this.

CH2M Hill sounds more like a formula than a company name, but this corporation has apparently perfected their own unique formula when also persistently obtaining lucrative contracts from FEMA and elsewhere. In Iraq, this global construction and project management firm joint-ventured with Parsons Brinckerhoff (a corporation that will appear in a later chapter) to provide support to the Public Works and Water Sector Program Office, which is a directorate of the coalition provisional authority's project management office. The total for that contract was $28.5 million in 2004. In Singapore, they'd built that countries deep-tunnel system. For the Panama Canal Authority's $5.25 billion contract, CH2M was the manager for that project. In Abu Dhabi, CM2 was selected as the project manager for the construction of "Masdar," a visionary city. Domestically, the decommissioning and closing of the former nuclear weapons factory in Rocky Flats, Colorado, was managed by them. The list could go on, but we'll add just a bit more information.

Obviously, none of these firms will return your phone call should you need repairs to a leaking roof, but although it may be surprising to see all these high-powered corporations having an interest in a seemingly insignificant enterprise in comparison to their more high-profile contracts, we need to keep in mind the essence of corporate greed that infests all of these entities. Also, we must remember that none of them would even consider accepting a contract to supply those trailers unless significant and easy profits were assured.

All of the above firms received a combined total of $3.7 billion to provide temporary housing to victims of hurricanes Katrina and Rita in the form of approximately 150,000 trailers and modular units, pretty-much evenly split between them. They had to procure them from any source available, transport them, and deliver them to a staging area before further transporting them to former home-sites or the places commonly known as Femaville, possibly from where you're reading this book should you still be suffering any consequences from the captioned corporations' lust for money.

Those particular contracts were in the range of $100 million each, but every prime contractor — those corporations— had cost overruns, bringing the total to over $500 million each. And so it went. According to FEMA sources and a Washington Post report in August 2006, FEMA increased those contracts to: $950 million for The Shaw Group in February of that year, $1.4 billion to Fluor in March, $5.75 million to Bechtel in July, and a projected increase to CH2M Hill for $530 million. Further, FEMA paid these firms approximately $1.9 billion at that time, and "obligated" an additional $1 billion in charges, forwarded to FEMA for processing.

You'd think that FEMA would simply reflect on Bechtel's performance in the Big Dig project in Boston, but then again, you'd also think that FEMA would simply go to the manufacturers of the trailers and modular homes and procure the units themselves, and then contract trucking firms to transport them to realistic staging areas. But that's apparently too logical for FEMA's taste or acumen to even entertain a rudimentary solution. Lots of money could be saved there. The cost of these staging-sites is appalling, but apropos to everything associated with the prime contractors.

The trailers and modular homes were purchased from anywhere they could find them, whether in "mom and pop" sales lots or much larger venues. Like a modern-day search for the Holy Grail, all the prime contractors scoured the nation for enough trailers and modular homes to meet the required number within each contract. A vendor named Freedom Roads in Lincolnshire, Illinois sold FEMA 2,000 trailers for a total profit of $16 million, and so it went. Basically, all the four prime contractors *had* to perform under their contracts, which stipulated that each unit had to cost under $20,000, including vendor's profit. So, some may have cost $10,000 or less, others cost a bit more, but either way most of them never had warm bodies occupying them. And now we will see *where* many of them wound up.

Utilizing the formula for Operation Blue Roof and debris-removal, and when calculating the profits of the above-captioned participants in this particular pyramid scheme, those profits may not astound you at this juncture, but the ineptitude of the process of obtaining trailers and modular homes probably will.

Using the Freedom Roads sale as an example, we can use $10,000 as the average price of a trailer. 2000 of them sold would come to $20 million, not including the vendor's profit of $16 million. That would equate to $1 million for 100 trailers, $10 million for 1000 trailers, $100 million for 10,000 trailers, $1 billion for 100,000 trailers, and about 1.5 billion for 114,341 trailers, which is the approximate number of units finally purchased by all four prime contractors. If we take into consideration the transportation of these trailers from all parts of the USA, the hundreds of personnel from each firm to provide logistics, and the feeding and housing of these employees, we can be *very-very* generous to allow another one-half billion (500 million) to reflect those costs.

Well, I'm not a trained mathematician, but that seems to leave about $700 million to be divided four-ways, or approximately $175 million each in profit. Not bad, I'd say. And we must also keep in mind that modular/manufactured homes were also purchased. You know, the ones you see on flatbeds along the highways that take up almost two lanes? Additionally, 25,262 manufactured homes were purchased at a cost of $902 million. It must be noted that though some may differentiate a modular home to a manufactured one, they are, essentially, the same type of structure. We'll be referring to them as "MH's."

Staging areas for the trailers and MH's were a prime source for wasted money and hidden profits for the contractors. As the system worked, and after the trailers were purchased, they had to be put somewhere, as each one wasn't immediately delivered to a site or ready-made trailer park for those who were waiting for them. As an example of the exorbitant costs that transposed to incredible profits, and as reported by the Government Accounting Office (GAO), FEMA spent an average of $30,000 on each 28 foot trailer at a staging site. In contrast, the cost of eight trailers at the Port of Beinville Park in Mississippi, escalated to an unbelievable $229,000, the same amount of money that could purchase a five bedroom, 2000 square-foot home in Jackson, Mississippi. Beside the initial purchase price for the trailers, peripheral expenditures went to items such as these:

1: Trailer purchase = $14,000

2: Maintenance cost = $4,000

3: Haul + Install = $12,000

Total = $30,000

For multiple trailers, their maintenance evolves to what's called "Group Site Maintenance." And for those eight trailers, the cost came to $174,000. I'm not sure how anyone could justify that figure, but I am certain that the prime contractors will find some justified retort to verify where that money actually went. Again, all of this *should* be a very simple procedure: A trailer is hauled to a staging site, it's installed on a pad or piers that elevate it off the ground (which many were not), and you post a few guards at intervals to prevent vandalism or theft. Additionally, and regarding the hauling cost, it doesn't make much sense to purchase a trailer or MH in California and truck it to Mississippi, but some, usually in lesser quantities, were also purchased in much closer geographical areas. As said before, the contractors bought them anywhere they could find them in the quest for that holy grail of government money. Thankfully, Alaska hasn't yet experienced a Katrina.

The town of Hope, Arkansas, was the birthplace of former President Bill Clinton, and was also the home of over 12,000 FEMA trailers that never experienced a warm body. As you may recall when saying I don't believe in coincidences, this is an exception to that rule. Added to those 12,000 trailers, there were approximately 8,300 MH's also stagnating in a 423 acre field adjacent to the local airport.

According to figures compiled as of February of 2007 by various sources, there were approximately 7500 MH's left and 11,800 trailers still in that field. The reduction of those units was due to government auctions that resulted in sales of roughly 40 cents on the dollar, and that comes to about $500 million. Staggering, is it not? Additionally, there were approximately forty-five personnel hired to maintain security and whatever else they did, plus the monthly lease payment of $25,000 that FEMA had paid to house those houses without a permanent home. Add to that the fact of placing those units in a floodplain, and the $5-7 million that FEMA paid to spread gravel in an effort to solidify the soil to prevent the units from sinking, and you get another example of how the contracting business is so attractive to those prime contractors who only see a bottomless coffer in which to dip into.

Yes, those contractors will retort that their profits as both "exaggerated" and "hard-earned," but the figures and information captioned are accurate and a slap in the face to every taxpayer who unknowingly subsidizes the recurring process of FEMA's pandering to these corporations that owe no allegiance to anyone or anything, other than to their bottom-lines of profitability.

We now know who makes what, how they do it, and most importantly, the cold-hard fact that none of us can do anything about it unless monumental changes are enacted in the contracting process. I'm not going to hold my breath for that occurrence, nor should you, but at the least, you will never look at another blue roof in the same way, or the debris blocking the access to your home, and you may even hate those travel trailers more than now should you've lived in one or still are. In that same vein, I also do not think that you'll ever look at a FEMA housing Inspector the same way after reading the next two chapters. Though in similarity to all the prime contractors we've briefly examined, that particular system takes-on a different form, for instead of tarps, trees or trailers, the disposables are human beings.

To put our previous figures into perspective in an overview, let's take CH2M Hill's contract figure for the seven contracts they were awarded for hurricane Katrina, which totaled $338 million. Assuming they'd adhered to the usual corporate goal of attaining at least a one-hundred percent profit, we could break it down to roughly $7 million per week via the time it took to clean-up the disaster. But even if we deducted half of that, it would still culminate in $3.5 million per week in profit. It seems that the more we unravel the former mysteries of gargantuan windfalls enjoyed by these pioneers of disaster, the more we realize the true value of what is actually received by those who pay their tax dollars for disaster services that beg for rebuttal and conscience. But we must remember that corporations have no conscience. In a perfect world, they would be required to offer answers to simple questions pertaining to facts outlined in this book. In our imperfect world, they are unfortunately protected by the very agency that purports to protect American citizens during times of natural disasters.

Truly, the age of apathy has descended upon us in rapid flurries of sucker-punches and jabs to the soul. Should the need for greed persist and prevail, the needs of the few will certainly disallow for the needs of the many. In a later chapter, we'll pose a scenario that takes place in the near-future. It is one of what could befall us all should multiple major disasters strike, but most importantly, it tells what could happen should FEMA not be there to assist.

11

HOUSING INSPECTION PRIME CONTRACTORS

"A CLEVER MAN COMMITS NO MINOR BLUNDERS"

JOHANN WOLFGANG VON GOETHE: 1749-1832. GERMAN POET/NOVELIST

    Parsons Brinckerhoff (commonly called "PB") and Dewberry Davis were the two prime contractors for FEMA's housing inspection services for many years. PB received its first contract in 1995, Dewberry in 2000. PB is still a prime contractor, but not in its previous multinational corporate form. In September of 2009, PB was sold to Balfour-Beatty, the largest construction contractor in the U.K., for $626 million. On October 31 of 2014, Balfour sold PB to WSP Global, a Canadian-based professional services firm, for $1.24 billion. The former giant of worldwide engineering firms is now known as WSP/Parsons Brinkerhoff. While PB was a multi-national — as are some other prime contractors previously discussed, Dewberry was the exception due to its mainly domestic contracts. PB and Dewberry were massive in size with about 20,000 employees, and the contracts both of these engineering giants undertook were immense, varied, and were all mega-profitable, as we'll see.

WSP/PB is still one of the current two housing inspection prime contractors, and it's still hard for me to believe that a foreign corporation has their fingers in the pie. In 2013, Dewberry lost its FEMA contract and was replaced with another multi-corporate entity, operating as "Vanguard Emergency Management." Many of Dewberry's personnel, both inspectors and supervisors, had gravitated to Vanguard in a type of musical chairs. Vanguard EM is a partnership of three corporations, two of them engineering + consulting entities. Atkins group is one of the world's leading design/engineering firms. The Louis Berger Group is a privately owned outfit that provides engineering/emergency management services, both domestically and internationally. The third firm, Tidal Basin, is an emergency management company, specializing in program/construction affairs.

FEMA's rule-of-thumb is to always have two firms as prime contractors for housing inspections so no one firm grows too comfortable within their position. It's a rivalry, of sorts, and there's no love lost. During the yearly refresher classes that inspectors are *supposed* to attend, PB was always referred to as "the other company," and vice-versa for Dewberry Davis. Stupid way for them to act, but maybe it's like the old adage "the only difference between men and boys are the price of their toys." In this particular case, the toys are green pieces of paper with pictures of dead presidents on them.

The former Parsons Brinckerhoff, based in New York, was the oldest engineering company in the country and had many large undertakings under its belt. They built New York's first subway system (the Interborough Rapid-Transit Line), and had partnered with Bechtel on Boston's infamous Big Dig project, whom, as you may remember from a previous chapter, was one of our prime contractors for the FEMA trailers. Mega-corporations usually have other companies, subsidiaries as it may be. For Parson's, one of them was Alltech, which controlled the actual inspection program. For Dewberry Davis, theirs was Partnership for Response and Recovery (PaRR), both of which will be the two principal sub-companies profiled in this chapter. We'll start with PB.

Prime contracting corporations often partner from time-to-time with others of that ilk for joint venture endeavors, much like an exclusive club reserved for the very-very rich. In the past, PB has partnered domestically and internationally with other firms, some of whose names you'll remember from the chapter about trailers. In Iraq, PB joint ventured with CH2M Hill to oversee $1.7 billion in public works and water projects that were *subcontracted* to four other firms, one of which was the Fluor

Corporation. In Singapore, PB also partnered with CH2M for the planning, design, construction and project management, for the $6 billion deep-tunnel sewage collection plant. In Kazakhstan, they'd partnered again in a $2.6 project to develop that country's oilfields. Bechtel is no stranger to PB either. Besides the Big Dig project in Boston, they teamed-up again in 1959 to build the Bay Area Rapid Transit System (BART) in San Francisco within the joint venture, "Parsons Brinckerhoff-Tudor and Bechtel." Though this is just a sampling, one can get a fairly accurate idea of the power and influence PB possessed, though currently diminished by virtue of assimilation to WSP Global.

In addition to that brief litany of corporate friendship, PB had also been the recipient of many FEMA contracts and is still *extremely* politically connected, cementing those relationships through years past via contributions of over $100,000 per year to both Republican and Democrat politicians. Even so, PB has not escaped the wrath of both workers and astute agencies during various undertakings. During the Big Dig in the year 2000, a Federal Highway Administration audit concluded that Parsons/Bechtel and certain state officials misled the Federal Government — which was funding part of the project — when accruing $2.2 billion in cost overruns.

According to state auditor Joseph DeNucci, $19 million of those funds was wasted on useless design work in the Fort Point channel section of the project because the two firms ignored concerns about unusually soft soil conditions in the area. A fraud and corruption investigation was begun jointly by the Federal Department of Transportation, the Federal Highway Commission, the Department of Labor, and the FBI's Public Corruption Unit. Senator John McCain launched his own investigation, blistering PB and Bechtel's representatives during hearings to discover the true reason for cost overruns and shoddy work. It's also noteworthy that directly because of faulty work on the Big Dig's "Ted Williams" tunnel, a thirty-eight year-old woman lost her life when driving through it, struck by a three ton section of fallen roof.

On the other side of the continent, the same type of problems existed for PB and its partners when contracted for the $7 million project to construct Los Angeles' Red Transit Line, a 4.4 mile stretch of subway envisioned to be the centerpiece of hundreds of miles of the city's metro rail system. In the end, lawsuits emanated, citing shoddy workmanship and payoffs pertaining to the sinkholes and cracking along Hollywood Boulevard and other locations. According to a Los Angeles Times newspaper article, an engineer named James Hamilton won a $200,000 settlement in a lawsuit against PB and its partner, Dillingham Engineering, after claiming he was fired for voicing concerns about health and safety violations. In another similar suit, a worker named Nelson McIntire alleged he was fired for exposing the threat of gas explosions and various other safety hazards on the site. In yet another lawsuit, Ben Pate, a former Metro Rail tunnel quality control inspector, was awarded $1.3 million by a Superior Court jury. In that suit, he stated that he was fired for not approving, what he deemed "shoddy and improper workmanship."

During an investigation by the Los Angeles Times in 1994, it was revealed that over the previous decade, members of the Metropolitan Transit Authority of that city accepted more than $500,000 in campaign contributions from subcontractors, loyalists and lawyers and other firms connected to Parsons Brinckerhoff and their joint venture partners. According to the report, Mayor Tom Bradley himself collected $45,000 from the contractors.

Not every project undertaken by PB is fraught with tales of corruption and inadequate workmanship, but it's beyond comprehension to understand the shady dealings and lack of fortitude on the part of this old and respected corporation that somehow found it necessary to resort to incidents such as those captioned. However, the point that needs to be taken into consideration is that even though a firm is large and well-known, the true common denominator for all corporate undertakings is profit. It would seem that the Big Dig, the Red Line project, and the Iraq contracts would be enough to satisfy even the most insatiable corporate giant, but this isn't the behavior of any of them, including PB. Amassing those billions of dollars in profits is the prime directive for these prime contractors. It may seem that the money to be made in the FEMA housing inspection program pales in comparison, but as we'll see when exploring the details of FEMA's home inspection program, those particular profits are nevertheless immense.

As opposed to the no-bid and open-ended contractual goings-on regarding the prime contractors discussed previously, PB's tenure is, and was, dictated by five-year contracts since 1995, but those have been subject to at least one "bridge-contract" that usually lasts for one year. These are issued when a problem arises in the bidding process, or when FEMA simply decides to do so for whatever reason. Five-year contracts are often bid for by much-lesser entities that have a difficult road to travel when trying to unseat PB, currently known as "PB Disaster Services" within WSP Global. An example of this was in 2007 when an engineering firm named "The Michael Baker Group" bid on the new contract.

Amazingly, Baker won it, but was eventually forced out via a protest appeal by PB, and which, as I recall, forced FEMA to institute a bridge-contract until the mess was straightened out. Again, and as said, PB is still *very* well-connected. They've won contracts since 1995, and it goes without saying that they'll win the next contract and those beyond, should FEMA's housing inspection program continue to exist in its current form. One can never tell what the future may hold.

Dewberry Davis of Virginia is also politically well-connected, and is a giant itself within the engineering field. Unlike PB's mammoth projects domestically and overseas, Dewberry's contracts are somewhat smaller and confined to stateside locations. Still, they've also partnered with a name that's familiar to us. In the 1999 Springfield Interchange Road Project in Virginia, they joint ventured with Bechtel, both acting as general managers and providing engineering services under a $676 million total contract. Unlike PB, Dewberry is of a much lower profile. As an example, the Interchange Project was completed on time, and no lawsuits or bad press emanated from it. Additionally, Dewberry has enjoyed other contracts with the Army Corps of Engineers and also with FEMA for its flood insurance program, providing technical services and mapping zones of probable susceptibility to flooding. Obtaining their first five-year FEMA contract for housing inspection services in or around 2001, they were also awarded subsequent contracts.

As an "upstart" in PB's eyes, Dewberry's PaRR superseded them in many areas as the years had gone by, and had attained equal stature, much to the chagrin of PB. For whatever reason during the 2004 Florida hurricanes, PB's inspectors seemed to come under much more scrutiny than PaRRs', and I remember the Sun Sentinel newspaper actually including pictures of PB inspectors and supervisors in one particular article, recognizing some familiar faces that were discovered to have past criminal records. While not being certain of why PaRR received less scrutiny, I'd venture to guess that PB wished an equal share of that publicity to be directed at their rivals. But one thing they'd both shared equally is the enormous profits from managing the home inspection program that differs greatly from the contract formats of most of the other prime contractors previously discussed.

In our effort to ascertain an approximate figure of their profits, we'll focus on PaRRs' 2005 hurricane season, specifically that year's Katrina, Rita and Wilma. Although Wilma produced roughly 418,000 housing inspections in its declared state of Florida, we'll compile our figures from Katrina and Rita so as to keep it simple. We can safely assume that PB's profits are similar, as FEMA usually allocates each firm an equal share of inspections; maybe it's their way of keeping the peace between the two. Each of these contracts includes many performance-based clauses, which is different from the other prime contractors we've previously discussed. For instance, in 2005, Dewberry's contract with FEMA totaled $54,895,019, but as we shall see, that figure alone *cannot* support the number of inspections performed. To avoid any confusion, we'll use the name PB when speaking about either their home inspection services or as a prime contractor in other fields. Dewberry will be PaRR in certain instances. The spelling for PaRR is correct, in case you were wondering about the lower case "a."

In 2005, about 1.8 million housing inspections were performed for Katrina and Rita, by both PB and PaRR. The breakdown is as follows in approximate even numbers:

264,000 for Hurricane Rita in Louisiana

351,000 for Rita in Texas

518,000 for Hurricane Katrina in Mississippi

700,000 for Katrina in Louisiana

95,000 for Katrina in Alabama

Since we know that FEMA tends to share the inspection workload with each prime contractor in fair fashion, the number of inspections completed by PaRR would be around 900,000. As each inspector was paid roughly $40 per inspection (I'm using round numbers) from PaRR (PB's pay was similar), we can safely assume that maybe $360 million was paid to those PaRR inspectors. Obviously, we're short about $306 million when deducting the $54 million from that sum, so where does the rest of that money come from? Since we also know that no one can predict how many hurricanes, tropical storms, floods or earthquakes will transpire in a given period, FEMA places a *dollar* value on each inspection, which was, as said, approximately $150 in 1997, but which was increased to $235 via the next 5-year contract.

Based on that latter per-inspection figure both prime contractors made about $210 million each. These are benign profits, as the initial $54 million generously attends to ancillary operational costs. But as the newest contract has less than two years to go, each inspection is *currently* valued in the vicinity of $500. And now they're making even more, it appears. Nevertheless, we'll concentrate on the past contract value of $235 per inspection, and how it was back then.

Since both firms always paid for the inspector's travel from home to the field and back again, we'd need to subtract airfares and travel costs for inspectors electing to utilize their own vehicles, of which each firm is adamantly cost-conscious of per both options. But even so, and for example, an airline ticket of $500 was basically the value of two inspections, and fifty-cents or so per mile traveled via personal vehicle with a mandated limit of 800 miles is a drop in the bucket. Regardless, that was the *only* expense incurred by PB or PaRR for its deployed inspectors, as most inspectors had to pay for car rental. All inspectors had to personally expend for hotel, food and gas. Management personnel in the field did not have to pay out-of-pocket for these necessities.

PB and PaRR had its own ladder of hierarchy, and this is where that $54 million was geared to support. Both firms employed a field operations manager, supervisors, field trainers who sometimes assume the role of supervisors, office personnel in Winchester and Herndon, Virginia, plus inspection reviewing staff in other locations, such as Denton, Texas.

Unlike the housing inspectors, each of those actual employees received a salary, except for the reviewers who made $12-15 per-hour. Supervisors made roughly $60,000 to $80,000 per year, plus incentives and per diems, which covered the basic costs of food, lodging and travel expenses. Trainers, who conducted the training classes, made approximately that same amount.

Besides an array of about a dozen supervisors, both PB and PaRR had one project manager and field operations manager. For the latter it was Lawrence Altman and Doug Frost, respectively, and for the former it was

Greg Reynolds and Ross Fuhrman. All were veterans of the housing inspection business, Mr. Reynolds was profiled in the Florida Sun Sentinel's 2004 articles as one among many with criminal records, that being a DUI, as I recall. Currently, Mr. Reynolds is the Project Manager for PB Disaster Services. For some unknown reason, PaRR's upper management was not subjected to that embarrassment, whether either sliding-under the radar gun or being clean as a whistle.

The supervisor's rise to their job description can often be traced to an association with the project/field operations manager on a personal level, much like all prime contractors do when aligning themselves with the right people in the right place. In the early 1800's of America's history, it was referred to as "the spoils system," particularly during the Presidency of Andrew Jackson. In this day and age we could refer to it as modern day nepotism. That nepotism usually coincides with the spoils enjoyed by privileged individuals in the right place at the right time, and the greater portion of hidden profits within the incentive-laden contracts between FEMA and PB and Dewberry were solely enjoyed by those at their pinnacles of hierarchy. While most inspectors live frugally, with mortgages and families to support, the higher echelons enjoy all the creature-comforts in communities reserved for the well-to-do.

The entire format of the housing inspection program resembles a type of Ponzi scheme, wherein the ones at the top of the ladder make all the money, while the ones at the bottom scavenge for the scraps allotted to them in apathetic fashion. It's the housing inspectors themselves who are the doormats of FEMA and the project managers and supervisors. Much like the factory worker whose daily output diminishes from day to day due to inhumane expectations from their bosses, so does the inspector experience fear in each disaster deployed to. If the project manager or supervisor likes you, everything will be well. If not, then everything you've sacrificed is for naught. And in the end, those unlucky souls find themselves questioning why they became a housing inspector that FEMA disassociates with in any avenue available, just because they are a subcontractor and not an actual employee of FEMA.

As such, the next chapter not only deals with that disassociation, but also about the actual housing inspectors — the subcontractors who perform the oftentimes daunting task of calculating the damage of your home in a federally declared disaster. They could be your next-door neighbor or an acquaintance. They could be your son or daughter who'd recently attended one of the many "classes" conducted nationwide by both PB and Vanguard, or PaRR in the past, the formers of which still constantly strive to maintain a database of available inspectors. Finally, they could be people much like me, who had performed thousands of home inspections spanning many years within numerous major declared disasters, while working for the mom-and-pops and for PB.

Each of the following chapters pertaining to FEMA's housing inspection program will be concise and detailed as per the format of this book. After reading them, you'll know more about how the system works than most any inspector who may arrive at your door.

www.femasbest.com

12

HOUSING INSPECTORS

"Don't judge each day by the harvest you reap, but by the seeds you plant"

Robert Louis Stevenson: 1850-1894/Scottish author

    Your favorite television program is the Weather Channel. It's watched religiously because this is how you make money. Your favorite websites are the National Hurricane Center (NHC) or The National Oceanographic and Atmospheric Administration (NOAA), because every potential storm has the possibility of increasing your bank account balance in rapid fashion.

For some, watching that television or rabidly perusing those websites, there is no emotion felt for the suffering about to befall nameless and faceless victims of a major hurricane, flood or tornado. For others, there's a tangible sorrow, because now they have to place the value of money earned in this disaster in the background. You remember the tear-stained faces of people sitting in front of what used to be their house during hurricanes Andrew or Katrina, and you still can't forget the families whose houses floated away during the mid-west floods of 1993. You pack your bags and wait for a telephone call that will jettison you to a place that will either serve to drain your emotions or fatten a bank account while not giving a damn about someone else's turmoil and despair.

You've been a FEMA housing inspector for many years, but you wonder if there's still a sane reason to leave your life for months and months when that "Standby" call or email puts your own life on hold. The memories of applicants for disaster relief that never got that relief grates on you like chalk on a blackboard, but you tell yourself that the best job was done and everything humanly possible was afforded to the one's you tried so admirably to assist. For the ones emotionally vacant, none of that matters.

Money: This is why you became a housing inspector, isn't it? Maybe it isn't.

The above descriptions of diverse characterizations amply identify two types of individuals performing housing inspections. Most of you who've experienced the pain and suffering associated with a major disaster and had applied for disaster assistance are familiar with them, and in-between it all are both good experiences and bad. Many newspaper reports, such as those in the Fort Lauderdale Sun-Sentinel during the Florida 2004 hurricane season, have seemingly portrayed virtually *every* housing inspector as a type of ogre to be mistrusted and chastised. But those reports, accurate in certain instances, are generally unfair and misleading.

As the grease that turns the wheel, it's the housing inspector who actually makes the system work or not work, depending on the viewpoint. As a subcontractor to either PB or Vanguard, or PaRR in the past, he or she enters the field with different personalities and reasons. For some, the inherent desire to help others in turmoil is equally paramount to the money made. For others, that money is the object that moves them from disaster to disaster, crisscrossing the country like vagabonds within a corporate system that reflects the mindset of the prime contractors for debris removal, blue roofs and trailers.

Applicants for disaster relief simply make a phone call or go online to start the process that results in a visit by a subcontracted housing inspector to their home, but applicants have no idea how this process actually works. As best possible, I'll try to make that easy to understand in this lengthy chapter in an effort to un-complicate a very complicated system. On this particular section of our journey, changes are the rule of the day, as we shall see

13

HOW ONE BECOMES A HOUSING INSPECTOR

"HAPPINESS CAN ONLY EXIST IN ACCEPTANCE

GEORGE ORWELL (ERIC ARTHUR BLAIR): 1903-1950. ENGLISH NOVELIST

In major newspapers or online sites or in radio spot advertisements placed by PB and Vanguard, they are the primary sources to obtain housing inspectors. Both PB and Vanguard employ a team of "Recruiters," usually comprising three to five people who travel the country in the ongoing effort to procure as many potential inspectors as possible. Usually, the advert's verbiage will heavily refer to FEMA, but in the end---and as we've briefly mentioned and will discover more about that later — the agency instead makes every effort to distance themselves from the very ones who perform these inspections. As well, many new inspectors are also found from word-of-mouth, that being an existing inspector who might pass the word to a friend, relative, or even to a stranger during a casual conversation at a bar or church.

Possessing a ravenous appetite that can be compared to head-hunting firms, the directives of both PB and Vanguard to maintain their database of qualified or semi-qualified inspectors is tantamount to their very existence, for without enough of them problems will certainly occur should an active hurricane season rear its ugly head or a catastrophic earthquake shake everyone's world. Everyone gets an inspector ID number after they attend a class. However, and in retrospect, I've never heard of anyone not getting either a number or a certificate. No one fails in these classes unless their brain activity rivals that of a lobster. Fancy-looking certificates are issued to everyone who's attended these eight-hour classes, propelling one to become an actual housing inspector. Much like currency that's not worth the paper it's printed on, this certificate is equal in value to the ego that oftentimes misuses it for selfish purposes, and of which we'll examine later.

Every year, year-after-year, these classes are held in major cities in order to maintain the database of inspectors to a high numerical level. As an example, Vanguard is currently holding classes in major cities throughout the year, same for PB. Each will have about 35-45 prospective inspectors attending, and this is typical. Typically, about 3,000 new inspectors enter the database yearly for Vanguard, and PB each. Why do they hold so many classes? I'll tell you, and this is from my experiences in hurricane Andrew, Katrina and 1989's Hugo, three of the deadliest and costliest storms to make U.S. landfall.

The work is demanding, but they won't say much about that in these classes. The idea is to paint a rosy picture that you're a type of blue-collar executive making his/her appointed rounds during a disaster. Unfortunately though, all it takes is the first deployment to understand that the work *is* long, hard, and extremely stressful. Not everyone is cut-out for this type of work, and the realities of the job become readily apparent on the first day. It's been said that the ones who survive are true Type-A personalities, and I can attest to that, knowing many interesting characters who've somehow survived longer than I. Though not a Type-A, I sometimes felt very close to joining that club from time-to-time.

    Averaging about five to six hours of sleep per night, and working sixteen-hour-days seven days a week, seeing and hearing nothing but despair and turmoil takes its unforeseen toll on you. Many times I'd forgotten what a normal life was. Day in and day out I existed only to complete my 12-14 inspections, unaware of what else was happening in the world and not really caring. Before that, I didn't have a wrinkle on my face or crows-feet, and all it took was one look in the morning mirror to realize the depth of damage I'd done to both my mind and body. Regardless, and much like some inspectors who I still call friends, money was not the primary motivating factor as was truly assisting those in need. Yes, one should receive compensation for their hard work, but the line between greed and obligation is wide. And this is why the dropout rate is so high, especially after a long deployment.

Both PaRR and PB knew that (and Vanguard currently) an inspector's tenure is usually about 4-6 years and oftentimes less, many of them reaching that "burn-out" plateau and losing the predilection to ever go to another disaster. To the supervisors, it's simply "Use them and lose them." There are some inspectors who actually *live* for disasters, a type of adrenalin junkies. I know a few of them that have been around for many more years than I, and they're still going strong.

Both PaRR and PB were astutely aware of that dropout rate, so is Vanguard, and this is one of the reasons that maintaining the database is tantamount to supplying adequate numbers of inspectors. For instance, should a major hurricane like Katrina make landfall, and a major earthquake strike almost simultaneously, FEMA would require that 8-10,000 inspectors be in the field. In comparison, the 2004 Florida hurricane season saw almost 4000 inspectors in the field, almost evenly split between PARR and PB. Additionally, both companies were astutely aware that not everyone can leave their lives at the drop of a hat to go to a disaster site, so they take that into consideration also.

If we take the numbers of people attending these classes, say from 2001, the databases of PaRR and PB — and now Vanguard for the past four years — it easily exceeds one-hundred-thousand "inspectors" who were issued an ID number. But that number also includes the many who've never been deployed and those who'd tossed their badge and gotten a real job. They'd waited and waited and waited for that phone call, but it usually never came. However, and should the scenario of two catastrophic disasters striking within a close time-frame, that may very-well change, should they receive an unexpected call from PB or Vanguard.

For a moment let's imagine another hurricane equal to Katrina, with new inspectors entering a system that takes many years to become knowledgeable of. Yes, there may be about 400 *seasoned* inspectors deployed — which is roughly the current number between PB and Vanguard, but they alone could never address the amount of applicants requiring expedient and professional assistance. As an example, there were approximately 4,000 inspectors deployed in the 2004 Florida hurricanes and about 3,000 during Katrina, all with varying degrees of experience. But as said, the longevity of inspectors is tenuous at best. And this is part of the problem with housing inspections: There are never enough who know what they're doing as opposed to the greater number who don't, and oftentimes never will. Additionally, there aren't many who even *like* what they're doing, and that's why they don't last long. Let's all hope that another Katrina won't strike. And let us also all hope that, somehow, FEMA produces a tangible and intelligent training program for all inspectors, for it's those inspectors who hold the key to keeping the system functional, or somewhat functional depending on your view.

In those classes attended will be pizza-delivery-boys and girls, retired schoolteachers and everything in-between. Very rarely will there be someone who has any prior experience in construction or related fields, and most of these prospective "inspectors" are both deluded in the belief they could actually perform the tasks necessary that may lie before them, and lack the foresight to understand that they'd be doing a disservice to the applicant who will errantly believe they'll know the difference between a rafter and a joist. In this particular aspect, FEMA, and their prime contractors' inability to supply qualified inspectors is severely lacking. With no end in sight to correct this most important facet in the housing inspection program, any profound change is difficult to prognosticate, given the agency's predilection to not address meaningful changes. To that end, it is *FEMA's* responsibility to demand of the prime contractors that they must supply the numbers of *qualified* inspectors FEMA requires to be deployed to a disaster. It's the old blame-game; FEMA blames it on the contractors and vise-versa. But in the end, the eventual loser is the applicant who had faith that the inspector who arrived at their door knew what the heck he or she was doing.

As we're now familiar about the pressure-packed experience of being deployed, and using my own experience as an example, the fact remains that *every* inspector prior to the year 2013 was a subcontractor to PB or PaRR, and *not* an actual employee of FEMA. As such, an inspector was not entitled to any peripheral perks such as workman's compensation, liability insurance or unemployment benefits. Each was described as an independent contractor, and as definitively outlined in the "task order" required to be signed before being allowed to perform inspections. This task order stipulated that you agreed to be in the field for a minimum of three weeks. If the task order wasn't signed, you didn't work. This included both experienced inspectors and new one's ("newbies," they're referred to as.)

Through efforts via my lawsuit against both PB and Dewberry to attain an employer/employee relationship, PB has agreed to do so. Conversely, inspectors with Vanguard are still classified as independent contractors, but are now reimbursed for hotels, cars rentals, gas, and a daily per diem. Good for that, but more work has to be done to correct that particular erroneous relationship that PB has wisely rectified.

In an example of Vanguard's independent contractor policy, should you be driving your personal car and get involved in an accident, a phone call to your supervisor will, at best, elicit a suggestion to call your insurance company. You'll be told to rent a car, and to return (transmit) the inspections in your computer (pad, we call it) if you're not able to get mobilized in rapid fashion. The reason for that is because every inspection *mus*t be completed within seventy-two hours from the time it enters an inspectors' pad. This facet of the program is a strict part of the overall operation, and is also part of the incentive clause in the contract between FEMA and PB and Vanguard — and PaRR in the past — that was discussed earlier. A sympathetic word may be offered by a field supervisor, but he (and they are virtually all male) will only be concerned about turnaround time, that being the 72-hour time-frame. Yes, this is a business and should is treated as such, but this does not negate the fact that *some* field supervisors are actual human-beings with feelings and are also under their own pressures relating to their particular job. In that regard, compassion oftentimes takes a backseat to their profits and job security.

We know that it's the housing inspector who makes the system function, but FEMA has a very low opinion of them, as said before, Many times have inspectors come into contact with agency personnel, and their comportment towards subcontracted inspectors is both rude and egotistical. Maybe it's because some of them were housing inspectors before the contracts were first issued many years ago and maybe not, but there's no excuse for that type of behavior. As the grease that turns the wheel, one would think that inspectors deserve at least a semblance of respect. The memories of brief interactions with these arrogant FEMA meatheads are hurtful. But they don't care about feelings.

On the badges all inspectors wear, the FEMA seal has sometimes disappeared only to re-appear, a constant reminder to contracted inspectors that they are the lowest echelon in the system. In 1999, that FEMA seal was prominently displayed. In 2004, it wasn't. Called in to the field office after the Sun Sentinel's expose' regarding criminal elements in FEMA's housing inspection program — including inspectors and some supervisors, every inspector was issued a different badge, but with the verbiage "under contract to the Federal Emergency Management Agency" in small red letters at its bottom that begged for reading glasses.

During that years Florida hurricane season, the negative publicity via the Sentinels rigorous and rabid investigation of criminal elements most likely added to FEMA's less than perfect attitude towards inspectors. But as one rotten apple spoils the barrel---or in this case more than one, the agency should remind themselves that without that subcontracted inspector they'd have to do the job themselves. And it seems that they finally understood that. The new badges have FEMA prominently displayed, DHS is also on it, and "Disaster Relief Official" is at the bottom of it in red letters. PB or Vanguard's names are not on it, which adds to its extremely official look. Nice badge. In the inside cover page at the end of this book, I've included a picture of one of my badges, from the good 'ol days, as it may be.

So how does one actually become an "active" inspector? The simple answer is either you are friends or neighbors with a field supervisor, have been one of the few who has excelled in the job and hold promise for the future, or you possess a magnetic personality that is so overwhelming that you're instantly deemed as a "keeper." What both PB and Vanguard (and PaRR in the past) looks for in an inspector to be continually called-out for deployments is the willingness to work long hours without complaint, adherence to the 72 hour turnaround time and maintaining excellent scores. This scoring system revolves around what we call "kick-backs," but is otherwise referred to as "Contractor Corrections" (Ccors) and "FEMA corrections" (Fcors). Additionally, there are "Quality Control (QC) scores that also have a decisive and direct bearing on who gets deployed or not. Simply explained, every completed inspection must be absolutely perfect, or else it will be returned to the inspector for corrections that must be attended to immediately. If not, this will impede consideration for future deployments. Like I'd said, this is a pressure-packed business. There's no room for compassion or excuses.

To further explain, PB and Vanguard, and PaRR in the past, have reviewers who peruse through each inspection. If they find something erroneous they send it back to the inspector, and which goes against that inspector's record as a Ccor. As mentioned, these reviewers are the folks who earn $12 to $15 per hour, and the majority of them lack any experience in the field of construction. Instead, they merely refer to a FEMA manual for guidance pertaining to the inspection protocol. In other words, not only do we have unqualified inspectors, but we also have reviewers who suffer thesame lack of wherewithal wherein they simply refer to a checklist written by FEMA personnel, who for the most part also lack basic knowledge of construction. I'd like to say this is a conundrum, but it begs to be compared to the movie *Dumb and Dumber*.

Once an inspection is sent back to the inspector and corrections are made via the reviewer's instructions, that inspection is then sent-on to NIPSY, where it is then reviewed by FEMA reviewers. And this is where those "desktop" Fcors emanate. It's reasonable to assume that PB and Vanguard reviewers should be held accountable for not catching any mistakes, since they are a virtual "Firewall" to prevent any kickbacks, but amazingly, and when FEMA discovers mistakes, PB or Vanguard reviewers are held blameless and it's the inspector who ultimately takes the heat. The first word that comes to mind regarding this is "unfair," but then again, everything in the FEMA system seems to be rigged. And now we have a much better idea as to why inspectors are constantly in fear, why there are usually never enough of them, and why they burn-out at such a rapid rate.

Many veteran inspectors had realized they were not being called-out as frequently as before. The reason for this can be partly due to the fact that not many major disasters had been declared since 2005, but also that both PaRR and PB — and Vanguard currently — realized that many of them *were* burning-out. To supplement the constant need for fresh meat, new cadres of inspectors were groomed to take their place. Some of these, in turn, have become old-timers. We can call this callous behavior or even economic cannibalism, but the fact remains that this *is* a business. There is no room for a human element.

Each inspector is told to periodically take refresher courses on websites. These online tutorials (OTM's) are designed to keep the inspector abreast of any changes in the guidelines, and it's also a prerequisite for getting deployed. However, this rule was never taken seriously by most inspectors in the past, for it was never a consideration in being called to a major disaster when numbers of inspectors were lean. Even as this book is written, I know three veteran inspectors whom hadn't done these tutorials, yet they had all been deployed to various disasters. Both PB and PaRR often had a difficult time in getting inspectors to agree to deployment for a variety of reasons. Currently, Vanguard is experiencing this same dilemma.

Primarily, the added pressure from FEMA to perform to a superhuman level has left its mark on the already weary minds of those who'd performed admirably for many years. Additionally, FEMA mandated — under a post-Katrina clause in their contracts — that PB and PaRR "flood the field" with inspectors in order to clear-out applicants in more expedient fashion, but which meant that each inspector received much less work. Vanguard is doing the same thing now, and many of their inspectors are extremely unhappy. In the past, some had refused deployment because the pay had not risen with the cost-of-living. Up until 2013 (before PB changed to an employee-employer relationship and Vanguard won the new contract from PaRR), about $150 to $200 a day would be spent on expenses, such as car, gas, food and lodging. As an example, if an inspector received 10-15 inspections per day, those inspections represented roughly half the amount necessary to receive what was called "quick-pay." To get that $1250, equivalent to 25 completed inspections, it took three days or more to qualify for it, thereby leaving the inspector to pay for expenses out-of-pocket for upwards of a week, taking into account the invoicing that had to be approved and the direct deposit bank transfer.

Adding to that scenario, and should an inspector have received too-many kick-backs, he/she might be told to do them over again or be released from the field. In that extreme case, every dime that was spent on expenses became virtually lost money, for rapid reimbursement was not in the vocabulary of FEMA, PB or PaRR and currently Vanguard, If the inspector had survived the onslaught of the first week, he/she would have to wait further to get paid for the inspections completed within a two-week period, and then have to wait for an additional ten days to receive any more money. The inspector was, and is, expected to carry the burden of initial expenses and to not complain. As said before, the ability to financially support oneself for this period is an important criteria to getting deployed, and FEMA and its prime contractors take this into serious consideration when ascertaining who goes to the field or not.

But, as mentioned, the year 2013 brought better news to inspectors. PB deemed all of its inspectors to be actual employees and not contractors. All inspectors are issued a debit card for expenses, which negates the need for significant personal funds. For Vanguard, their inspectors are still subcontractors; they are not issued a debit card, but *are* reimbursed for their expenses. However, the first reimbursement doesn't occur for roughly two weeks. After that, it's about every ten days Both PB and Vanguard pay a GSA per diem, which is anywhere from $50-80 per day. Hotels, rental cars and gasoline are paid for (PB), or reimbursed (Vanguard). Working for the latter firm still entails self-funding, as Vanguard's reimbursement program takes time. For all the work I'd done when starting an inspectors association (PAFI) in 2007, and filing lawsuits against PB and Dewberry with the intent to classify all inspectors as actual employees, I feel happy to have at least been a part of that change. Within that emotion, a subsequent chapter details my efforts, which had a profound effect on my life, albeit both positive and negative.

Starting in 2006, every inspector was required to submit fingerprints to facilitate a full criminal background check, via the FBI. Emanating from the 2004 Florida hurricanes that uncovered many inspectors with criminal pasts, FEMA mandated that this be done. Unfortunately, the background checks were not infallible, and many times the fingerprint samples were not cross-checked with the Automated Fingerprint Identification System (AFIS). In order to accomplish those background checks, PB and PaRR had *contracted* that service to a private firm, and those past results were proven to be both disturbing and questionable.

I actually know inspectors who'd met a representative from these private firms in places such as Starbucks. The representative had a suitcase with fingerprint cards, had the inspector fill out forms, and took their prints over a nice latte. The cost of this was about $50, which the inspectors paid for. In one instance relayed to me, an inspector who'd had charges filed against him for domestic violence in August of 2007 was deployed to the California wildfires in October of that same year. Though this isn't an isolated incident, it nevertheless provides insight into the faulty mechanism in place at that time. Currently, and rightfully so, background checks *are* invasive and thorough, and private firms are not involved in the process. It takes a few to several months to get badged, and no stone is unturned by the Department of Homeland Security. One friend of mine commented that DHS knew more about his deceased father than he did.

We went on a little tangent there, but it's an apropos place to include information for anyone thinking about becoming a housing inspector. Since there will be more about the intricacies of housing inspections in the following chapter, we'll close this one.

And so, should you somehow rise to the middle-to top tier of the call-list, it will be because you've met the criteria described before or are just plain lucky. It takes many years of performing these inspections to get to the stage of really knowing what you're doing. Much like anything else in life, practice makes perfect. But no matter how good an inspector becomes, change is always the order within every single day of that stressful occupation, which we'll now further explore.

14

HOW AN INSPECTION WORKS

"APPEARANCES ARE A GLIMPSE OF THE UNSEEN"

AESCHYLUS: 525-456 BC. GREKK DRAMATIST/POET

Every inspection in the FEMA system is controlled by the Individual and Households Program (IHP), and the information taken during that inspection is stored in the computer we call a "pad." But before that inspection gets issued, a series of events must transpire. When I'd first started performing inspections in 1989, we had no computers. Instead, we used paper forms. It was simple but effective. If the current computer system ceased to function during a disaster, FEMA would *have* to revert to those paper forms.

You, the disaster victim, calls tele-registration (1-800-621-3362) or applies online, and you'll answer all of the cursory questions asked. Sometimes you'll be immediately declined for receiving an inspection for a variety of reasons, such as adequate insurance coverage, duplicate applications from the same address, or insufficient damage as you describe. Should you meet criteria and receive a nine digit application number for an inspection to be issued, the actual process is as such:

1: The inspector comes to your home. His/her pad has an installed program called an "Automated Construction Estimator" (ACE).

2: The completed inspection is communicated electronically by the inspector to either Vanguard's or PB's reviewing headquarters in Winchester/Herndon, Virginia, so those reviewers can check for any deficiencies before sending it to the next step in the process.

3: If the inspection passes the reviewers checking-systems, the inspection is transmitted to the National Processing Service Center (NPSC ("Nipsy" as we call it) via FEMA's National Emergency Information System (NEMIS).

4: NPSC notifies "Other Needs Assistance" (ONA) staff of any peripheral assistance required, such as medical needs, storage expenses or funeral expenses. ONA then reviews the application for any duplication of benefits, which might constitute willful fraud on the part of the applicant. If so, it will be flagged for further review.

5: After the review process by NPSC and ONA, the applicant is notified by USPO mail of the decision to award disaster relief or not. If the application is approved for a grant, no repayment is required, according to FEMA information. If a grant is not awarded, the applicant is sent an application for a Small Business Administration (SBA) loan. Further, the applicant is also notified within that same letter of his/her right to appeal the inspection. Should that applicant decide to proceed with that appeal, it will be inspected again by another inspector, but *never* by the original inspector. Should the same determination result after the appeal inspection, there is no recourse available, and the applicant will receive another letter of denial. It's a done deal at that point.

To explain a bit more about each of the above sections of the inspection process, FEMA *is* on constant guard for instances of fraud. That may seem like a misnomer within all the fraud that *does* go on virtually undetected, but to not at least have some safety measures in place would certainly cause the system to completely buckle-under. In another chapter on our journey, we'll see how easy it is to get government money once it's learned how the system can be "worked," and that many have mastered.

Item # 1 is the most important of the five, as the inspection itself will primarily dictate if you get assistance or not. Even though every inspector is instructed to always tell applicants that "we don't have any part of the decision-making process," that's not entirely true. Should you ever ask that question to an inspector after he/she has completed the estimation of your damages, you can rest assured that, in fact, your inspector *is* the core reason of getting a disaster relief check or not. A good rule of thumb to follow is to make sure your inspector takes at least 25-30 minutes inspecting your home, and 15 minutes and maybe even more than that if your damage is severe. If the inspector rushes in-and-out and appears to only want your signature on the privacy act statement (90-69 it's also called), then *immediately* call the FEMA helpline number and tell them exactly what's transpired. Never-never confront the inspector, as this will only work against you. I recommended calling the helpline immediately because if you wait until you receive a letter of denial, then FEMA will construe your complaint as simply one of "sour-grapes." Remember, FEMA's not entirely brain-dead.

Nine times out of ten you'll be issued another inspection, hopefully with an inspector that *will* take the necessary time to address your needs. Above all, FEMA is extremely sensitive to applicants' complaints, and they are adamant about providing excellent customer service, just like your friendly neighborhood television repair shop or whatever. The last thing that FEMA (supposedly) wants to hear about is an inspector not doing the job, and is only concerned about making as much money possible within a day's work.

In the old days, if anything would cause an inspector to get fired this most certainly would have been the reason. But that was then and this is now. For both PB and Vanguard, their subcontracted "Runners" perform inspections in this exact fashion. We'll be addressing those Runners as we go along in this book, and will be explaining their importance in regard to attaining certain numbers of completed inspections within PB's and Vanguard's contracts with FEMA.

Item #2 is the system employed to check the inspector's report of your damage. Certain criteria are adhered to during this reviewing stage of your application, and reviewers are trained to spot any abnormal line-items that warrant any corrections before sending them to NIPC/FEMA review staff.

PB's and Vanguard's reviewers basically act as a firewall, as they try to detect any anomalies before transmission to FEMA. Typically, a phone call to the inspector from a PB or Vanguard reviewer will attend to any necessary changes, but more detailed mistakes in that inspection or the inspector's inability to timely address the corrections will cause it to be maintained in the system, therefore prolonging the processing of your disaster relief check, should you qualify. This will also result in negatively affecting the inspector's performance score via any kickbacks, but that's not your problem. Every inspector is instructed to *never-never* allow a returned inspection to sit in a pad, as this will also prolong that all-important turnaround time for PB or Vanguard, whichever is the inspector's contractor. Sometimes, albeit rarely, the inspector may have to go back to your house to make those changes, and that certainly may not bode well for your faith that he or she had performed a good job for you to begin with. However, and to be fair, good inspectors are entitled to a few of these in his or hers career, and in relation to the job's frenetically hectic schedule.

Items #3 and 4 are the middle and last stages of either getting a grant or not. The inspection has been approved by PB's or Vanguard's reviewers, and it now has to pass FEMA's. Should the first reviewer have missed something, then FEMA will return it to them, asking for certain corrections. For the inspector, this will mean that an Fcorr will be noted on his performance score and the inspection has to be corrected. For you — the applicant — this will mean more time elapsing for that possible grant, and you probably won't be inviting that inspector to dinner any time soon if you are not awarded funds.

But as much as the inspector may be to blame, we must keep in mind that FEMA's rules for conducting inspections whimsically changes, and that's why every inspector is required to listen to the "broadcast line," wherein messages are sent to him via phone. Oftentimes there are up to a dozen of these messages per day and it's mind-boggling. Continuous failure to check these broadcast messages is another reason for dismissal, as not keeping abreast of changes within the inspection format will *again* affect the turnaround time. However, I've experienced---as most inspectors have also — the instance where you either can't reach the broadcast line because of technical difficulties or a change happens just after last checking the line and only noting the latest ones heard. Some mistakes aren't necessarily the fault of the inspector, but rather by FEMA's predilection to not abide by the adage "If it ain't broke don't fix it."

Item #5 is obviously the most gut-wrenching for those that really need expedient assistance. The previous steps have passed through the system and the final determination will be mailed to you within 7-10 days. Should you be denied, you always have the option of filling-out the SBA form enclosed with your letter and maybe receiving a low interest loan. Should you receive the grant, it's not required to ever be paid back — per FEMA's standard information — and they'll most likely never come back to check that you've actually used that money to make all or any repairs. Conversely, if you have received a denial letter, then the process of appeal is an option to seriously consider because, and as mentioned before, the core ingredient of garnering disaster relief funds is the inspection itself.

No, the inspector *does not* have the consummate power to decide if you get an award or not, but what he puts into the pad has a direct effect on that outcome. Nevertheless, it's very possible that all of your damages were not recorded on the pad, whether by an inexperienced inspector or a veteran's human error, and that alone may warrant an appeal inspection. But one must keep in mind that filing for another inspection will *not* necessarily fatten your award check, and may, in fact, result in the opposite. Many times, applicants have been under the mistaken assumption that getting an additional inspection will result in obtaining more money, and many times has that same applicant regretted that decision when notified by FEMA that some of those funds have to be repaid via that second inspection. Once again, whatever information the inspector records in the pad will essentially dictate whether you receive a check or not. I must clarify that if you do not meet the financial requirements, what's in the pad is a moot point.

We now have a good idea of how an inspection works, but we still don't know about what's in that pad which holds the key to getting assistance or not. Let's now see what's in it, and what's in the mind of the one who controls it.

15

THE INSPECTION/THE INSPECTOR

"WISDOM CONSISTS OF THE ANTICIPATION OF CONSEQUENCES"

NORMAN COUSINS: 1915-1990. AMERICAN EDITOR

When an inspector first arrives at your home, questions will be asked of you in an effort to determine that you actually own the home or are the legal renter. Within this initial, but most important stage in the inspection, an award will hinge on whatever documentation is presented to the inspector. No award will be forthcoming should you admit that the home is not your primary residence (NPR), and when stating that that you *do not* spend any days over six months per year there. Upon that statement and upon your signature on the privacy act statement, it will send that inspector to the next appointment. Sometimes, that admission, per an inspector's question on the telephone, will not require your signature per FEMA guidelines. Some veteran inspectors still forget to ask the applicant that question when calling the night before to setup the inspection appointment. Let's just qualify that mistake as the byproduct of fatigue and stress.

By telling the inspector, on the phone or in person, that the house is not your primary residence, it will negate the need to check your damages, as he/she will note an NPR on the pad and $45-50 was made in a matter of minutes. Even so, the inspector *cannot* designate an NPR *unless* the applicant reveals that information. FEMA will do their due diligence and find that out, sometimes anyway. In a later chapter about fraud, we'll delve deeper into the lies and theft that goes on-and-on-and-on. I must add that when an applicant applies to FEMA, that question is supposed to be asked by whomever they speak with at Tele-registration or answers that particular question on the website's form. But, of course, these are the same folks that will tell you that every inspector is knowledgeable in construction, a blatant lie.

Should you not be an NPR, and once you've proven that the house is legally yours or that you've proven that you are the legal renter/occupant, the inspection can then proceed. Every inspector is different in the way they handle an inspection. I used to address all the exterior damage after obtaining the owner/occupancy documentation, or getting verification of occupancy from a renter. Ideally, FEMA prefers inspectors to ascertain ownership with a copy of their insurance policy, the reason for which is so they can have an avenue for keeping track of duplicate payments should a grant be awarded. Second best is a mortgage payment book. If that fails to be produced, a title will suffice. If that's not available, then a call to the local tax office by the inspector will document ownership. For occupancy verification, whether for an owner or renter, every inspector is required to view a telephone or electric bill in the owner's name with that address, or, ideally, a driver's license with that same information. If an applicant lacks any of those, then virtually any piece of mail with that applicant's name and that address will suffice. Those are called "Merchant Statements."

Amazingly, inspectors had been required, in the past, to assess renters' exterior and interior damages (called "Real Property" or "RP" damages), even though the renter will *never* receive grant money from RP damages, but could receive a grant for "personal property" (PP) damages, such as furniture and appliances. I can't begin to tell you how many applicants have unknowingly expected that they'd receive money for their landlords' house or apartment.

Let's imagine the numbers of renters who'd actually believed they'd receive money while watching the inspector measure walls and ceilings, never knowing they wouldn't get a cent no matter how much damage their rented house or apartment had suffered. Many inspectors had felt very badly about the fact that they were deceiving these folks, but they couldn't say anything about it to the applicant. But now, that particular cat is out of the proverbial bag.

Many an inspection has been performed without noting what's called "Deferred Maintenance," and many a homeowner has been awarded more money than actually deserved, possibly due to the inspection of that pizza-delivery boy/girl or that retired schoolteacher. Simply, deferred maintenance — or "PE" (Pre-Existing) — is anything that happened *prior* to the storm/hurricane/flood that existed *before* you applied for disaster relief.

Years ago, on the Post-Inspection screen on every inspectors pad, was a box with drop-downs, listing items of possible pre-existing damages, such as walls, roof, floors and so on. Some applicants will admit that there was prior damage, and others will not. Nevertheless, an experienced inspector — a veteran with many years in the field, knows how to differentiate prior damage and those caused by the disaster. Alternatively, an inexperienced inspector has been the reason that many applicants have been awarded more money than deserved. And for those applicants, Christmas came early.

As falsely reported in various newspaper articles since the advent of the 2004 Florida hurricanes and Katrina in 2005, an entire bedroom *is not* subject to an entire replacement just because the bed itself was damaged. The same holds true for other furnishings, such as living rooms, wherein a complete set of new furniture will not be supplied by FEMA should just a sofa or chair be affected. No dollar amounts are actually on the pad, but FEMA has a dollar value for each item, from televisions to refrigerators, from children's toys to clothing, and this value also changes from city to city.

For instance, say in Louisiana, a bedroom replace is $2495 and lower for a repair, which could be for a slightly damaged bed, table or chair, or both. A bathroom or kitchen replace could $862, and that's based on such things as towels, toiletries, pots/pans and flatware, and not the RP like sinks and toilets. In California or New York, a bedroom replace could be $4,000 or higher, succinctly because those items are more expensive to replace in a more affluent area.

One of the most expensive items is clothing, and it's the one item that FEMA does *not* want to give you because of the cost, the gray area involved with ascertaining actual loss, and the fact that other relief agencies such as the Red Cross has programs to supply those clothes. Years ago, many inspectors were listing this clothing loss blindly, and FEMA started to clamp-down on this around the year 2005. Each set of clothing, varying somewhat from locale to locale, has a value of roughly $800 to $1,000. If you multiply that by the hundreds-of-thousands who'd received a check for clothing, the total would be astounding.

Many years ago, the standard question we were instructed to ask was "Do you have three changes of clothing?" If the applicant answered no, then you could list clothing replace on the pad. However, multiple sets could also be listed, should the damaged dwelling (DD as we call them) have additional family members in need of clothing. In these days, the question is "Do you have enough cloths to wear?" Simply, if the applicant is wearing clothes at the time of the inspection then he or she doesn't have clothing need. According to a much-debated instance of about ten years ago, PaRR's project manager was quoted as saying on the broadcast line: "Don't give away any clothing unless the applicant comes to the door naked." No, I didn't hear this myself, since I never worked for PaRR, but I knew inspectors that did hear it when checking their broadcast lines.

Now, I'm not suggesting that you try this in order to get that $800 to $1,000, but if you do, remember that a *good* inspector will always look in the closets under the auspices of checking for damage. Besides the clothing, generators are another item that's undergone significant scrutiny, mainly due to the ease of obtaining that $836 during the 2004 Florida hurricane season. Under the new guidelines, FEMA will *not* award any money for generators unless certain parameters are followed. The main criteria is a true medical need, which would include an applicant requiring one to power a device, such as a breathing-machine or to charge a battery for an essential wheelchair. However, an applicant with diabetes who needs a working refrigerator to store his/her insulin may not necessarily be construed to be a worthy recipient of a generator.

To me, it's totally amazing and wrong to deny a diabetic's needs, but when one does the math pertaining to hundreds of thousands of these units multiplied by $836, FEMA's oftentimes reluctance to provide funds for them is, in their minds, warranted. One bad apple spoils the barrel, as it's been said. But ultimately, FEMA's Other Needs Assistance (ONA) personnel ultimately decide that award, when requiring the applicant to supply medical records to substantiate their claim.

The core avenue to get assistance is to *prove* that the generator was actually a disaster-related/medical need, whether when purchasing a new one or an existing unit that was damaged by the storm. How do you do that? Simple: FEMA always abides by something called an "Incident Period," which usually encompasses a time-frame of two to three days before the federal declaration to about thirty days, and sometimes more, into the disaster. Should you provide the generator receipt to the inspector that shows you'd purchased it within that incident period and you are actually using it to supply power for a proven medical need (meaning it's out-of-the-box, hooked-up outside, wherever), then you may qualify for the money. Every inspector is instructed to *not* list the unit on the pad should it still be in its carton or does not appear to have been used. Many inspectors still make that mistake.

We'll be looking into those generators a bit more, but let's continue with the inspection itself. To start with, intricacies of the pad itself will be explored. Although the laptops were replaced a couple of years ago with tablets, they're still called pads. Old habits die hard. For those who've had an inspector at their home before, you'll remember them constantly touching a pen-type device to the pad's screen. Tap-tap-tap at sometimes blinding speed, it gets to be an instant reflex after many inspections per week. From room-to-room that inspector goes, constantly moving his head to observe everything of importance within a particular space. Of course, this would describe a *good* inspector, for it's been commonplace in the past for some of them to never even enter the damaged dwelling. Nice money for them, bad experience for you.

The pad has graduated from the old ACE 1's to ACE 2, to ACE 3 and now to the Ace 4 Tablet. The latter pad was supposedly designed to limit the amount of work for the inspector in an effort to accelerate the actual inspection's time, but in retrospect this effort has failed because performing an inspection is now more cumbersome. In truth, the reason was to slow-down inspectors, forcing them to take more time during an inspection. One step forward and two steps back.

The pads themselves are of a much higher quality and are much lighter and smaller, but many inspectors miss their predecessors that were far-less complicated. As usual, the pad has numerous screens, each for a certain purpose. The registration screen is utilized to take down insurance information, ownership documentation and the like. A screen for "Comments" is also on it, used by inspectors to note anything of importance on its onboard keyboard. Always, they are instructed to never allow the applicant to sneak-a-peek at any screen, for the information may not be agreeable with the applicant. This may include the abbreviated-type verbiage, "gen prch non-ess/gen not used dis nds," which means the generator purchase is non-essential/generator and has not been used for medically-related needs.

Other examples of this verbiage would be dictated by a particular situation, but the comments are always noted in this unique type of shorthand which all inspectors are instructed to use but are never really trained in how to write them. No, they didn't learn this in the "classes," but more often than not are learned via those Corrs, wherein a reviewer will either download the inspection back to the inspector or call him/her to clarify comments made. As of a few months ago, and because many new inspectors do not know how to properly write comments, every inspector, including veterans who *do* know how to write them, must use drop-down (pre-written) comments. In itself, this initially inhibits the performance of veteran inspectors who had previously never used the drop-downs, but after a while it becomes a reflex action. And this is yet another example of inane changes, one step forward and one step back.

An interesting facet of comments is when an inspector feels that an applicant is lying about damages. Any comment such as "applicant is lying" *cannot* be noted in the comment screen, but due to some changes, that are addressed at the end of this chapter, an inspector *may* make a notation, such as "app stmnts nt reflecting viewed dam," which means that an applicant's statements about viewed damages conflict. Succinctly, this alleviates the inspector of a possible Fcorr should that inspection be re-inspected by Quality Control personnel. Additionally, the inspector may be required to "Flag" the inspection, via a button on the top of a screen, thus alerting FEMA to potential fraud.

Inspectors, especially veterans, do not welcome any added responsibilities. For that $35-$45 per inspection earned, many tasks are required to perform an honest and complete assessment of a damaged dwelling. To compound it with the additional task of ascertaining if an applicant is being truthful or not extremely stretches the limit of both an inspectors' knowledge and acumen. I want to stress that there is *no* instruction or training in the classes about detecting applicant fraud, but there should be. Yes, I believe that most applicants are forthright and honest, but there will always be the ones continually beating the system for their own benefit. Unfortunately, this is something that will forever be a part of the FEMA inspection program.

For that $35-$45 per inspection that's paid — or underpaid while under-appreciated, that sum is not adequate for the work undertaken. Further-on in this book is a chapter about two days and nights in the lives of two disparate housing inspectors, one good and one bad, so to speak. Per that chapter, the reader may glean a far-different view of that inspector who calls you at night and arrives at your door the next day. A *good* inspector wears many hats. They have to be personable, caring and efficient, while enduring the stress that requires working long hours and suffering the constant and daily barrage of changes to the inspection program that must be expediently adhered to. Stress emanates from many instances during a work-day.

In an example, an applicant may call FEMA to complain, whether justified or not, about the inspector's rude or uncaring demeanor, or relay that to the QC inspector who follows-up that inspection. There have been times when applicants have complained about an inspector for no valid reason, and times when applicants thought that by complaining they'd get special treatment. Remember, FEMA is *very* concerned about customer satisfaction and deals harshly with those who pose a threat to their reputation. They *do not* care about the welfare of the inspectors who essentially make the entire system work, or oftentimes not work. Instead, they seemingly make every effort to accelerate that inevitable "burn-out" that we'd spoken about before.

During those sixteen-hour days seven days a week, the inspector has to remember that they are *not* investigators, that it's not *their* money to award, and that every effort be taken to comport themselves in a highly professional manner. When asking the applicant questions, a knowledgeable/veteran inspector will usually nod in the affirmative, even while noting in that comment screen that something is not subject to consideration for an award.

So as you're telling your inspector about how you've lost all your clothes, or that you've used that generator that's still in the box, the appropriate notation will be logged in the comment screen. Again, this is not taught in classes, but is learned either by watching experienced inspectors or asking questions. These days, however, veteran inspectors aren't as willing as in the past to offer assistance, mainly because they themselves are bombarded with the job's stress. Yes, even in the inspection business, apathy has unfortunately taken root. And for that, I can totally understand.

That same demeanor may often *seem* to mirror FEMA's comportment, when you, the applicant, tell the inspector about the big-screen television that was soaked by wind-driven rain through a broken window, or when it was inundated by the floodwaters that entered your home. FEMA does not care about what type of TV it is/was, and they don't care how many got damaged. Money for one unit may be awarded, but *only* one, as it is an essential item that the applicant needs in order to stay abreast of pertinent news broadcasts that may affect the safety of the home's occupants. This holds true for a radio as well, among other items deemed by FEMA to be essential. Yes, the inspector may ask you about that television in the bedroom or the family room, but it's only for the purpose of completing the inspection according to FEMA's guidelines. The same holds true for other personal property, such as refrigerators and other kitchen appliances, vacuum cleaners, et cetera. Furnishings are another example of how damaged or destroyed items are compensated by FEMA.

Your "Family Room" may have also suffered the effects of a storm/flood or other type of damage, but FEMA does *not* recognize this area to be essential, so whatever PP has been damaged or destroyed, and even though the inspector is dutifully noting them all down on the pad, no repair or replace funds will be considered within the total scope of the inspection. The same holds true for an office or hallway, as these two areas are also considered non-essential. However, any real property damage *will* be addressed in the review process for all those captioned rooms, as they may affect the habitability of the entire house. Additionally, and although a bathroom is classified as an essential room, most inspectors fail to address the PP in them, such as towels and toiletries and so-forth. Similarly, many inspectors don't ask the applicant if any PP was damaged or destroyed in the kitchen, which is also an essential room. Pots and pans and the like can all be addressed by FEMA, should the inspector have the wherewithal to ask about them. Folks, just make sure your inspector asks.

One particular flaw in the inspection program pertains to furniture that was damaged or destroyed during a flood. As it is, some people can't afford the nice beds that others can, and consequently have to lay mattresses on the floor. Yes, we can understand that, but it would be a miracle for FEMA to also understand. During a flood inspection, certain guidelines exist for determining damage, and the most important is the "Waterline" that all inspectors are required to locate. A waterline is the telltale epitaph of exactly how much flooding there was, and this waterline will dictate to the reviewers — augmented by the required pictures taken by the inspector — if the damage warrants an award. As a prime example of the program's faults, we can take the bedroom, where mattresses (beds) were on the floor.

For example, the inspector notes on the pad that three-inches of water had entered the house, but all the beds have been destroyed and are listed as replace. After uploading the completed inspection to review, it comes-back as a Ccor. Why? Because FEMA will say that with only six- inches of flooding, the beds can't possibly be damaged or destroyed because most beds are elevated by at least six inches. To fix the correction, the inspector has only one alternative to ensure that the applicant has a chance to receive funds for those beds, and that would be to explain the situation in the comment screen with something like: "beds=mattresses on flr/pre dis." This would tell FEMA that it was a pre-disaster condition, but many times this has failed to work, frustrating many good inspectors in their intent to assist a needy applicant. This particular problem has to be corrected in the guidelines, and I think the best course of action to take, should this situation mirror your own, would be to tell FEMA about the mattresses on the floor upon registering for assistance. Hopefully, you can help to change policy by doing that, as well as helping many others. In lieu, there are other ways you can also help.

When the inspector asks how many occupy the house, there's a pertinent reason for this question, and a very important one that FEMA needs an accurate answer to. During the registration process, you're asked to quantify the number of people living in the house, their ages and social security numbers, the latter if available at that time. This is asked not only to find out how many live there, but to also ascertain if any children or infants are residing in the house. In the program, items such as toys, cribs, strollers and the like are listed on a drop-down screen on the pad. No, it's not that FEMA is overly concerned about your children, but it's also a way to track an inspector's diligence.

Many times has an inspector not bothered to view the "Occupancy Screen" on the pad, which would tell him/her that children/infants *are* members of the household. Sometimes, kids are out-and-about for whatever reason, and that invisibility---plus the inspector's failure to either ask the question or fail to look at the occupancy screen — may result in FEMA either not awarding any funds for their damaged items or delaying them until the inspector is notified by reviewers that he'd missed infant items and/or children's toys. Sometimes, those items are out with the kids on a weekend visit with relatives, the stroller's in the car and so-on. Nevertheless, it's up to the inspector to ask the proper questions so that no mistakes are made. Before 2003, children's toys and infant items were not even addressed in the ACE program. My first experience with it was during a deployment in that year, and I remember all of us inspectors being very confused as to the rules regarding them, and those rules seemed to change almost daily.

Another scenario would be that the children weren't listed on the screen, either through an applicant or Tele-registration error when first applying, or the inspector failing to ask that question. And then you may have to appeal the inspection. Another reason for FEMA's question about the number of occupants, lays within yet another common mistake among inspectors. For instance, should the registration screen list two occupants and the inspector doesn't ask how many bedrooms are actually occupied, instead assuming that the husband and wife share one bedroom, which may not be the case, then he'll note on the pad that one bedroom is occupied, thus alerting FEMA that only one bedroom's PP should be addressed. I've encountered this situation many times, and always felt uncomfortable when asking that question. Often, the husband or wife meekly say that two bedrooms are occupied and make an excuse such as she or he snores at night, or whatever quickly comes to mind.

I'd guess that after learning about how the inspection actually works, you may find yourself inspecting the inspector. If but for nothing else, you at least have the knowledge that may prove to your benefit. Good lessons to follow for all applicants. But there's more.....

FEMA doesn't care whether your roof is tile, copper, shingles or rolled roofing or solid gold panels; all they want to know is the *exact* square-footage of damage. An insurance company will usually replace the entire roof, but this isn't so for FEMA. In the pad, this is listed as "Roof Replace," and includes removal of the damaged portion. If an entrance door is damaged, it doesn't matter if you'd paid $500 or $1000 for it, for all they'll allow is maybe $100 to replace it. If swollen from water saturation but it still somewhat closes, the inspector will use the drop-down "Door Trim/Refit." So-on-and-so-forth, FEMA's inspection program is a bare-bones product, utilized to restore the home to *habitable* condition, meaning safe, sanitary and functional. The same bare-bones dictum holds true for debris.

As previously explained, FEMA is just concerned about debris actually blocking your entrance or access to the house, and this would include your driveway. The same holds true for damaged trees that are leaning precariously and pose a threat to either the house or its access. However, a leaning tree that is *touching* the ground is designated as debris removal and no longer considered for tree removal, two other dropdown items on the pad. Yes, I know that won't make sense to the greater portion of you, but again, FEMA's rules are somewhat inane. The rules don't stop there. You should find this very interesting.

FEMA's system for tree removal dictates that a tree that's less than eighteen inches in width (at the widest point) qualifies it as "One Tree Remove," and anything over eighteen inches is a "Two Tree remove." This is why inspectors are instructed to measure each tree. Now *you* know. Time after time I've been asked "Why are you measuring the tree?" In reply, I'd simply say that I'm required to do that and don't know why. Well, back then I couldn't tell the applicant that FEMA pays about $1,000 for each 18 inch or under tree and double to triple that for one above that measurement, but I think I just did now. Also, insurance companies typically do not address tree damage, which is why many homeowners with insurance apply to FEMA for it. Even though an applicant has paid $10,000 to have a tree removed, FEMA will not necessarily match that figure, as they have their own figures that dictate those costs. This situation holds true for homeowners without insurance.

Interestingly, a crew of out-of-state subcontractors, working the South Carolina floods of late last year, (DR # 4277 in 2016) were overheard in a restaurant, saying that their crew of eight had made about $250,000 for about a month's work. Some applicants were getting incredibly high quotes to remove even one tree. One particular elderly applicant was quoted $40,000 to remove one tree that measured thirty inches in diameter, which was leaning on her home. Disasters have a habit of bringing out both the best and worst in people, and this is a perfect example of the latter.

Debris that meets FEMA's criteria *may* also have a bearing on your award, and this sometimes backtracks to our prime contractors such as AshBritt, Shaw, and their multi-layers of subcontractors collecting that debris you'd painstakingly piled in front of your home for removal. But if handicapped or elderly, and you have to hire someone to collect it from your front yard or access, then the rules change. During an inspection, should an inspector not see any debris, they're supposed to ask if you had any debris removed from the house or its access. If you did, then having pictures and/or a receipt that shows that expense may fatten your award. Since you're now aware of the approximate costs for debris removal in a previous chapter, you also have a good idea how much FEMA will pay you for that expenditure. To clarify, FEMA *does not* care about debris in your backyard unless it inhibits your access to a back door. Same rule applies for trees in that location that don't pose a threat to the house.

So the next time an inspector is measuring a tree or trees on your property, ask him/her if it's over or under eighteen inches in width. I'd like to see the look on that inspector's face, but I'm certain that yours will have a wry grin. Most certainly, the inspection process is an all-important stage in determining if you get assistance or not, and there's one segment of it that either seals the deal or not. Some of you may be familiar with it and some not. Either/or, most don't really know how it actually works.

This particular big-ticket item that FEMA very rarely approves for an award is "Clean and Sanitize" (Cln/San we call it), which describes a situation of sewage-tainted standing water or its residue in a room or basement floor that requires attention. The presence of black mold is also criteria for an inspector making this call. The value of this item is $1,500 to $2,000 for an average-size house, and that cost is based on a professional crew coming to a home and treating the floor after cleanup with appropriate chemicals. Years ago this was often given to applicants without much resistance by FEMA, but now it's very rarely approved, even though FEMA currently requires inspectors to include that line item on their pads.

Even though inspectors have to list the square-footage of areas to be cleaned/sanitized, FEMA expects the applicant to attend to the cleanup and sanitation themselves, using common bleach or store-bought solvents. In the past, however, some inspectors had been able to side-step this on some inspections, mostly for elderly or handicapped applicants, by adding in the comments screen, "prof cln/sn nded/elderly app nt abl cln/sn = ess nd," or substituting "handicapped" if applicable. Either way, this tells FEMA that the applicant is unable to perform the task, and consequently has a chance of getting that money included in their award. Inspectors rarely ever know if an applicant is actually successful in getting an award, but the ones who really try to bend the rules for the deserving are content with knowing that at least they'd tried their best.

Out of all the screens on the pad, the most important one is a "Post Inspection" format where the basic question is asked if the applicant feels a need to move or relocate due to storm-related damages. This is a required question to ask an applicant, and it's amazing that some inspectors still don't do this. Specifically, your answer will augment what damages the inspector had logged in the pad, but it will also tell FEMA that you feel unsafe or safe living in the house. Within that, one should be aware that the actual damages *are* the guiding force behind what's selected in the dropdown on the post inspection screen: Home Unsafe yes/no. Now, if your damage is minimal, say less than five square-feet of roof replace, or a sticky entrance door, then your reply of "I feel unsafe living in the house" won't fly with FEMA. But if your damages consist of a sizable portion of roof, broken windows, floors and the like, then that same answer could fly. Automatic calls for home unsafe are those leaning or fallen tress we'd discussed earlier, electrical damage and plumbing, as examples.

If awarded any funds due to a correct and verifiable home unsafe call, you'll get about three months rental assistance, based demographically according to a region's economic indicators. It might be $480 per month in Louisiana or $240 in Puerto Rico, for instance. Many have continued to live in their homes after receiving this money, opting to use it for immediate repairs or basic family sustenance, but I've never heard of FEMA asking for that money back in that instance. Most applicants face the daunting task of surviving the aftermath of a storm, which is often worse than enduring the storm itself and, luckily, FEMA is not usually of the volition to double-check after one gets an award that has passed muster with FEMA reviewers or quality control.

Yes, applicants *are* supposed to use that money for its intended purpose, but in times of disasters the rules have to sometimes be bent or broken. Many applicants go a bit further in their effort to purposely utilize these funds for whatever else they may require, and I've even heard of applicants buying boats or taking vacations. However one may choose to rationalize that comportment, it's fraudulent, but I do understand why some who are awarded a grant might be forced to use that money for *basic* necessities. The worst part of a storm is its aftermath. Unless you've experienced one, there is no way you'd understand.

Another very important screen is the "Unmet Needs/Miscellaneous Purchase," which is also cause for an inspector to be either harshly reprimanded or fired should he/she exhibit a pattern of inattention to it. These important questions, much like the home safe/unsafe, are required to be presented to an applicant. Any medical/dental need or funeral expense as a *direct* result of the disaster must be noted, and even if your false teeth were broken when slipping on your wet floor, it would be considered. Also, any purchases such as generators, chainsaws, wet/dry vacuums and de-humidifiers must be addressed for possible reimbursement. Of course, receipts must be shown, or else it's a moot point. Pictures of receipts must be taken by the inspector with the pad's camera, and his/her inspector's number with the word "Verified" must be written on that receipt. You might be an honest person, but FEMA's rules are stringent and rigid when it comes to disbursing their money. And that is a cruel joke when considering what we've so far learned in portions of this book.

So now we know about the importance of the pad's home unsafe dropdown, the unmet needs and the basic ins-and-outs of an inspection and the inspector. Still, there are a few more things to explore. Then it's on to the next chapter.

Most applicants may think that once an inspector leaves their home and transmits the inspection to the reviewers, via an Internet connection on the pad, that it's a done deal. But some applicants get a second telephone call from a different type of inspector. This is "Quality Control" (QC, we call it). Within the contract between FEMA and PB and Vanguard, and PARR in the past, it's mandated by FEMA that roughly 3% of all inspections are followed-up by these quality control personnel. However, *you* are not mandated to comply. That 3% has apparently increased of late, the result of many new inspectors in the field replacing the one's either burning-out or dropping-out. Regardless, I believe that it's an important segment of the inspection program; if no quality control existed, then the entire system would certainly suffer. Most housing inspectors absolutely hate this part of the process. Part of that may be ego-based, I surmise, for no one likes to be checked-up on and have their work torn apart. But most certainly, some should be checked on more than others. As said before, there are good inspectors and bad.

Around 2008, the QC system changed in its grading for all housing inspectors. Before, it was based on a percentage up to 4.0, but now it's regulated on a one-to one-hundred system. Within this new guideline that Senator Joe Lieberman and GAO were a major part of altering through their efforts of attaining the best job done by over-worked inspectors, the end result is invariable added stress for them. Always, it's the actual housing inspector that takes the heat for FEMA's inability to realize that without them, no applicant for disaster-relief would *ever* get assistance in the present inspection format.

FEMA conveniently relegates rigid quality control dictums in haphazard and inane ways, If they were truly adamant in controlling costs and performance, every prime contractor would be devoid of their fat contracts that only serve to weaken an already economically burdened USA. Meanwhile, the corporate spoils system employed by FEMA, and its converse penchant to maintain the highest level of customer-service, has somehow evolved to a degrading exhibition of mistake after mistake and inability to recognize the true reasons for administering disaster relief.

www.femasbest.com

Once again, it's the subcontracted housing inspector who is held most accountable. Always, the pressure is omnipresent. Maybe that's also the case for the applicant, but to fully understand the process of what it takes to get an award is very difficult to grasp. And that's one of the reasons I've written this book.

When you receive a call from a QC, you have a choice to arrange an appointment or tell him or her that you're not interested. As said before, you are under *no* obligation to meet with that person. But should you decide to see the QC, the downside *may* be that any mistakes the inspector made may result in getting a letter from FEMA saying you owe them funds, maybe because the inspector (new inspectors usually) listed damages that were not present, for instance. Yes, letters of this type from FEMA have actually been sent to applicants, and as we shall see when relating some instances of FEMA wanting money returned.

Always remember that QC inspections are *initially* about the inspector's work and not about your award, should one be received. There is absolutely no upside for you unless you had an inspector who'd obviously not done a thorough job, but there could be that downside mentioned. Either way, it's for the applicant to decide how they prefer to handle it should that QC inspector call you. Also, please keep in mind that the QC inspector may sometimes be accompanied by an actual FEMA QC person, which means that even PB's or Vanguard's, (and PARR's in the past) QC inspectors sometimes get QC'd. Round-and-round we go, folks. Seems there's no end to the multi-tiered layers of redundancy, eh?

In relation to FEMA wanting back funds, many people who'd been awarded grants have received those letters and all are/were absolutely dumbstruck as to what they'd done wrong. Well, they *didn't* do anything wrong, but are simply caught-up in the system that's severely broken in many ways. And this has happened since even the 2004 Florida hurricanes. An award is a "grant." A grant is money that does not have to be paid back, plain and simple. Conversely, any SBA assistance is a loan that *has* to be paid back. So why are some applicants getting letters from FEMA, demanding that some—or all funds be returned to them? The answer isn't as precise as it is coincidental, but I can give you a couple of examples.

An elderly woman, a renter who'd applied for and received an inspection for a declared disaster in 2004, started to get letters from FEMA within a year, stating that she owed $1,122.60. When she was awarded over $5,000, the thought never occurred to her that she might have to pay some of it back. When telephone calls to FEMA produced no recalcitrance on their part, she asked an inspector if they could write a letter to FEMA in an effort to sort it out. After looking through her papers and documentations, letters from FEMA and the Department of the Treasury, (they actually collect the money) The Inspector agreed, extremely upset that something like this could happen to an honest and hard-working individual who'd been renting a home. Whether luck was on his side or not, she never again heard from FEMA or the Treasury. But then, another similar occurrence came to light soon thereafter.

Her niece, another renter, and as well a hard-working mother with two children, came to him after realizing her aunt wasn't being further harassed by FEMA or the Treasury. Same scenario: An almost $6,000 grant awarded and they wanted $1,216.37 back. To top it off, and when initially meeting with her, he asked her about the inspection itself, and if the inspector actually entered the house. She'd answered "no." He also asked her if she had a visit from anyone else from FEMA, and she'd answered "yes." To backtrack a bit, those same questions were asked to her aunt, who'd also said that the inspector had never even entered her home. She never received any more letters from either FEMA or the Treasury Department.

From the above two examples, both the aunt and niece had bad inspectors, both had QC inspections, and both were renters. Now, I'm not saying that FEMA is purposely targeting financially- struggling renters, but the fact is that the greater numbers of applicants *are* renters, and always have been. Another fact is that there are many thousands of cases like this, both in the past and currently, and involved/involves both renters and homeowners. There appears to be no sane reason to award a grant to any honest individual and then ask for all or part of it back. When as a child, this type of behavior was that of an "Indian-giver." As an adult, I'd call it baleful. But we must remember that ever since FEMA fell under the umbrella of The Department of Homeland Security (DHS), budget-cuts for disaster-relief have been the norm, and roughly four out of every five dollars appropriated to the agency is purportedly redirected to anti-terrorism programs. Basically, disaster relief is no longer FEMA's prime directive. In another chapter, we'll explore what that directive might actually be.

In July of 2006, The United States Senate Committee on Governmental Affairs, chaired by Connecticut's Senator Joe Lieberman, made recommendations to FEMA regarding many of this book's previously-captioned sections in the inspection process. Among them was the need to limit excessive awards for furnishings, require that inspectors be trained to report fraud, modify guidelines to establish reasonable values for destroyed vehicles, and to revise criteria for determining that a home is unsafe or uninhabitable.

Those suggestions were just a part of the committees' mandate. In fact, some were actually adhered to by FEMA, such as more intensive background checks for housing inspectors, increasing the number of quality-control inspectors, and reviewing/revising existing guidelines under which clothing awards are made so that those awards are made only for truly eligible applicants. Other and equally important recommendations were not considered by FEMA, and this is certainly apropos for anything in government. In the long run, FEMA's ability to completely purge the system of all fraud and the resulting billions of dollars wasted is a fanciful pipe-dream. Yes, some changes have been enacted to correct some aspects of the disaster assistance program, but those changes are equivalent to simply placing a bandage on the wound. In the end, nothing can completely stanch the flow of blood flowing from it.

A long chapter this has been, and I think it's time to continue to the next. But I'm still going to include a short subchapter specifically pertaining to homeowners who apply for disaster relief and have an insurance policy. Once again, FEMA's comportment has grown harsher since Florida's 2004 hurricane season, and most certainly, since Katrina in 2005.

www.femasbest.com

16

THE PRATFALLS OF HOMEOWNERS INSURANCE

FEMA's rules regarding the issuing of awards to homeowners with insurance differs greatly from those without. The Agency's policy--- an underlying assumption as it may be — is that assistance to businesses and individuals should first emanate from insurance. As outlined in the Stafford Act, I'll quote that segment: *"The President shall assure that no such person, business concern, or other entity will receive such assistance with respect to any part of such loss as to which he has received financial assistance under any other program or from insurance or any other source."*

As stated in a 2006 report by "The Center for Catastrophe Preparedness and Response" and echoed by many others of the opinion that FEMA's regulations pertaining to homeowners insurance is both inane and contrary to its position as the preeminent agency to address disaster relief, I wholeheartedly agree with that opinion. Amazing as it may be, hundreds of thousands of homeowners adversely affected by a disaster are left waiting- and waiting-and-waiting for their insurance adjuster to assess their damage, and often can't even get any substantial relief from FEMA while they endure that interminable period of frustration and turmoil. While they wait, homeowners without insurance are oftentimes immediately afforded assistance. Most certainly, there are solutions to assist homeowners with insurance in appropriate fashion, but that's up to FEMA to consider.

When experiencing these insured homeowners' frustrations while inspecting their homes, I'd always thought that an equitable solution would be to allow funds to be awarded so as to provide the applicants expedient relief, and for FEMA to simply wait for their insurance settlement to be ascertained. From then, FEMA could do the math and either deduct or supplement whatever grant amount they received or to appropriate any tax refunds due them for the duration of the monetary discrepancy. Of course, that's maybe too uncomplicated for them, as it seems they prefer more complicated answers to rudimentary questions. To this day, many applicants still mistakenly believe that FEMA will pay the difference between what their insurance awards and the actual costs for repairs.

Simply put, it is FEMA's stated policy to encourage homeowners to obtain the necessary insurance, but they fail to realize that some policies have been cancelled due to multiple claims---or that some can't afford the premiums. However, some relief can be attained in certain other ways included in the FEMA system. For one, if your policy does not include "additional living expenses" (ALE), then the inspector should note that on the pad, If so, this will alert FEMA to your plight should the home be unsafe/uninhabitable, and you may receive some temporary rental assistance funds. Another avenue is the medical, dental and funeral line-items, and any expenses incurred *after* the storm for storing personal property. Again, should your home insurance or health policy not cover any of these, you *may* gain some relief from showing the inspector those records. Should receipts not be available at the time of your home inspection for anything you wish to claim, then FEMA may accept them either by fax or in person at the Disaster Relief Center (DRF), as long as they are received in a short time-frame from first applying.

Another pratfall of home insurance, and very familiar to many applicants who'd filed a claim for their damaged or destroyed home, is the premeditated compunction for insurance companies that didn't list the true cause of damage (COD). It must be noted that in Louisiana, less than thirty-percent of homeowners carry flood insurance. The primary reason for this is that it's financially prohibitive — Louisiana has a very high unemployment rate — and many homeowners can't even afford to enroll in the National Flood Insurance Program, (NFIP) the cost of which is roughly between $150 and $750 per year. And this is a state where much of it is barely above sea-level.

Concerning the National Flood Insurance Program, it must be noted that through the erstwhile efforts of politicians such as Senators Bob Melendez, Cory Booker, Charles Schumer and Kirsten Gillibrand, FEMA has agreed, as of March in 2015, to re-open approximately 144,000 flood insurance claims emanating from Super-Storm Sandy. This does not exclude the approximate 2,000 claims under litigation. These claimants have stated the belief that they were victims of fraud, by virtue of suspect engineering reports. To that end, these politicians have promised to hold FEMA accountable to its oversight responsibilities. Let us all hope that transpires.

When deployed to Katrina, I well-remember the frustration of some homeowners when told by their insurance company that they were covered for wind-driven rain (WDR) but not for the flooding, which according to the adjustor was the true cause of damage. Recognizing the true COD when learning that the lake water surged to affect the houses across the street but then retreated, I'd ascertained that the initial damage *was* caused by flooding, but that the *major* impact was caused by winds buffeting an already weakened structure.

Thankfully, at least one applicant was able to convince their insurance company — using my inspection as a guideline — that the true COD was caused by wind. However, this probably wasn't the case with most folks living on that particular street abutting the lake. The same could hold true for someone without wind insurance but has flood coverage. Either-or, many insurance companies seem intent on cheating their policy holders. Should the insurance company hold firm in their opinion of a COD, then FEMA may grant an award since certain insurance coverage not exist. But if their income is too high, no award may be available. Instead, an SBA loan would be their only alternative. Remember, the current cap amount under the Stafford Act for a grant is roughly $32,000, but it can be tweaked a bit from time to time.

The preceding factual account is an example of a housing inspector actually doing the job in the best possible fashion. Sure, it would have been easy to simply do the inspection without taking the time to study the situation, but that would have adversely affected the very ones you're trying to help. After all, haven't they been through enough? No, I'm not saying that my concern is not indicative of other inspectors, for it is, but not enough of them seem to really care about the applicant. This results in some of the bad press, and upset applicants who rightfully direct that anger to the ones sent to assist them. In the end, and as said before, some inspectors are totally in it for the money.

Some of the duties of an inspector have been outlined in this chapter, but the job itself entails much more than so-far described. Within newspaper reports during the 2004 Florida hurricane season about the vast sums of money supposedly made by these mostly hard-working folks, the truth is far from that, and as we'll now see.

17

TWO DAYS AND NIGHTS IN THE LIVES OF TWO INSPECTORS

"IF YOU HAVE A JOB WITHOUT AGGRAVATIONS, YOU DON'T HAVE A JOB"

MALCOLM FORBES: 1919-1990, PUBLISHER AND POLITICIAN

There are many people who work long hours within uncountable job-descriptions. The common theme is the fatigue and stress associated with those jobs. One may be working in the factory standing on his/her feet all day or night, a carpenter under deadlines on a building site, or a real estate agent desperately trying to close a deal. For those involved in the FEMA housing inspector services, they experience that fatigue and stress on a non-stop level and with virtually no proper rest. For those sixteen hours every day and seven days a week, every inspector sacrifices their health, and sometimes even their life. A story surfaced in early 2008 about a long-term inspector who died in March of that year because of many deployments to flood disasters, and consequently being exposed to the omnipresent black mold that's the signature of that type of disaster. Certainly, that sad occurrence caused concern for the many of us who've been exposed to it also. In a later chapter, other stories of that ilk will be told.

As mentioned before, many media reports tended to portray the daily work-life of an inspector as one of easy money earned for minimal effort. So far removed from the truth is this opinion that I couldn't begin to gauge the distance between that fallacy and the facts. In truth, it's not only the most grueling job that most have ever undertaken, but it's also the most addictive. When speaking about the Type-A personalities earlier, I was absolutely serious. Adrenaline junkies may be a more apropos description for those particular inspectors. For them, that rush emanates from watching a disaster looming on the horizon when watching the weather channel on TV, or tracking a storm on the websites of NOAA or the NHC, and then to soon be living in a storm's aftermath. But after the first few days of deployment, the reality of that new environment takes its toll on even seasoned inspectors, and any initial excitement fades away with each home inspected, where all you're greeted with is despair and stress.

For practically everyone who works over forty-hours per week, the law stipulates that one must be paid an overtime wage. Everyone except the FEMA housing inspector, that is. As said before, they were, for many years, not employees but rather subcontractors. It was a convenient and profitable arrangement for PB and PaRR together with their parental pariahs Parsons Brinckerhoff and Dewberry-Davis, within a systematic endeavor to promote fear and debilitation to housing inspectors who mostly don't have a clue and which has been purposely instilled, oftentimes not so subtly. Before PB's first contract in 1995, small companies such as Vulcan and Suncoast and Computer Science Corporation were user-friendly ("Mom and Pop" operations FEMA called them privately), treating the inspector with respect and dignity. Each inspection paid $22. There were no computers, no consummate pressure, and the job always got done. Inspections were performed via a simple paper report, a few pages at most. Stress wasn't a factor because no one was forced to that level of emotional debilitation. Back then, there weren't many inspectors as there are now, but a core-group was always at the ready, loyal to their job and the cause that went with it. In the end, Vulcan and the rest were superseded by Dewberry and PB, through both the latter's political connections and their combined inherent corporate mindset.

As of three years ago, in an attempt to attract more inspectors to the field, PB offered debit cards to their cadre of inspectors to offset peripheral expenses such as hotels and car rentals, and even offered per diems, health insurance and 401k'S. Nevertheless, and even within this new employer/employee relationship that was due to my lawsuit against them, current inspectors are nonetheless dissatisfied with the pay and the suspect behavior of the supervisors still ensconced in nepotism that favors certain inspectors.

Most current inspectors with PB or Vanguard make roughly $35 to $45 per inspection. Experienced inspectors only make that higher amount. As an example of the disparity in pay within the industry, an insurance adjuster would be paid between $1500 and $2500 dollars for the same type of inspection, but would also make a percentage of the total amount of the claim. That adjustor could conceivably make upwards of ten thousand dollars for that inspection. Given that those inspections take more time because insurance firms require more customer attention, adjustors routinely perform no more than three inspections per day. Conversely, FEMA expects their inspectors to perform the same duties, but to visit a minimum of eight houses per day.

In a disaster that creates hundreds of thousands of applicants, or even in a disaster of lower magnitude, the rigid mandate remains "to get 'em done." And that means at all costs, even to oneself. Those sixteen hour workdays every week, for every month the specific disaster warrants, results in hectic activity that demands about 70 to 90 inspections to be completed each week by each inspector. Literally, when in the field there's very little time for personal pleasures. Your life is put on hold. Time is measured not by the hours in the day, but by how many inspections have been done.

Usually, it takes a few days to get adjusted to the area you're inspecting, being assigned that turf when getting your first down-load of work on the pad. Sometimes it's ten or twenty applicants, but in a major disaster 40-60 is not uncommon. Upon arriving to the field office that's always in a hotel, the frenetic pace is always apparent and oftentimes unnerving, even for seasoned veterans of the doom-and-gloom that inevitably awaits them after receiving their government-issued computer and attending a briefing that outlines the guidelines for that particular disaster. Confusion, however well-hidden, is etched on the faces of newbies who have no idea what to expect, except what was told them at the class or classes they'd attended. And those classes are a joke. It's unbelievable that PB and Vanguard refer to them as training classes. Try to go to one yourself to see what I mean. Log onto the PB Disaster Services website or the Vanguard EM websites. Enroll in a class. You'll be amazed.

The new inspectors of today are a far cry from the veterans still working the field. Wearing their FEMA badge around their necks as if they've attained a Walter Mitty identity, these newbies mostly have no knowledge of home construction, and many of them exude an air of superiority, maybe because of their nifty FEMA badge. Nevertheless, they resemble deer in headlights, no matter how they try to mask their true emotions. In the old days, veteran inspectors oftentimes greeted each other as if at a school reunion, and ego-based affectations were rare. In many ways, I miss the old days. We were called "Regulars." We were the ones always called to the field. We were like a family.

Yes, there are two distinct types of inspectors: Those who are in it for the money, and those who equalize the dollars with the inherent desire to truly assist others. For the latter, some have stayed in disaster areas after being released from deployment for the sole purpose of helping applicants rebuild their homes or keeping track of their special needs, and without monetary compensation. Guam is a good example, and where some friends of mine were deployed in late 2002 for Super-Typhoon Pongsona (pronounced Pong-son-wa). Two of these individuals, now no longer inspectors, took it upon themselves to make certain that folks with dire needs were taken care of. They knew the system was faulty, even back then.

In Guam, most of the houses were rudimentary in construction, but they were *homes* to the ones that lived in them. Invariably, they were wood-frame, barely so, and sheeted by the rippled galvanized tin that you sometimes see on roofs. The floors are dirt but sometimes not, and a single light bulb may hang from a suspended wire to illuminate the entire living area that would rival that of a closet in a Beverly Hills mansion. In these types of disasters, the reason why one becomes a housing inspector becomes both self-evident and impacting in ways uncountable. For the ones devoid of compassion an compunction to assist those in need, I believe that flipping burgers may be a more equitable solution to their vocational limitations.

And so, in the following chapter, the nights and days will begin for David Morse, the inspector with a big heart and morals embedded in his soul. And for the one with only apathy and greed to propel her on a road of deceit, the nights and days for Lauren Robbin will also begin. The following are fictional examples of how it was in 2004 and how it is now. Interestingly, not much has really changed.

INSPECTOR # 1

EAST COAST FLORIDA, AUGUST 30, 2004

All the tasks are finished at the field office. The next order of business is to locate a motel or hotel in or near your assigned area so you can setup shop and begin work, should time allow. If enough daylight doesn't permit any work to be accomplished, then the prerequisite telephone calls must be made this evening, and you carefully try to gauge the number of applicants to call. Although you've always averaged 14-16 per day, it's always better to do only 8-10 for the first so as to get adjusted with the new guidelines to avoid any kickbacks. After twelve years in the business, starting when you were thirty-years old, you know the gig well.

You've worked for the mom and pops, and then for both PaRR and PB, but this time you're with PaRR. You're thankful for the addition of 'Street and Trips" on the pad that both PB and PaRR have incorporated into them, for in the old days all that was available were zip-code maps from book stores or from local chambers of commerce. Getting that map was the first thing done after getting the first download in the field office, or as you waited in your room where it was located so as to keep fully abreast of everything happening. But for today, your first download is fifty-two applicants and it's time to hit the road. The music is turned up on the rental car's radio. It's a Christian alternative station. It's always good to keep God close at hand.

After over two hours of searching, and after seven motels that were packed with guests or refugees from Hurricane Charley, you finally find one that has an available room. It's not a mainstream place like Red Roof or Holiday Inn, but it has a telephone, a three-foot by two-foot desk and its chair, a television bolted to the wall above a small dresser, and most importantly, a semi-comfortable bed to try and get a reasonable night's sleep on. It has no kitchen, but another motel room with one may hopefully be found in a few days. Living on fast-food has its limits, and restaurants are out of the question since there's no time for that luxury. For now, this is how it has to be. You throw your bag on the bed and start to devour the first of two hamburgers hastily purchased at McDonald's. The pad is set on the desk where the telephone sits idle for now. The television is your only link to the real world. You look at the pad's list of applicants. A couple of tiny drips of ketchup and mustard fleck the screen that will dictate your life for as long as you can survive the mayhem yet to come.

The pressure builds, for you are expected to "get 'em done." The names on the screen are faceless victims that you'll meet in about eleven hours. It's now eight-o' clock, and you're not allowed to call applicants after nine. You feel like a zombie after a five hour flight and three more at the field office, and appear as one while briefly staring into the mirror to the left of the television that's blaring news reports that FEMA has come to town. Pressure: no matter how many times experienced, it's never an art that will be perfected. The chair is pulled-out and the sound of your cracking bones rises above the pulse-tones of the first number dialed.

After spending over an hour on the phone, six appointments are made, the first at seven-thirty in the morning. Two applicants told you they couldn't meet because they had to work, and no matter how you tried to convince them of the importance of getting their inspection done they wouldn't budge from their stance. "It's a federally declared disaster," you'd said. "We're here to help. I'd really appreciate if you can be at home." Your hands are tied because if persisting too much, the risk of them calling FEMA and complaining about you is too great a price to pay. One complaint and you'll either be sent home or be put on alert to tone-down your delivery. It never fails: folks calling FEMA to get an inspection and being told that an inspector will be contacting them within seven to ten days, or maybe before that, does no good. And as you recharge your pad and camera, provided so a few required pictures can be taken of every house inspected, the thought occurs that the old days are gone but not forgotten.

Before, you'd felt like you were actually helping people. Now, you feel more like a vacuum cleaner salesman. Why can't FEMA simply tell them that they *have* to be at their home at the appointed time the inspector asks of them? The answer is simple: "It's the inspector who takes the lumps," you whisper. The days of the moms and pops are remembered, when the job was easy and not stressful. But now, the big corporations have seemingly sunk their teeth into the meat of your mind and body. The job can be best compared to a street-corner prostitute's experience on a night devoid of Johns.

You brush your teeth and pull back the sheets of the bed that sags in all the wrong places. A phone call is made on your cellphone to your wife who's worried about you, but whom also knows that you're a both a veteran inspector and a good man. She sends her love and you go to sleep, wondering what the day will bring, because most every recent deployment has been a disaster within a disaster.

At five-forty-five you're awoken by the cellphone's alarm. At best, seven hours of sound sleep was attained. For all the many disasters you've done, it's always the same at the beginning; that pervasive feeling of trepidation.

A hot shower is taken and you dress. The pad, camera and chargers are packed in a small black over-the-shoulder bag, and you wonder what the day will bring as the door is opened to a new sun rising. The car you're driving is $330 per week, reflecting the inevitable shortage of rentals in major disaster areas that always inflates prices. The motel is fifty-six bucks per night, and you mentally add-up your weekly expenses including gas, food and ancillaries as you driving to applicant number one.

The first inspection takes almost forty minutes to complete for the elderly couple whose six-hundred square-foot home, owned for the last forty years, now looked like part of a war zone. The roof was split in half by a two-foot diameter tree. Three others of similar size were leaning precariously in front of the house, threatening to hit it at any time. You record eight "Tree Removes" in the pad, following the rule of eighteen inches, and feel validated for the three leaners because it would be construed as an impending danger, should that inspection be QC'd. Unfortunately, you couldn't list the uninsured house as "destroyed" because the core of the structure was intact and could be rebuilt. The rule of thumb is "one wall standing = not destroyed." In a way, you think, it might be better for them if their house *was* destroyed because they might get the cap set by the Stafford Act. Nevertheless, they'll most likely get substantial assistance because they're both living on social security checks.

You wish them well as you finish the inspection, and silently hope that the award, that they'll most likely get, will fix the 360 square-feet of roof damage and the interior damage it also caused. The motel down the road will be their home for a while, and you know that the wheels of the FEMA freight train often move slowly and methodically. The next inspection is driven to. You feel the emotional drain rapidly taking root.

By noon, three more inspections were completed. The car is parked under a shade tree near a 7/11, where you bought a sandwich and a Coke that had to be finished in five minutes to make it on time to the next applicant. The broadcast line was called to see if any changes in the inspection guidelines transpired, and so far there were none, itself a rarity. A quick review of the completed inspections is done and uploaded to PB review, keeping in mind about that all-important turnaround time that the supervisors and project manager are always rabid about. The last bite and liquid are finished and it's on to the next applicant. By one o' clock or so, cold-calls to applicants will have to be made to get more inspections done. About six hours of daylight remain to get in some more work. Luckily, the distance between applicants has been less than a half-mile. For that you're thankful.

Every area assigned is different. Sometimes it's inner-city, sometimes the suburbs or a combination of both. Inspecting homes in rural areas is always the toughest assignment; too much driving time and limited amounts of inspections to do because of the great distances between applicants. There were times when less than one-hundred dollars was made daily after expenses — not including income taxes that have to be paid — but the job is the job. Yes, it's important to make money, but there are sometimes more pressing issues. Your cellphone rings and you switch it to speaker while driving. It's one of the applicants who had to work today, telling you her boss gave her some time off and she's home. She asks when you can be there. The appointment is set for two to three o' clock, abiding by the standard guideline of always giving an hour cushion so as to not get anyone upset and risk a complaint. "Get 'em done," you whisper.

The next applicant has similar damages as the others done today: Typical hurricane mayhem of fallen trees, roofs with gaping holes, leaning or fallen trees on the house and its driveway, debris littering maybe a front lawn, and always, people suffering from distress and confusion. The family of six included the wife's elderly mother, who proudly said she was ninety-one in a barely inaudible whisper. Her name is Mildred. She reminds you of your own mom who passed away when about the same age, and every effort is taken to somehow get her medical needs taken care of.

Her wheelchair needs a power supply in order to recharge it, so the generator the husband had bought yesterday morning at the local Home Depot is an essential need. As well, it's a necessity to power the refrigerator that's needed to keep her insulin from spoiling. At least in your opinion it is. You know that the reviewers may kickback the inspection because FEMA is often sticky on the subject of refrigerators being an essential need for medications or the like, but the risk of any kickbacks pales in comparison to the comfort and survival of someone who's probably gone through much more in her life than you ever will. A comment is made in the pad: "gen = ess nd/ref = ess nd/elderly/disabled app insulin dep." You remind yourself that the system isn't infallible, especially in a major disaster when both PaRR and PB reviewers and FEMA's are inundated with inspections and confusion reigns within their own job descriptions. Maybe this will be one of those times when luck will occur. All you can do is hope.

The home is insured, but Robert or Barbara, the husband and wife, weren't able to reach their agent. According to their policy that you've read, they have ALE, so their motel bills won't matter to FEMA. You feel like telling them not to count on an expedient return telephone call from their agent but you don't, and instead hope they don't become victims of insurance companies' predilection to collect policy-holder's payments without offering help promised upon signing on the dotted line. For FEMA, a trailer won't even be offered, and maybe that's a blessing. The thought of this entire family being crowded into one of those deathtraps grates on you as the husband signs the 90-69. You shake his hand and tell him to call you should he need to, but caution him to not say anything to FEMA about that. He asks you why in puzzlement. You reply that you're not allowed to do so.

In agreement by a nod of his head, the family of three adults and three children, ages six to twelve, waves to you with hopeful smiles as you open the door of an over-priced rental car that will have to take you to hundreds more applicants that believe the lies of both FEMA and insurance companies that really don't give a damn. The ignition is turned and Jillian, the eight-year-old with a face of an angel and trust in her eyes, runs to you with a drawing she made while you were doing the inspection. With a smile, the crayon drawing of a house with an angel hovering over it is gently taken from her quivering hand and you pat her on the head, telling her that everything will be ok. You drive away from the house that was once a home and pull the car to the side of the debris-stricken street, staring at what she drew as a tear forms in your eye. You fight the urge to cry because veterans don't do that sort of thing, but you still do when reading what Jillian wrote in her best penmanship available at this most difficult time

"Thank you mister fema man for helping me and my family."

A deep breath is taken. The next inspection is three blocks down. Your cellphone rings and you answer quickly, seeing your wife's name on the LED. She asks if you're ok, and you keep a brave-face while answering in the affirmative with an upbeat voice that sounds somewhat congested. You hope she won't notice, so you cut the call short by telling her that you're a few minutes late for the next inspection. The mantra is to get them done and so you will. But as well, any way you can bend the rules for the deserving ones will be done. For the ones you know are trying to work you, the opposite will transpire.

The house is in fairly good shape as you pull into the driveway virtually devoid of debris on its front lawn and driveway. A stocky man with arms folded is waiting. As the car door is opened, his brusque words offer a glimpse of how difficult and taxing this inspection is going to be: "It's about time you got here," he says. "I got some damage on the roof and inside. Let's get it going, okay?" You extend your hand to him and introduce yourself. He shakes it quickly, says his name is Bill, and wipes his hand on a plaid shirt with slightly more wrinkles than on his face. The time on your cellphone is one-o-six, and you told him last night you'd be here between one and two, but some folks treat you like they own you, thinking they're entitled to abuse both you and the system that pays easy money. A deep breath is taken as you follow him into the house, noticing that a few roof shingles are uplifted and a tree is leaning slightly at the far-corner of the property. "Get 'em done," you murmur.

When sitting down at the kitchen table, he tells you that he's retired and had cancelled his homeowners insurance policy a few months ago, citing the continuing premium escalations and the fact that this area hadn't been hit by a major hurricane in years. "Anyway, *FEMA* owes me for all those years I paid taxes, I figure," he added, anger evident in his voice.

After the registration information is recorded in the pad and he signs the 90-69, the exterior of the house will be inspected, for that's how you've always done it. Some inspectors do the interior first, but it's better to gauge the outside damage to qualify whatever was affected inside. Deferred damage can't be overused — even though you want to — and everything must be done correctly. The pervasive feeling that Bill will try to bully you into getting an award that doesn't merit his apparent minimal damage grows omnipresent while walking with him around the house, and as you measure it with the thirty-five foot tape that's one of the most important accessories in your inspection arsenal. He's asked if there are any medical needs or storage expenses or dental needs or funeral expenses, and Bill gruffly says that his back hurts him and he may have to see a doctor. "Slipped on the damn kitchen floor this morning because of the water from the roof-leak," he complained. You respond with an affirmative nod of the head and a concerned look on your face, but you know he's milking it for all it was worth.

On the notebook tucked underneath your arm, the three square-feet of uplifted shingles are written down, and to be transposed into the pad once inside the house. A lot of mistakes are made by many inspectors who take the pad outside, the sun's glare making it sometimes virtually impossible to correctly record exterior damage. Lessons learned the hard way are the most remembered; Five Ccors on the first day of a deployment two years ago almost ended his career as soon as it started. It was a very hot and sunny day, with a one-hundred-percent chance of a mistake.

At the front of the single-story ranch type house, a picture is taken of it, one of three that are required every inspection. Before 2004, all that was necessary was to record the electric meter number or the gas or water meter if the electric one was unreadable either due to moisture or at a height that required a ladder. And just then, as if Bill was reading your thoughts, he said "You going up on the roof to check out those shingles? I'll get the ladder out of the garage." It's explained to him that any damage is observed from ground-level, and he gives an exasperated look, rolling his eyes to the sky. "Whatever," he says. "Just get it all down. I think I might need a whole new roof." Nodding your head in affirmation, you proceed to the far-end of the property, being careful to comport yourself professionally and patiently. As every day is different, so is every applicant. Good and bad, greedy or not, they all have to be dealt with fairly. For Bill, he will also receive what he deserves.

The twenty-foot or so tree leaning near the house is measured. Twenty inches in diameter: Big enough to cause major damage to the house should it fall that way. As such, that tree will be noted as an impending but not imminent danger. You wonder if he's seen houses like Jillian's family, but you know that he wouldn't care. That's the way it oftentimes is in the aftermath of disasters: people grabbing and grasping for anything they can get. You walk with him back into the house and ask if he's bought a dehumidifier, generator or chainsaw, and he replies that a chainsaw was purchased this morning. You ask to see it, and it's on the garage floor with the carton next to it. You have the distinct impression that he expects to get reimbursed for it and he probably will. However, there will be no award for the tree. Sometimes less is more.

There's a small section of ceiling sheetrock that's stained from the seven uplifted shingles above it, but nothing significant. Bill will probably get a denial letter from FEMA via very minimal property damages, but he might a couple of hundred for the chainsaw, and he'll probably file for an appeal inspection. Hopefully, he won't complain about you, but one never knows in the world of disaster assistance. He signs the 90-69, and a tentative handshake is finalized by an attempt of getting information about the inspection as you both walk outside.

"So what do you think? How much will I get? Lots of damage here."

"I have no idea about money," you reply. "All I do is collect information."

"C'mon—c'mon, you know." Bill is about one-step behind. You can feel the tension in his voice. "You gonna' let Fema know about that kitchen floor and my back?"

"Sure will. And I wish I knew about how much money, but I don't have a clue," you say while opening the car door. "I'm sure you'll get what you deserve."

The car door is shut and the ignition turned. You remember what was noted in the comment screen about Bill's medical malady that doesn't exist: app med nds = non dis related/app states slipped on flr post dis.

From experience, this had to be done to circumvent folks like Bill saying to FEMA that the inspector didn't address his medical claim when no award came for it. Also, simply by using the word "stated," it tells FEMA that his claim may be suspect, and that even if he did slip it was not directly caused by the storm. Amazing it is how some people conveniently forget about the many uses of towels, you think while wryly grinning.

At one-forty-five on the dashboard clock you pull the car over and open the pad, picking-out names from the screen that lists applicants' registration dates. With FEMA, it's the most important guide to use when mapping out a day's work; the oldest ones have to be done first and so-on down the line. You write down five telephone numbers and corresponding names in your notebook, because it's more convenient to do it that way so you don't have to open the pad every time you call. If four are reached then it's ten completed for the day, the field supervisors that are tracking your completed inspection uploads will be happy, and you can maybe get back to the motel by six o' clock. Tomorrow will be better. Always, the first day is the worst.

Amazingly, four out of the five were at home, and appointments are made. These remaining inspections must be performed quickly but efficiently, as you don't want to get back to the motel in the darkness of night, which is always depressing. And then you suddenly remember that an exterior picture of Bill's house was not taken. With exasperation and frustration, a U-turn is executed. Problem is, you don't want to see Bill again, especially under these circumstances, and you certainly don't want embarrass yourself by admitting a mistake was made. Taking a picture of *any* house would be a classic mistake committed by many inspectors new and old. QC is big on those pictures, and an obvious attempt of forgery would be met with a low score and a call from a supervisor. With a deep breath you slowly approach Bill's house that's about twenty-feet off the street. You stop, quickly snap the picture, and step on the gas. To avoid passing the house again, three left turns are taken, bringing you out to the main road and out of sight from Bill's house. A catastrophe averted, you promise to never let that happen again, but know that it may, for no one's perfect, especially in times of disaster.

By five-forty-five, you pull into the motel lot and park in front of room number sixteen: Home away from home and who knows how long for. The ignition is turned off and you reflect on the day. Nine completed inspections. Not great but not bad. The last three were of medium-range damage, the applicants were thankful to see you, and none of them tried to claim anything they shouldn't. All had one or two trees leaning towards their houses, all had purchased chainsaws, and all would hopefully get the tree-award that's always a popular way for inspectors to reward honest applicants.

The car door is opened. Pad and camera and chargers are carried to the room that is unlocked with a free hand. You place them on the desk and turn on the television, wondering what's happened in the world you used to live in. Beneath it, you sit at the desk and recheck the last six inspections, making sure that the day is absolutely free of kickbacks. The growl from your stomach makes you think of a home-cooked meal that's light-years away, but tonight it will be chili and a couple of burgers from the Wendy's down the road, all washed-down with a couple of bottles of water that will stanch the dehydration felt from being in the sun most of the day. The inspections look fine and are communicated as you make the sign of the cross.

The best time to reach applicants is between six and seven, so the trip to get food will have to wait. The day is far from over. A new list will have to be mapped-out for tomorrow's inspections, completed 90-69's have to be logged on the invoice sheet, the broadcast line checked once again, and telephone calls to be made. With a little luck, you can go to bed by ten and get about seven and half hours sleep to make sure tomorrow's work is as good as today's. With ten done, the goal will be for fourteen inspections, starting he first one at seven and ending at six. From now on, eleven hours of inspections seven days a week will hopefully be the norm, a total of fifteen to sixteen hours every day, including all the other required tasks. For a moment, you remember how some inspectors worked beyond daylight hours, performing inspections in the dark with only a flashlight to view damage. You can't recall any of them being released for that, but it's one of the most serious infractions one can commit in the field. Numbers. It's all about numbers.

Before falling asleep, you'll speak with your wife and kids while bracing yourself once again for the onslaught of tomorrow's doom and gloom. You wish the world was a placid place with no hurricanes, floods or earthquakes, but nature provides no relief or respite from them. Only

www.femasbest.com

FEMA can allocate that. Unfortunately, it's never enough for those who truly deserve it, but it's sometimes more than enough for the abusers who don't deserve a dime. And within that thought, the work at hand must continue. You recall seeing another inspector today, as she was gong the opposite way on a secondary road, knowing that because of the familiar PaRR signs on the windows of her car. You wonder if she's a newbie or a veteran, and didn't recognize the brief glimpse of her face. Still, you wonder how her day went and how she's handling the pressure. But for now, your own tasks must be finished. "Get 'em done, David," you mutter.

INSPECTOR # TWO

EAST COAST FLORIDA, AUGUST 30, 2004

At a corner booth in the Holiday Inn's Italian restaurant, you eat bites of Fettuccini Alfredo and take sips of red wine while talking on your cellphone. Your boyfriend still wants to come to visit, but you assure that everything's okay and that the first day of this disaster was excellent. With twenty inspections done by five o' clock and all of tomorrow's appointments made, life couldn't be better. You tell him that at this pace, one-hundred-fifty inspections could be done every week for a total pay of six-grand, which would come to twenty-four thousand every month, but you're hoping to make even more. Of course, you both agree, this dream job wouldn't have happened if your father hadn't been old friends with a veteran PB inspector who'd retired a few years ago.

You laugh and smile at something cute your boyfriend says and the conversation is interrupted by another call, its familiar number displayed telling you that it's important. You say goodbye and tell him you'll call later. You say hello to whoever is calling from the field office. He tells you that you've done a great job and, that you, Lauren Robbins, are the top producer for inspections completed today.

The day that went so well is now getting even better, for he's asking if you're able to take fifty to sixty downloads three times a week because of your work today. In the affirmative, the answer is a resounding "yes" that echoes through the restaurant. You smile a sweet smile to the other patrons, probably wondering if you were just proposed to, and in a way, you were. Much like a marriage made in heaven, the money that will be made from this hurricane will far exceed the last outing a few months ago, your first deployment. He tells you that two-hundred-thousand applicants have applied, and roughly four-thousand per day will be applying in the weeks to come. With that much work available, he adds that the tightest areas will be assigned to you, which includes condos, but mostly apartment buildings like you already have in your pad. You say goodbye and take a generous sip of wine, toasting your father.

With a good meal finished, a one-dollar tip is left for the waiter who'd failed to fill your water glass as quickly as expected, even though you'd told him that you're a FEMA housing inspector. Just like everyone who applies for inspections, no one appreciates all the hard work entailed with performing damage assessments, like when dealing with stressed-out people and having to walk into bug-infested houses. You know that it's their fault to begin with because they'd either depended on their insurance companies or never took the time to board-up windows and doors or to make sure their roof was strong enough because FEMA would be there to bail them out. "Leeches on society," you mutter, and take the elevator to your third-floor room. Although paling in comparison to your bedroom at home, it would have to do. "Guess I'll have to suffer a bit," you say, crinkling your eyes cutely while opening the door.

The big-screen television is tuned to the soap-opera channel, just as you'd left it when going to dinner. Your Gucci purse is gently tossed on the plush double bed and you head to the bathroom to freshen-up, the memory of the many sweaty hands shaken recalled. You still feel their sweat that an entire package of sanitary instant-wipes failed to eradicate, and make a mental note to buy some more first thing in the morning. Your hands are thoroughly washed and dried, and the scent of perfumed soap surrounds you while fluffing the pillows and lying on the bed that feels like a cloud. The remote is turned-up, and in the shadow of another type of mayhem, you reflect on the day that was much better than good. You think about your plan that could only be described as pure genius. It might result in doing at least sixty inspections per day. Money: It's the reason you're here.

The gigantic four-story apartment building you've been working — that should have been demolished years ago — had roughly thirty units on each floor. Minus the twenty knocked-off today, that complex would provide a daily twenty-four-hundred-dollar profit for twenty days or so. In theory, fifty-eight thousand could be made in less than three weeks, and you become a legend. Besides that, the assigner promised you even more of these types of apartment buildings.

From what was experienced today, virtually all of them were mirror-images of one another; the same number of bedrooms, bathrooms and exact floor-plan. But it's not possible to reach the record-books all by yourself, and that's why you'd arranged with the young son of an applicant to knock on doors ahead of you so as to get the applicants ready for the inspection. The forty-dollars agreed upon for the day's work was maybe being too generous, but well-worth it. Besides, his family needs every dollar they can scrounge for after the hurricane broke every window but one in their pigsty, and maybe they were broken before.

Every applicant appeared like they were born homeless. Every apartment stank of either greasy hamburger or body-odor. You wonder how people could live like that, but know that they don't care about anything but a handout from FEMA every time a storm comes to town. As you click the remote to the local news because the soap operas are as boring as every applicant you'd seen today, a promise is made that not one of them will get a dime more than they deserve. No sense wasting money on dirt-bags and freeloaders. And besides, the less you give to them will reflect on your own standing with FEMA. Way too many inspectors give-away the farm, as the supervisors had said at the briefing.

The anchorman on television looks like he's wearing a wig and you laugh at his idiocy. The laughter diminishes to a wicked grin as he interviews victims of the hurricane who complained and cried about losing their homes and jobs. Thankfully, your first deployment taught you valuable lessons about lame excuses for not preparing properly or evacuating to safety.

"So what if you don't have a car," you say, staring at the image of an elderly black woman holding a dirty kid in her arms.

You reflect with pride about studying the OTM's on PB's website, learning everything there was to know about becoming a successful inspector. You silently send kisses to your father for arranging private sessions with his friend, the former veteran inspector, so that you'll be the best. In the right place or the right time, or maybe just because you're a very pretty girl, FEMA's idea of making sure that women are a big part of the inspector program has been both opportune and invigorating, in the financial sense. "Life is great," you say, and smile.

You continue watching the ongoing banter about all the destruction caused by Hurricane Charley with disgust, and harbor no compassion for any of them because it was they who chose to live on food stamps, the WIC program, and anything else that came to them without a price. For you, it hasn't been easy either, even at the young age of twenty-one. There was the accident that wrecked your Porsche — a graduation gift from your dad, the decision to drop-out of college because everything they'd taught had bored you, and the constant battles between both parents during their divorce. "And they think they have problems," you whisper, watching the image of a trailer-trash family whose crap-hole of an excuse for a home got reduced to the rubble it should have been in the first place.

Tomorrow, you'll be harder on the leeches than you were today. No more whining about the television that got wet but still works, no more complaining about beds that got wet because they weren't beds but just mattresses on the floor, and no trying to shake my hand because I'll say I have a cold and don't want to pass-it-on to you, but what I'll really mean is that it'll save me some money from not having to buy more sanitary wipes so I won't get sick and miss work that will wind-up costing me money. "Dirt-bags," you mutter, standing to undress for a good night's sleep.

At the spacious desk in the far corner of the room, just to the left of a large sliding-glass door that offers a view of a city largely without lights, you glance at the stack of triplicate 90-69 forms that will be separated when you feel you're up to it; One copy for you, one for PB, and one for FEMA. Maybe tomorrow or maybe the next, the most important thing is to get a good night sleep so you can unleash the type of justice an inspector should administer to the ones who live off the government.

Another trip to the bathroom satisfies the nagging feeling of germs remaining on your hands. Your sparkling white teeth are brushed to a gloss that rivals a blinding flash, and a black silk negligee is slipped on while you stare into the mirror at a self-made twenty-one year old business woman and sex goddess. The light is switched off. The television is turned off. You try not to think about the disgusting people and the vile apartments you'll be visiting tomorrow, and instead think about all the money you'll make. And while falling asleep, you remember the car that passed you today: A male inspector that had PaRR stickers on his car's windows. You wonder if he's inspecting houses or apartments, and you hope he's a newbie so he doesn't soak-up any of your workload. Of course, if he was with PB, you could arrange to have him transferred, but your connections only go so far. "I hope your car hits a freaking telephone pole," you say.

The last image in your mind, before falling blissfully to sleep, is of you being congratulated for breaking the all-time record for most inspections done in a day. "Get 'em done, Lauren," you say, smiling sweetly.

INSPECTOR # 1

LOUISIANA, AUGUST 28, 2016

DR 4277

When entering the lobby of the Homewood Suites Hotel that offers a free breakfast buffet and affords a peaceful respite from the day's work, you reflect on how much things have changed during the past twelve years. No longer does David Morse have to stay at cockroach motels and live like a refugee. You're being paid an hourly wage of twenty-five dollars per hour, time-and-a-half for overtime, receive workman's compensation and health insurance, your car, gas and hotel are paid for, and you get a daily per diem, which in this location is fifty-one dollars. You've elected to work for PB because of the benefits that Vanguard doesn't offer, but are still unhappy about the meager money made that pales in comparison to the old days. The old days: gone but not forgotten.

In the last seven days you've done fifty inspections and have worked roughly eighty-four hours, taking into account the telephone calls to applicants. Including overtime pay and bonus for performing an average of seven per day, you've made about three-thousand-eighteen dollars. Yes, you think, that might sound like a lot of money to many folks, but taxes will be taken out, and more importantly, what's been taken out of your psyche after so many years of doing this job could never be explained to a casual observer. Ten years ago a normal week's worth of work would be ninety to one-hundred inspections at forty-four dollars per.

Although this job is in your blood, and although you love to help folks in need, the applicants of these days aren't like the ones in the old days. They seem to be greedier. And as you pass the front desk and return a friendly hello the clerk, who maybe recognizes a tired person in need of a good night's sleep, the thought creases your mind that you've finally reached the burn-out plateau. But even though you try to relegate that thought to your fatigue, the fact remains that your days are numbered. You really don't

www.femasbest.com

want to do this anymore.

From time to time you'd thought about switching over to Vanguard where you still maintain many friendships with inspectors from the PaRR days, but you've heard that they aren't much better at providing enough work to make it worthwhile to leave your home and family for extended periods. And besides, they don't offer any insurance, which is important at your age of fifty-four. You recall the inspectors of the past who'd lost their lives or had gotten seriously ill while doing this job, and that thought is what sticks in your mind as you press the elevator button for the second floor, to your home away from home. It's been another hard day, and at the age of sixty-three you know your days are numbered in this business of disaster-relief that you once loved, but has totally morphed to disaster capitalism. And as the elevator doors open to the second floor, it feels like you're about to walk a green mile to your room.

Putting down your pad on the table in the small but efficient kitchen, you're thankful for the positive changes to the program, such as the pad incorporating a camera, a better mapping system, the ease of invoicing your pay on it, and the lightness of the unit as compared to the laptops of before. In some ways, it's gotten easier, but the job has somehow gotten harder. You retain fond memories of the ACE 3 computer program, but this new ACE 4 is slower, which somewhat prevents you from performing your normal fourteen to sixteen inspections per day. But that was pre-designed, according to your information gleaned from rumors that FEMA was resolute in finding a way to prevent mercenary inspectors — the runners — from spending barely ten minutes in a DD for the sole purpose of accumulating profits at the expense of applicants. Yet, there are still some who do upwards of twenty-five inspections per day, making one-thousand dollars daily. And yes, those types were always in the program, but it pisses-you-off that they've never been reprimanded or fired. But you also know the gig: supervisors turning a blind eye for the sake of attaining mandated FEMA production numbers under the contract, and FEMA happy for those numbers any way they can get them. Hypocritical at the least, it just proves how low the program has sunk.

You recall that the FEMA website tells applicants that an inspection will be performed within ten to fifteen minutes, but the supervisors dictate that an inspector should take between thirty and forty minutes to perform that inspection. You close your eyes in frustration, but then manage a slight smile within the knowledge that you've never spent less than thirty minutes at a DD, even when there was no discernable damage. You always did your job, even when you could have made a runner's money.

As you settle into a comfortable chair and turn the forty-inch flat-screen TV on via the remote, hoping that the runners will one day have to pay the ultimate price for their dereliction of duty, CNN is reporting on the destruction of the floods you're now working. Even though the damages you'd so far inspected were minimal, you've been around long enough to know that the media tends to blow-up these disasters for benefit of ratings. And as you look at the pictures of flooded neighborhoods in other areas of the state, you think about the telephone call received this morning between inspections. It was an old inspector-friend from the PaRR days but is now with Vanguard, also here in Louisiana but assigned to different counties.

He'd told you that the female runner who you both refer to as "The BItch" is still racking up numbers after all these years and still getting away with it. You both tried to laugh about it, but the laughter was hollow. Sometimes in life, one has to accept the fact that injustices will prevail. And as you change the channel from the mayhem to a sports channel, you recall her being fired from PB after she'd gotten a DUI when in the field several years ago, being fired from PaRR after a time there, and somehow she'd passed the intense background checks to continue working at Vanguard. You wonder if she's just lucky or if she has some friends in the upper echelons of management, and decide it must be the latter. As well, another runner, this one with PB, is accumulating big daily numbers also, according to your own information. This is the guy who started his career with the mom and pop outfits before PB and PaRR, and who'd actually was working as an illegal alien, being from Canada without any documentation.

You're stomach growls, reminding that you haven't eaten since this morning's breakfast downstairs: cereal, a banana, toast and orange juice. On the way to the bathroom to splash some water on your face, you decide to microwave a couple of the five frozen chicken pies you'd bought at the supermarket after work yesterday. And while looking into the mirror, it seems that you look a bit older than yesterday. You think back to the twenty-four years you've been an inspector, and wonder how you've survived all the turmoil, the stress and the tedium. You've earned well over a million dollars for the eighty or so disasters you've been deployed to, and it comes out to be about fifty-thousand per year after taxes, which isn't much, given the difficulties always encountered with the job.

Luckily though, you've had the extra income from your construction company, specializing in decks and other small jobs, keeping in mind that disasters can happen at any time and finishing a job is the most important thing, in life or in business. You've paid off your home's mortgage, have over fifty-thousand in the bank and in some investments, and have no credit card or other debts. Your wife still teaches at the high school, the kids have all gone to college and have their own careers and you silently thank God for all of those things. The plan is to do this for a couple more years and then hang it up at age fifty-six. Hopefully, that plan will be realized, for with each passing deployment the job gets more stressful.

The pies are put in the microwave, and its clock says it's only five-fifteen. You think back to the days when you'd get back to your cheap motel room at seven-thirty or later, make appointments for the next day, do your paperwork and finally eat at ten o' clock, either a microwave dinner or take-out. And within that thought and a slight smile, you extract a stalk of broccoli you'd also bought, in the spirit of healthy eating. After dinner, phone calls will be made for tomorrow's inspections. You'll try to do twelve, but know that ten is no problem, given that you spend about thirty to forty minutes at each house. You'll hit your first app at seven in the morning, the last at about four-thirty. Unfortunately, you have mostly owners, which always take more time to inspect. You think about the Bitch, and try not to get upset at the thought of her making at least twice the money you make, but feel solace in the knowledge that you're doing the job correctly. It's the only way you know how.

You'll be through making calls by eight o' clock, then watch TV on the bedroom's forty-incher. And as you take the first bite of dinner, you feel like you're walking a very long green mile while wondering if you'll survive any more years of this, even though the perks have made it easier.

"Time will tell, David," you say, and take a deep breath.

INSPECTOR # 2

LOUISIANA, AUGUST 28, 2016

DR 4277

Another successful and profitable day is self-congratulated as you pull up to the four-star Marriot hotel's entrance at five o' clock and stop in front of the valet's kiosk. His name is Paul, a nice-looking twenty-something who's been enamored with you ever since first checking in. And because of that, and because you've been telling him for the past few days how tired you are, he's offered to park your car for you. He opens your door and you slide out with your pad and notebook in hand, giving him a seductive smile while thanking him for his excellent service. But beneath your smile, you chastise him for being such an idiot.

As you enter the lobby and press the button for the second floor, you chuckle when thinking about feigning tiredness when Paul opened your door. In reality, you're as fresh as a daisy, even after doing twenty-six

www.femasbest.com

inspections today in about eight hours; all were renters except for the two owners that had required some drive time. You feel like complaining to the assigner about giving you those two apps that wasted precious time, but deferred not to for now. Besides, you don't want anyone to think you're a bitch. Anyway, tomorrow will be even better. You're just hitting your stride.

As usual, all the apps were the same greedy and needy types, and even though you've been doing this job for over ten years your feelings have not altered towards them. In fact, you hate them even more. You think about the two years of inactivity when fired from PaRR and PB, which had cost you at least a hundred-thousand dollars, and hate the ones who hated you because you're so good at your job. But it's a testament to your fortitude that you'd survived everything they'd thrown at you. In the end, FEMA needs inspectors like you to produce those big numbers. You know that and so do they, but you've promised yourself to curtail your drinking, at least while driving. No need to tempt fate, even with your dad's connections, which somehow didn't fix the problem of those two years' inactivity. You recall how mad he was, but everyone makes mistakes, you'd kept telling him.

He'd never understood your need to be independent, always the type to do things your way. Yes, he might have helped you with his connections, but you're the one doing the work, figuring out how to maximize the profits and doing the job the way it should be done. FEMA doesn't really care about these crybaby apps even though they say they do, so why should you? It's all a scam in the end. You're just playing the game also. No harm in that. What do you care about the idiot inspectors out there doing their measly ten to twelve a day? They are who they are and are where they are because of their sheer stupidity.

And here Lauren Robbins is," you say, shrugging your shoulders, and then opening the door to your plush room.

It's an apartment, actually; a nicely furnished living room with a fifty-inch TV and a large mahogany desk, a full kitchen, a comfy bedroom with another fifty-inch TV. Compared to the old days, you're living in the lap of luxury and making over a thousand dollars a day. Life is good, and will continue to be so, you opine, as you put the pad and notebook on the desk and pick up the menu to see the choices for dinner. The salmon with asparagus and salad looks good, but the filet mignon does also. You decide on the salmon, thinking that it's the healthier choice. At forty-six dollars, not including tax, and you're daily per-diem of fifty-one dollars, even if you go over a bit it doesn't matter. What matters most right now is perusing your applicants on the pad and making a list of the thirty-two leeches on society that you'll be calling for tomorrow's inspections. In a passing thought, it's wondered if you should give the room service waiter a bigger tip than last night. You decide to give him two-dollars, twice as much.

Room service is ordered, and they said dinner will be delivered in about an hour and a half, just enough time to make the calls. You set your pad on its stand, smiling at the ease of it all. Each appointment takes about three minutes, within your short but concise monologue perfected through the years. Besides checking listing them as "Scheduled" on a screen, the names are written on a notebook, numbering each one. You give them your name and tell them that FEMA has you listed for an inspection tomorrow. You never take no for an answer, even when the applicant says they have to work or whatever lame excuse offered. However, and following the rules, if the app can't be there then you tell them anyone in the household over eighteen years old can suffice.

Each renter is told to have their driver's license or utility bill ready to view — or anything with the apps name and address on it. For owners, a driver's license and insurance or tax documents must be readily available. You tell the renters that the inspection will take about ten to fifteen minutes, the owners about twenty to twenty-five. Your credo is to take no prisoners. You are the warden of all these malcontents, who cry when their house gets damaged by a storm and expect the government to help.

"Pitiful," you whisper, walking to the fully appointed kitchen.

A bottle of vodka and a bottle of cranberry juice are taken from the refrigerator. Together with a tray of ice cubes from the freezer, all are set on the counter. A hefty portion of vodka is poured into a glass with some cubes, the juice added to it. Back at the desk, hearty sips are taken in preparation for the task you hate most about this job: getting the idiots to be at the DD to get their inspection. You hate even speaking with them, much less having to see them. Luckily you have a way of never having to shake hands with them, saying you've just gotten over the flu. "Who knows what diseases they have," you reason. "Some of these places aren't even fit for pigs."

Taking a breather after twenty-eight calls including several voice mails left, and while refreshing your drink two times, you smile at the system you've perfected to allow the numbers accumulated daily. Since quality-control re-inspects the first ten inspections for every inspector's hundred, and for each succeeding hundred, the trick is to take reasonable care for those first ten. Though never knowing if a Vanguard QC inspector has a FEMA QC with him, — "That freaking ride-along bastard," you say when thinking about them — caution must be adhered to. But after that first ten, you're free to run wild, knowing that the next ninety inspections won't be re-inspected. And just to be extra cautious, in case someone can't count properly, you sometimes take care for the first twelve of each hundred.

For inspections on owners who are safe from the QC number-zone, sometimes you don't even ask the unmet needs questions or walk all the rooms, but you always list some damages as deferred maintenance not caused by the storm, even if you know that the storm had caused them. DD's are rarely measured, instead just taking a guess that's usually near the actual square-footage anyway. But you do always see an insurance policy if they have one, and a driver's license or utility bill. After all, that's a part of the job. For renters, especially in an apartment block, the same square-footage will be for a one bedroom unit, a two bedroom and so on. And for those renters, even if they have no occupancy verification, you simply get their landlord's telephone number and add that info on the pad.

"Easy-peasy. I'm a genius," you say, and dial another number while looking at the pad's clock. At six-thirty-two, all appointments are made. You'll hit the first one at eight, complete the twenty-eight apartment building apps by two o' clock, maybe a bit earlier. The four pain-in-the-ass owners will take another two hours, including drive time, but you'll be back at the hotel before five o' clock. Should, at some point, you're assigned more owners than renters, the new Rapid Damage Assessment app on the pad makes inspecting an owner almost as easy as a renter. The RDA does all the work, calculating the floors, walls, electrical and doors, and all you have to do is to figure out the furnishing damage. Even for a twenty room house, you can do the inspection in twenty-five minutes. Sure, it would take longer if you went into each room, but no one's the wiser, unless it's the first ten of each one hundred inspections, of course.

"Uhmm, maybe twelve," you say while shutting-down the pad, and then stretching your arms outward. "Not bad for a thirty-three year old bombshell. I bet I could have made even more money if I went into modeling. Oh well."

The thought occurs that since FEMA has dictated that both PB and Vanguard must deploy a certain amount of inspectors to each disaster — "flooding the field" is the term — the days of expecting to be out for months at a time are long gone. New inspectors don't seem to last long these days, and both contractors are continually trying to fill the ranks. And it's because of this that makes it tantamount to complete as many as possible within the first three to four weeks. Even so, at this rate, you'll do at least six-hundred inspections during those weeks for a grand total of about thirty-thousand dollars. Taxes will have to be paid, of course, but luckily for you your brother is a very good accountant.

You know that the apartment blocks won't last forever, but also know that the supervisors and the assigner will most likely give you tight areas for the apps who are owners. They'll give you houses on the same street, others on nearby streets. In those cases, very rarely would you even utilize the mapping system you'd perfected, combining a Google pin locater and GPS. You miss the mapping systems that PaRR had and PB has, and figured that Vanguard is just being cheap for not buying license to a mapping system. But even so, and if the renters get lean, you can easily do twenty five owners in ten hours. "It's such a pain in the ass doing owners," you complain. But then you smile, mentally counting the money you'll be making.

The knock on the door signals that dinner is served. A thick wad of bills is taken from your designer jeans and a couple of singles are peeled-off. And as you open the door with a seductive smile to the nerd who wears a stupid smile, you thank him, take the tray and close the door, and imagine that he'll have a wet dream tonight.

The tray, with its stainless steel dish-cover and top-end silverware wrapped in a large red napkin, condiments placed neatly on a corner, is set on the coffee table.

And as you take the first bite of salmon, you feel like the luckiest girl in the world.

"A princess, actually," you say. That's what your father always calls you.

18

THE SUPERVISORS

"If you can't get the skeleton out of your closet, then teach it to dance."

George Bernard Shaw/American playwrite7/26/1856-11/02/1950

For both PB and Vanguard, a bevy of supervisors are also deployed to a declared disaster, and the usual number is about twelve of them. Virtually all of them were once inspectors, virtually none of them has had any formal managerial experience prior to their ascension to the position, and their job description basically entails keeping track of each inspector's daily output, their Fcors and Ccors. Nepotism still runs rampant within their ranks, oftentimes favoring certain inspectors for myriad reasons, but sometimes simply because they were good friends during their own days in the field. In many ways, the good ol' boy system remains alive and well.

Albeit generally appearing to be friendly and nice individuals, their sole mandate is to preserve their own stream of money from the work of the inspectors they're babysitting. Each supervisor makes the equivalent of twenty daily inspections, which for Vanguard equates to $900 per day. For PB, their supervisors are within the same range of daily pay. Additionally, all supervisors' expenses are paid, and they are usually sequestered on the floors of hotels where access is enabled by a special keycard. Some of these supervisors can trace their beginnings back to PB's first contract, and others go back to the mom and pop days, such as with Vulcan, Charter and Computer Science Corporation (CSC). All of them know the system well, and have the acumen to adapt to the many changes they've experienced through the years. For lack of a better description, they are consummate pros.

But even though it sounds like a cushy job, the stress of it shows on their faces. Many of them look older than they should, just like their former brethren who are still working in the field. Some of them are unhappy with the system and its constant and oftentimes idiotic changes, while others don't care as long as long as they make their money. And at just under thirty-thousand per month, there are those that will agree with that latter mindset. With the added stress of this current contract, up for bid in less than two years, there stands a good chance that Vanguard will not be awarded the next contract, due to its subpar performances in recent disasters.

Conversely, PB, being a FEMA favorite and continuing to be the more professional model, will most likely be one of the two recipients of that next contract. Regardless, one must remember that Vanguard is basically PaRR # 2, and as such, its supervisors have simply moved from one outfit to another. Should Vanguard ultimately lose the next contract, these same supervisors will most like enact a different version of musical chairs, whether to outfits like The Michael Baker Group, Pilot, or several others who have tried to garner the contract in the past. It remains to be seen, however, if FEMA ultimately decides to continue to align itself with contractors. In lieu, I'll be addressing that possibility later in this book.

These supervisors are in the field before inspectors arrive, and are the ones who setup the field offices, always in rapid fashion. Computers must be shipped from the home offices, logistics completed, multiple conference rooms prepared for briefings and other needs. It's an amazing process that through years has been perfected. In that sense, these supervisors are great at their job. However, during the course of a disaster, the human element oftentimes intersects morality. But as said before, there really is no morality in the FEMA program up and down the line. This is merely another aspect of disaster capitalism.

Added to the supervisor's stress is that fact that each prime contractor, under a certain clause of their contract with FEMA, which contains many performance incentives, must complete five-percent of the assigned applications FEMA releases to them within three days. In other words, if fifty-thousand have been released, then twenty-five hundred must be completed within those three days. And this presents another problem: how to get two-hundred-fifty inspectors to complete ten clean inspections a day when most of them are either new or have only been deployed one or two times. For PB, they have about two-hundred-fifty seasoned inspectors and can do that. For Vanguard, the number is less, maybe half of PB's. This contract clause is the core problem preventing Vanguard from usually attaining production goals, and it goes back to the lack of training and the occasional instances of the bad behavior of supervisors to inspectors. Because of that, although not primarily, it augments the decision of many new inspectors to never again be deployed.

As said, these supervisors are invariably former inspectors who'd simply attained their positions by being close with project or field managers who, in many cases, were themselves former inspectors. For Vanguard, that would include men such as Dennis Brown, Jaime Ceron, Dennis Pollack and James Constantello. For PB, that would include Mark Parr, David Kerr, Bob Kamer and Mike Trumbull. Regarding the classes to "train" new inspectors, Jaime Ceron usually conducts them for Vanguard, while Bob Kamer does that for PB.

Vanguard's current field operations manager is John Botero, and Chris Walker is the current project manager. Botero is a former veteran inspector from the days of Hurricane Andrew, and Mr. Walker is a retired Air Force officer, whom I've heard is doing a good job and understands what inspectors endure, even though he was not one himself. During 2016, Vanguard underwent many personnel changes in both field operations management and project management. Kevin Hamby, for instance, was project manager for only a few months, but due to his heavy-handed approach, as I've heard, he didn't last long. Hamby was never an inspector. To clarify, supervisors are subservient to project managers, in the hierarchal sense. Project managers answer only to corporate.

Though not certain if any current supervisor or manager is engaged in blatant favoritism, the fact remains that they are all still allowing the runners to accumulate inspection numbers that would be impossible to attain if they were actually doing the job correctly. This is the preferred way that both PB and Vanguard attempt to meet the performance clause of completing the five-percent within three days. And that is so wrong. If FEMA is aware of this scam, shame on them. If they are not aware, then now they know. We shall see if they act on it.

From a prospective of basic intelligence, Vanguard, for instance, has somehow failed to assemble a suitable cadre of experienced inspectors, even though they offer reimbursements for hotels and rental cars, gasoline expenses and pay a daily per diem. The fact is that new inspectors are constantly being rotated-out, as many of them become quickly disillusioned when unceremoniously thrust into the field after little training. In addition, many experienced inspectors are uncertain of any future decision to be deployed, the reason of which emanates from lack of an adequate volume of daily work. And why is there a lack of work for many of these inspectors? Simple: some supervisors favor certain inspectors for varied reasons, even though they aren't any better at the job than even another veteran.

Another reason is FEMA's bright idea of "flooding the field" with new inspectors. And yet another reason is that virtually all supervisors condone the immoral and unethical practice of allowing the runners to accumulate large numbers of inspections for the sole reason of abiding by the contractual percentage clause with FEMA previously mentioned. One would think that corporate upper-management also knows about this practice, but if not, and should Vanguard lose the upcoming contract, they'll have no one to blame but themselves.

And it's within this particularly twisted segment of the FEMA program, also due for a major overhaul, that we understand the true nature of a supervisor's role. But compared to some supervisors and project managers before them, these guys are angels. A prime example is a former project manager for PB, named Jim Soucy. In my mind, he was the epitome of corruption within the ranks of supervisors and managers, and one who I'd suffered from personally, both before and during hurricane Katrina.

During Katrina, and while working sixteen hours a day seven days a week in Mobile, Alabama, and with a lung infection that was slowly getting better, I became concerned about Mr. Soucy moving me to another area, which would add more stress for me and inhibit my recovery from the infection. While mentioning my concerns to another veteran inspector friend, he told me that if I wanted to stay in one area, guaranteed, I would have to send Soucy, who distributed the work, cash money in an envelope to his home address in Ft. Worth, Texas. The alternative was that if I didn't send the money I'd risk Soucy sending me to other areas and curtail my inspection numbers, my applications of apps, to a minimum. I couldn't believe I was hearing this and had no idea this sort of thing was going on, or could exist. As it were, this was only my third deployment for PB, so I looked at it as an educational experience, albeit a diabolical one.

I sent Soucy the money with my name and inspector number, but less than one week later he called me to say he was moving me out of Mobile, I responded by telling him I had sent the money. "Well, why didn't you say that in the first place," he replied, and laughed heartily, as an old friend would do when sharing a funny story. I'd thought about how much money he was making, and calculated that if he was taking bribes from one-hundred inspectors for even five disasters, than he'd be pocketing about three-hundred grand, tax-free.

In the end, a project manager or a supervisor can make or break an inspector in many ways. If I didn't comply with this payola scam, my career would have been short-lived. I paid. I stayed. In retrospect I wish I hadn't, but I needed the job. This is but one facet of the power they hold. This is only one aspect of the misuse of that power.

During that same disaster, a call from the broadcast line sent shivers up my spine. The female voice issued a directive — obviously coming from upper-management — that little or no assistance should be given to the black population in certain areas of Prichard, Alabama. She outlined the roads encompassing that area. I couldn't believe what I was hearing. To this day, I wish I had taped that broadcast. Later that day, I remembered what a PaRR supervisor had said during a flood disaster in Puerto Rico a few years before Katrina.

"The only thing wrong with Puerto Rico is that there's Puerto Ricans living there," he'd said with a smile.

Several inspectors heard that statement, and a few of them relayed it to me at that time. I have to think that there must be many more instances where a supervisor or project manager had uttered similar disparaging remarks lacking any professionalism or human emotion. Despicable barely describes his statement about Puerto Ricans. I was going to include this inane statement in the chapter titled *Inane Quotes*, but thought it was more apropos here.

While working Prichard, I had wonderful experiences with those good folks, many of whom had lost everything in the hurricane. In lieu, I disobeyed the broadcast directive. Every subsequent inspection I performed was done correctly and honestly, but I must admit there were instances where I was overly generous. Nevertheless, and since FEMA can award money or not at their discretion, many of the folks I inspected were denied anyway. I felt bad but there was nothing I could do except to tell them that they had the right to apply for an appeal inspection, one that I knew in my heart would also be denied. However, and after getting back home after my deployment, I decided to do something. Calls to Senator Ted Kennedy's office resulted in no action taken but was understood, as I'd later found-out that he was gravely ill at that time. Undaunted, I contacted Senator

Harry Reid's office, but they were not interested in the black community of Prichard, Alabama. To this day, I feel bad for those folks. To this day, I still feel the powerlessness I'd felt. And because of those lingering feelings, I decided to embark on a path that would ultimately lead to a class action law suit against both PB and PaRR, and which will be addressed in a following chapter.

In fairness, I must point out that not all supervisors and field and project managers are the devils incarnate. Rather, some of them hope for positive changes within the system, but nevertheless have to protect their own livelihoods. It's my hope that through this book's information, they will become empowered to help enact those changes.

www.femasbest.com

19

SCAMMING THE INSPECTOR?

"There's nothing better than a good, blind referee."

Raymond "Bobby" Louis Heenan/ professional American wrestler, 11/01/1944-

At this juncture we've addressed the daily routine of inspectors, which oftentimes seems to be a vocation filled with frustration for the honest ones and a monetary windfall for the dishonest, specifically the runners spoken of, and like Lauren Robbins in a previous chapter. Other immoral practices also exist, maybe purposely designed to augment gargantuan profits for the corporations acting as prime contractors in FEMA's inspection cadre. For lack of a better word, it equates to cheating inspectors of funds they'd worked for but will never see. Much like the good supervisors who seek a positive change but are afraid to rock the good ship FEMA, which may result in termination of their jobs, many good inspectors are also trapped within the conundrum of living in a world where right and wrong are merely words in a dictionary.

As also said at the beginning of this book, in addition to the lengthy and tireless research I've done on the subject of FEMA, significant information is still currently relayed to me by both veteran and new inspectors. Some of them had previously joined my "Professional Association of FEMA Inspectors" (PAFI), and all of them have been promised anonymity, because if it became known that they were ferreting timely information the end result would be their firing and blacklisting, thus preventing them from pursuing their livelihoods. Following, are some examples of how inspectors are possibly scammed. I say *possibly* because even though my information is deemed accurate, I will nevertheless leave a tiny window of doubt. However, I'm the type of individual who does not believe in coincidences. I want to use the word "probable," but will defer.

For ease of understanding, I will numerically list these possible scams.

1: During the daily routines of inspectors, and even the runners, there is always the incidence of an inspector failing to make contact with an applicant even though due diligence is taken to do just that. Yes, the runners will fudge those attempts, but for this instance we'll concentrate on the inspectors who do the job correctly.

When an inspector cannot initialize voice contact with an applicant, that inspector is required to visit the applicant's house (the DD) and post a notice on it, and should the applicant not answer a knock on the door or a buzzer. Thereafter, that inspector is additionally required to call that applicant three times per day, at different intervals, such as eight o" clock in the morning, two o' clock in the afternoon and seven o' clock in the evening. After three successive days of trying to reach that applicant, and should they not respond to the notice posted on the DD or the telephone calls, then that inspector is required to upload that application to Vanguard or PB review personnel as a "No Contact" (NC's). The exact times of the inspector's telephone calls for those three days must be listed and, if not, review will send it back as a correction to be further addressed. This process expended by the inspector takes roughly 40-50 minutes total, figuring in the time it took to drive to the DD, the time to post, the time to make those three calls a day for three days. Essentially, that time is *worth* the time it would take to perform an actual inspection, which is approximately forty-five dollars.

But as recently reported, not many inspectors have been paid for their NC's. Per memory from my own deployments, and even in the memories of inspectors working past disasters, not getting paid for at least some NC's is beyond comprehension. Usually, in the past, we were paid for about sixty-to seventy-percent of them, but now it appears that something else may be preventing those payments which, apparently, could be added to the corporate bottom line.

Should one do the math, two-hundred inspectors with five NC's each on a particular disaster deployment (which is the normal amount) would total five-hundred NC's. At roughly $500 per inspection — the amount paid by FEMA to PB and Vanguard under the current contract — that results in a one-million dollar profit for PB and Vanguard. Multiply that figure twice, and it becomes two million. Multiply that by ten disasters and that figure blooms like a summer daisy. But how long has this been going on? Although not certain, it seems like a few years at the least. Basically, we may have a scam that affords both PB and Vanguard added profits to their already inflated contract. And if so, both PB and Vanguard will hopefully be held accountable.

2: This is a twofold possible scam. As such, I've combined them for ease of understanding.

For as long as I can remember, every inspector had ten-percent of their total pay held back for a period of forty-five days, and this still holds true. Ostensibly, this hold-back was to ensure that any Fcors committed by the inspector, and not sent back to him/her before leaving the field, would be deducted at the per-inspection rate. But the truth is that, unless in very unusual circumstances, those Fcors *are* sent to the inspector within a few days. In the circumstance where an inspector has left the field and an Fcor *is* late to be reported, then another inspector will re-inspect the DD — and *he* will get paid for it. This is usually called a "Desktop" Fcor, which can be issued months later after leaving the field, and since certain FEMA personnel are tasked with reviewing virtually any inspection that presents any potential red flags. Nevertheless, before an inspector leaves the field, his/her computer is checked by office staff to see if any Ccors or Fcors are present on the pad, and that inspector then has the opportunity to fix it on the pad without having to visit the DD again. It sounds like all bases are covered, but the excuse to hold back pay doesn't appear to hold water.

If one does the math, two hundred inspectors doing one-hundred inspections each and making $45 per, each inspector would have $450 withheld. But Vanguard or PB, in that scenario, would be holding $90,000 for one-and-a half months — and making interest on that money. Saying that doesn't sound fair is only revealing the tip of the iceberg. So, if we double that number of inspectors, and maybe double the number of inspections each completed, then we have an amount that gets close to a half-million dollars. And when we multiply that by, say, five disasters, another windfall for Vanguard and PB is revealed. In that scenario, they get more than two-million.

Fcors — FEMA corrections — are issued by both PB and Vanguard QC inspectors and contracted QC inspectors (in-house inspectors). The former is usually also field inspectors when not doing QC work, but the latter is not affiliated with either PB or Vanguard, except for their QC work. For lack of a kinder word they are mercenaries, because they *want* to issue Fcors and because that validates their job description. If they don't issue a large number of Fcors, then they aren't doing their job. The firm they work for is "Institute for Building Technologies and Safety" (ITBS) and is based in Ashburn, Virginia. Conversely, the in-house QC inspectors are, albeit rarely, lenient in their reports, but only if they don't have a FEMA "Ride-along" with them when doing these re-inspections, as that FEMA person will be stringent and totally without mercy.

Fcors were always issued in the past, but they're apparently now being given out like penny candy, thus inhibiting FEMA's own purpose, which is to expediently and effectively close-out a disaster. For instance, if an Fcor is issued at a late date, then that applicant can't get the help he/she applied for until it's fixed. And in the case of a "desktop" Fcor that's issued months later, then that applicant who's already received assistance might have to pay back money to FEMA. I have seen this happen many times, and it's criminal to blame an applicant for FEMA's inability to run their program efficiently.

www.femasbest.com

It's been apparent for the last few years that FEMA has increased their focus on issuing Fcors, and it seems that they are purposely setting-up PB and Vanguard for ultimate failure. As recently as three years ago, before the latest contract, Fcors were not being issued in the high numbers they are now. The average inspector currently performing two-hundred inspections is being issued an average of five-to-ten Fcorrs, oftentimes more, especially for newbies. When an Fcorr is issued to an inspector, it generally means that the inspector made a mistake in his inspection that exceeded FEMA's $500 limit. As an example, this can happen if an inspector fails to address a bathroom vanity that needs replacing, the sheetrock behind it, the floors it sat on, or In another scenario, if the inspector failed to ask the applicant the all-important unmet needs questions, such as medical or dental needs caused by the storm or funeral expenses or storage needs. In either case, an Fcor will be issued, even if everything else in the inspection itself is correct.

When saying that FEMA may be setting-up PB and Vanguard for failure, I mean that FEMA has been seeking an alternative to the present system for inspections, and has been studying more efficient ways to do so for many years. At the end of this book, I will expand on that. But for now, the fact remains that most every inspector has no idea that the ten-percent scam or the Fcor scam is going on, or has gone on. With this information, it's hoped that some questions will be asked and palatable answers will be forthcoming. However, I'm not holding my breath.

3: This is a multi-faceted one, but should be included as it's been reported in several instances. We know about the competition between the prime contractors of the housing inspection services, and that to keep their cadre of inspectors intact requires that they all make decent money for their hard work. But this is usually an impossibility to attain, and many inspectors gravitate from one outfit to the other in the search for a bigger paycheck. Though not as often as years ago, there are inspectors who still do this switching within this particular version of musical chairs, and per my reports, it seems that PB inspectors are the ones mostly switching. Their main complaint is that PB is holding back work once that inspector approaches the number of weekly inspections that will result in a bonus, or extra pay via that incentive number of inspections. As in the ten-percent situation, this is yet another example of a corporation holding the bottom line of profits sacred, and above any semblance of morality.

When these reports came to me, several inspectors also relayed that PB threatened to take their badges if they defected to Vanguard. But that's an impossibility because it's a federal badge, does not have PB's name on it, and there's no written rule that stipulates an inspector can be held hostage by PB — or for that matter Vanguard. Basically, the two apparent and possible scams captioned appear to be fear-based, because each contractor needs all the experienced inspectors they can muster. It will be interesting to see if PB changes their tune on these, but once again, I won't be holding my breath.

4: As we know, the pay scales for PB and Vanguard are different, but are somewhat equal pertaining to the pay per inspection. However, that is only viable when a PB inspector reaches his weekly incentives, and we know about that from scam # 3. For this one, we'll concentrate on Vanguard, because most of my reports concerning this are about that outfit.

Vanguard has different levels of pay, from $35 to $45, depending on experience. The few inspectors who have contacted me have said that although they've performed between three thousand and five thousand inspections in their career, going back to PaRR or PB, they are still getting paid the lower amount of $35, the same that a brand new inspector gets paid. And that is not fair by any stretch of the imagination. Apparently, Vanguard has been saying that they can't retrieve those inspectors' records, even though they have their former badge numbers, and their personal records. Nevertheless, what Vanguard is *not* telling them is that The National Emergency Management Information System (NEMIS) has all of these records. I've advised them to call, but they are afraid of causing problems that might result in getting blacklisted and losing their jobs. I hope that when this particular infraction comes to light, they will be paid retroactively for all their hard work.

5: In what could be the greatest scam of them all is what happens at the beginning of every inspector's life: The class or classes attended. As opposed to the old days when classes were held at a cheap motel, the ones today are held at four-to five-star hotels. You will have a very nice lunch with wait-service, eat with expensive silverware, wipe your mouth on a napkin that looks like a small blanket, and generally be treated like royalty. Your class instructor will act like he's your older brother and tell you about all the money you will make, that you will have a very cool federal badge with which to impress your friends and family with, but will also tell you, albeit judiciously, about some not so nice things.

He'll tell you about the Fcors, but not in entirety. He'll tell you that you will have support staff to help you on your way to a fine career in the field. He'll impart that you will stay at fine hotels like the one you're in now, that all your other expenses will be reimbursed, (in the case of Vanguard) and tells you that the quality and quantity of inspections and good customer service are to be the mandates in your new career. But what he doesn't tell you is that trying to accomplish those two things will be very difficult, and as we know after assimilating the chapters previously read.

Potential inspectors are found by a team of several professional recruiters, employed by both PB and Vanguard. These recruiters post adverts on various contractor sites, and sometimes even advert on the radio. In between these efforts is "word-of-mouth" information about these classes. But whatever form of fashion brings these newbies to the classes, the fact is that about 80% of them will never be deployed, and of those remaining, about 10% might become decent inspectors, for however long they last, that is.

The classes themselves are presented in "power-point" fashion, wherein the instructor, for instance Bob Kamer with PB or Jaime Ceron with Vanguard, has a large screen behind him, which displays the various screens on the pad. The instructor guides his class from screen to screen while explaining how to perform an inspection. If you've never seen a room full of deer in the headlights, then you should sign up for one of these classes. So after that nice lunch and a couple of fifteen minute breaks, members of that class have become acquainted with the proper way to perform an inspection, and within roughly seven hours! Of course, and should they even be called for deployment, they still have to have a team-leader, do two to three inspections for several days and get them reviewed. And if they pass muster, they are released into the field where most of them again become more confused. It's a vicious cycle, and this is why both PB and Vanguard — and PaRR in the past — always had difficulty keeping a professional cadre of inspectors at the ready.

I'm not certain if there's other possible scams being committed, but I'm betting there are. I hate to hear about things like this because the job is hard enough without taking unwarranted hits. Yes, the job is very demanding, but it's also dangerous, and as we shall see in the next chapter.

20

DEATHS & ILLNESSES IN THE FIELD

"Our dead are never dead to us, until we have forgotten them."

Mary Anne Evans, pen name George Eliot/American novelist 11/22/1818-12/02/1880

Besides being an extremely stressful vocation, an inspector is also faced with many hazards during his/her day. From dog-bites to entering houses with four-foot high black mold on the walls to walking on spongy floors of mobile homes or old structures that many inspectors have fallen through, from checking fuse or breaker panels in flooded basements to working in areas with gang activity, these are but a few of the life-threatening situations encountered. You will never learn of them though the FEMA website, due to their general apathy towards inspectors, but the incidences spoken of within this chapter have only been known to some inspectors and most every supervisor. Sans example # 3, the common denominator in the following stories is the apathy displayed by both FEMA and the contractor the inspector worked for. Once again, I will present them in numerical order, but am only presenting a partial list of the sad tales of inspectors trying to do their jobs at the risk of life and limb.

1: In 2003 during DR # 1501 in Puerto Rico, a veteran inspector with PaRR, named Ron Houston, and who was aligned with me during my lawsuit against PB and PaRR several years later, was involved in an automobile accident while driving to the field office in Ponce. After receiving rudimentary medical treatment at a local hospital, he was airlifted to a hospital in the States, wearing a "Halo" due to his head and spinal injuries. There was no official statement by PaRR or FEMA. There was no help offered by either of them. Left to personally incur extremely high medical expenses, and not able to work again, he suffered for many years. To date, no one is certain if he's dead or alive. Ron was a good person and an excellent inspector.

2: An inspector, deployed to Detroit in the early 2000's, went into a basement during an inspection. There was a large dog chained in the corner, but the owner assured the inspector that he couldn't get free. The dog got free and mauled the inspector's leg. After almost two years of therapy, that inspector's leg was nearly normal. According to my information, he never again worked as an inspector. He had to cover all of his medical expenses. There was no mention of this incident from FEMA or PaRR.

3: A veteran PB inspector from the early 1990's to the early 2000's, named Beth Mortimer, who I personal knew, passed away almost a decade ago. She had always done the job to the best of her ability, and was an extremely nice person. While she was ill, rumors persisted that she became ill due to the toxic mold she had breathed during her many flood disasters, even though sometimes wearing cloth masks she'd purchased at her own expense. Though that rumor was never proved correct, it was an apparently nice gesture of PB's to annually fete an inspector who'd gone beyond the call of duty during a disaster. It's called "The Beth Mortimer Award." I'd like to think PB's heart was in the right place and hadn't done that for the sake of some good publicity, but I still have my doubts.

4: A Texas inspector, deployed to hurricane Katrina, ended up in the emergency ward of a Mobile, Alabama hospital due to a lung infection from breathing in the black toxic mold present in the homes he inspected. His wife came to his bedside from Texas within a matter of hours, but he passed away that evening. After taking him back home for burial, and devastated at his death, she became suicidal after the trailer she and her husband shared was repossessed. Penniless after paying her husband's medical and burial bills, and with no hope or hint of salvation from her misery, she cut both of her wrists. Luckily, a neighbor coming for a visit called 911 and she was saved. Nevertheless, this poor woman wound-up in an insane asylum. Once again, FEMA nor, in this case PB, never offered help or condolences.

5: A PaRR inspector, working a flood disaster in Detroit in the early 2000's, knocked on the door of a DD he had made an appointment to inspect. The applicant opened the door and started to beat the inspector on the head with a hammer with one hand, and tried to grab the inspector's pad with the other. The reason for all this was that the applicant thought that the pad printed checks. The applicant was arrested. The inspector suffered severe head injuries and, per rumor, never again returned to the field.

6: A father and son team, working hurricane Katrina, had high hopes to make a good wage and to assist the victims of that disaster. The result of their efforts proved to be a nightmare.

Upon arriving to the field in two separate cars, and each receiving large downloads of applicants of approximately sixty, they had a very difficult time finding a hotel or motel room as they were all full with disaster victims seeking refuge. The son told his father that he would sleep in the car, albeit knowing that the streets were unsafe due to looting and rampant crime. There was no alternative, he had told his father.

The father told his son he would spend the night looking for a room, and to park the car at a 7/11 they had purchased food at earlier. The father, feeling his son would be comparatively safe at that convenience store that offered outside lighting and a security guard, said that he would be coming-by early in the morning to have breakfast and continue their search for a room together, should his efforts to find lodging prove to be unsuccessful. Upon arriving at the 7/11, he found his son dead on the car's back seat. He had died during the night by leaving the car running, succumbing to carbon monoxide poisoning. Per my understanding of this event, PB's only response was a frail apology, and asked the father to return his son's computer. They then asked the father if he wished to continue working.

Of all the stories above, that last one hit me hard in the personal sense. I thought about the non-disclosure agreement we all had to sign upon arriving at the field office, essentially preventing us from conveying stories such as the ones captioned. I searched for words to describe the heartless comportment of the prime contractors, PB and PaRR at that time, and could only find apropos verbiage in the words "Immoral" and "Evil." While fomenting human misery in the name of profits, the entire FEMA system is fraught with misinformation when purveying themselves as saviors, and while committing what constitutes abuse in the workplace. And it is partly because of stories such as these that I filed a class action lawsuit against PB and PaRR.

As previously noted, PB or PaRR did not ever offer any safety equipment, such as proper masks or ventilators. Due to this, I had contacted OSHA to bring this to their attention. After numerous complaints to them, OSHA's response was that they could do nothing because all inspectors were subcontractors and not employees. But to this day, even as all inspectors with PB are now deemed as actual employees, no safety equipment is offered. For Vanguard — PaRR # 2, those inspectors are still deemed as subcontractors. It is my hope that designation will change.

To this day, there are inspectors in the field who get sick from breathing mold, get injured in various ways, but continue to work because they need the money. Most are afraid to complain for fear of losing their jobs, but some do complain and never again elect to be deployed.

As said, there are many other stories of inspectors' deaths and illnesses in the field, but those instances are not confined to inspectors alone. For story number seven, we shall see that FEMA's apathy extends to even their part-time employees, specifically one who worked in the Disaster Relief Center (DRC) during the Typhoon disaster in the Pacific island of Saipan (a U.S. possession in the Northern Marianna Islands) in late 2015

7: In August of 2015, FEMA "reservist" (a part-time employee) Thomas

Stilwell, of Georgia, became ill while working at the DRC. Hospitalized locally, and with medical staff unable to exactly isolate his dire condition, he passed away within days despite the valiant efforts of medical staff. His family, at their own expense, traveled to Saipan to retrieve his body and return him to Georgia for burial. To my knowledge, there was no mention of his death on the FEMA website. Conversely, the governor of the Northern Marianna Islands, Eloy S. Ines, issued condolences to his family and asked islanders to offer prayers.

I wanted to add something to further describe this despicable comportment displayed by FEMA, but will defer. But as we can now fathom, anyone working for FEMA — or contracted by them — are simply to be used to the fullest. There is no humanity in their system, no room for it. From inspectors to reservists, you're basically on your own, and all while operating under the assumption that you are making a difference for the betterment of mankind. And that may be the biggest lie.

21

AMUSING ANICDOTES + INANE QUOTES

Being a FEMA housing inspector in a major disaster leaves little room for levity, but in every deployment there nevertheless are humorous stories and mindless utterances that serve to break the tension. Whether transmitted via email or a telephone call, the lighter side of applicant's antics somewhat buffers the serious nature of the job where even a smile is oftentimes hard to produce. Although there will never be a television show called "Applicants Do Funny Things," I think it would do pretty well in the ratings. A show called "People Say the Dumbest Things," however, would most likely eclipse it.

From Barbara Bush in Houston's Astrodome to the applicant that thought an inspectors' pad had the ability to print-out checks, the sheer lunacy of it all defies logic. But as we already know, there's no real logic in anything associated with FEMA. Think it's time to get a laugh or two. I could use one myself. We'll start off with some insanity from the field, experienced by myself and fellow inspectors who shared their stories with me through the years.

Anecdote #1:

In a wealthy New York suburb during DR # 1724, an inspector drives up a long tree-lined driveway to find himself in front of a three story brick mansion with no apparent damage from the severe storms and flooding. An elegantly dressed forty-six year-old woman (the inspector knowing that because of the information in the Pad) emerges from the front door upon hearing the car pull-up, and motions for the inspector to follow her along a path alongside the house. The inspector tells her politely that he needs to take down her information first, but her adamant attitude prompted him to accede to her wishes.

"You need to see what happened out in back here," she ordered, briskly walking with the inspector in tow a few anxious feet behind her.

"You have damage back here?' it must be bad, he thought.

"Darn right it's bad. I'm supposed to have a party tomorrow and it's a mess. I'm expecting FEMA to see to it immediately!"

They reach the back of the house. The perplexed inspector quickly surveys the structure. Not seeing any damage, he says the only thing that came to mind.

"Everything looks fine."

"No-no," she impatiently said. "Down there." She pointed to an Olympic-sized swimming pool, placid water not affected by the rains, clear blue and ready for a party. He followed her down about ten steps with landscaping on either side that would be the envy of many. At the end of the pool, she pointed to the opposite corner of it.

"So now what am I supposed to do with those?"

"With what?"

His voice was calm but he was now very wary. What was next, an attack with a kitchen knife deftly hidden under her flowing red dress? The inspector thinks about going back to his car to call a supervisor, but decides to tough-it-out. She motions with an index finger that goes back and forth almost faster than the eye can see. Her voice became more exasperated with each step they take to the far end of the pool.

"Look at these! What am I supposed to do with this mess?" She pointed to the pile of towels, white but wet. He wanted to kick them in the pool but didn't want to get stabbed.

"Do you have a washing machine and a dryer?" The question seemed innocent enough to him, but to her it was an affront to her intelligence, or so it appeared.

"Sir! I have two washing machines and two dryers, but I refuse to place these filthy rain-soaked towels in my expensive appliances! Do you know how much bacteria and filth rain-water carries with it? I need these replaced immediately!"

"Miss," he said, keeping calm as possible but watching for a sudden movement for the knife, "FEMA doesn't do towels or swimming pools."

As soon as he said those words, the mistake was instantly realized. But it was too late. She went off the deep end, unfortunately not in the pool, which would have afforded him a hasty exit to his car and safety. As he retreated to her advancing steps, menace and malice in her voice, the duty of a good inspector was evident.

"I still need to inspect the house, Miss. I'm required to do that," he said. Looking over his shoulder to make sure he wouldn't trip on a step walking backwards.

"There's no God-damn freakin' damage in the house you simpleton!" Unlike the lady she initially appeared to be in that very expensive-looking dress, she was rapidly reverting to the verbiage of a harlot in a Saturday night bar. She was only a couple of feet away from his face and he could smell her breath. Hot-dogs, he thought, grinning and almost bursting out laughing. But that was yet another mistake.

"Oh, so you think this is funny? What kind of inspector are you? I'm calling FEMA!"

"I'm doing the best I can, Miss, he replied, reaching the top step and back-peddling rapidly towards his car. Besides reaching relative safety, it would be a race to the phone that he'd win.

The ignition was turned and he backed out of the driveway, glancing to the windshield a couple of times to a woman in a red dress whose arms flailed helplessly at the sky, as if to demand divine intervention. At the next block, he pulled to the curb and called his supervisor, telling him of the bizarre interaction in a breathless voice that may have sounded that he just narrowly escaped the wrath of a serial killer. Thankfully, the supervisor understood and instructed him how to send the inspection in. With that information, he carefully noted those instructions on his comment screen: "WVO = app refused inspec. App-towel only inspec. App = nt allow inspector entr dd." Basically, the inspector withdrew the applicant for an inspection, that she'd only applied for towel damage, and that she did not allow him into the house.

Suffice to say, this particular inspection is still a cause for laughter whenever it gets repeated, but not necessarily so for the soft-spoken veteran inspector who actually experienced it. We won't elongating every story as we did this one, but there are others of equally strange behavior from applicants that can't tell the difference between FEMA and Santa Clause, as the following will attest.

Anecdote # 2

Yes, there actually was an applicant who'd thought that the inspector would "cut" her a check via a magical program that the Pad possessed. It happened in DR # 1482 in Tennessee, and the very nice elderly lady who gave the inspector a nice lunch of chitterlings and gizzards was promptly regurgitated in the bathroom just before he left. Although the inspector told her that his upset stomach was due to the stress of the job, he thought she knew the truth when saying, "Can't jump and don' know what a good meal is, right darling? So when's the guy with the good computer comin' to give me my money?" The inspector checked back with her ten days later when he was again in the neighborhood doing other inspections, and she told him she got "a fat check" and that he needed to gain some weight. Politely declining another offer of lunch, he wished her luck and left with this particular story I'm now able to share with you.

The title of this chapter may not relate to this next story, but it's still somewhat amusing, in retrospect at least. Still good friends with the inspector who'd actually experienced this totally bizarre behavior on the part of an applicant, we both find that the humor exceeds the seriousness of the situation at this point in time when recalling the episode. From this next story, we might fully realize that the job of an inspector is not without its dire perils.

Anecdote # 3:

It seemed like a normal inspection, but it soon became evident to the peaceful and mellow inspector, while sitting at the kitchen table with the husband and wife applicants, that he was in the wrong place at the wrong time. While the inspector was being handed the insurance documents, the husband's face grew red, his voice bellowing curses as he threw his chair against the wall and blocked the entrance door with his body.

"You're not fu***** leaving here until you cut us a check! You God-damn hear me?!"

"Sir, I'm here to help you," the inspector said, not knowing what else to say as he gathered-up his pad and camera and stood from his chair with fear in his heart and terror on his face.

The wife pleaded with her husband to calm down. The more she tried the angrier he became. The husband blocks the door with resolve and the wife tries to explain to the inspector in a quivering voice that they'd been undergoing extreme financial hardships. More curses directed at the inspector. The wife tries to calm her husband. The inspector turns his head to the back door and wonders if he can make it in time. The wife shoves her husband away from the door and yells to the inspector: "Now! Get out!"

Like a racehorse that sees the finish line, the inspector bolts to the door and opens it to the freedom that, seconds before, seemed impossible. Running the fifty-feet or so to his car, he glances back and fully realizes the depth of his predicament. The husband is about twenty-feet behind him, a baseball bat in his hands held like a home-run hitter focused on hitting one for the record books. He's yelling at the top of his lungs: "You son-of-a-bitch! Where's my money! FEMA sucks! You suck!"

From out of the blue, a miracle occurred in the form of a neighbor alerted to an impending disaster within a disaster when most likely hearing the loud voices emanating from the house and outside. In a flying tackle that would have made any linebacker proud, the husband was subdued, giving the inspector the time to get into his car. While backing-out of the driveway he glanced ahead, observing the wife in a kneeling position on the front lawn, her face buried in her hands. The neighbor covers the body of the husband, the baseball bat thrown well beyond reach of an irate applicant intent on inflicting bodily harm on the one that could have helped.

In closure to this somewhat disturbing but still humorous incident, this inspector still thanks God that he suffered no injuries, at least to his body. My personal and initial predilection when hearing of this story would have been to prosecute, but I also remembered that virtually everyone affected by a disaster, however relative in scope, succumbs to behavior detrimental to their immediate salvation and converse to their normal patterns. As such, it's up to every inspector to understand that they are the ones that frustrations are directed towards, and oftentimes wrongly so.

The anecdote captioned above, that's not entirely indicative of the ones to follow, may hopefully serve to augment the crux of this chapter. We may have an idea about the dark-side of the inspection system, but the true shadow of substance will be studied in-depth later in this book when we'll learn their origins. As FEMA may stand for many things, suspect and otherwise, the one thing they've never done is to support their subcontracted inspectors. As the "grease that turns the wheel," I'm particularly thankful that some inspectors still have the latitude to recognize the difference from an actual plight from an effort, however inventive, to obtain money not deserved.

From another personal experience via a veteran inspector, and one that I still remember with a smile, the following inspection with an applicant who'd reminded of the long-past television character "Grizzly Adams," is still etched in my mind.

Anecdote # 4:

In the rural areas of Oklahoma, where my inspector-friend was deployed for DR # 1482 via an ice storm, his first inspection of the morning was about fifty-miles away from his motel. As said before, in the old days there was no *Streets+Trips* mapping system on the pads, and the first stop after our field office briefing being a visit to a bookstore or chamber of commerce to get a zip code or county map with which to find or way around. Regardless, this particular applicant was so polite when my inspector friend had to call him several times to get exact directions to his house, just like most of those folks in those two counties he'd covered. Of course, his interpretations of exact differed greatly from the inspectors. After a few rounds of "go down the road a bit and you'll see a fence, then down-a-ways you'll see a wooden post" and so-on. He met my friend at a crossroads of two dirt roads that led to somewhere only left to the imagination. Dressed in blue overalls and with a gun on each hip, he exited his pickup truck that was hard to believe it was once new, and shook my friend's hand till it hurt. His first question was unexpected.

"You hungry? Just fixed some grub. C'mon, follow me."

Down the dirt roads and taking lefts and rights that made my friend totally lose any sense of direction remaining, they pulled into a driveway where a house sat on wooden pilings, and which resembled that of Jed Clampett's in the Beverly Hillbillies television show. Once inside, the applicant kept interrupting the inspector's questions about his damage and requests to see his ownership documents, explaining that since it took so long to find him he had only about a half-hour to get to his next appointment. Seeing he was getting nowhere, the inspector called the next applicant on his list to say he'd be a little late, and he said that there was no problem with that.

As he ended the call on his cellphone, a large bowl of meat, potatoes, carrots and onions in a thick amber broth was placed in his hands. A large silver spoon was stuck deep in its bowels, a heavily buttered slice of white bread ceremoniously slapped on top with a hand that looked like it hadn't been washed in days. With no way out unless he wanted to appear rude, he took the first bite, silently praying he wouldn't contract food poisoning. The meat was a stringy brown and though assuming it was beef, a little voice prompted him to ask what it was.

"Like it, huh? Yep, been eatin' that meat for quite a while now since times got tough. Simmer it in special sauces and stuff. Butcher it myself too," he said proudly, after slurping a big spoonful of the stew. "Game is game." he said. "Not too much game in the winter," he added, digging his spoon into the bowl that was twice the size of my friend's.

The "game" was hard to chew, but my friend finished most of it and the applicant threw the leftovers back into the large pot on the wood-burning stove. The inspector started getting down to business, asking for the ownership documents for the house and occupancy verification, authenticating that via his driver's license. He started the inspection, finding no damage while going from room to room. They went outside to inspect the exterior, and while walking past a small open shed, the inspector noticed a rectangular wooden table inside. On its apparently blood-spattered top were two butcher knives, and what looked like body parts of small animals. His stomach heaved and he felt like throwing up when realizing what he'd eaten, knowing that when seeing the long tails of rats.

He wanted to yell and scream at the applicant, but thought the wiser as he quickly finished the inspection. Although it took every bit of courage to again ask what the meat was, and hoping that he was way-off base for assuming he'd eaten rat stew, the question flew from his lips.

"Tastes like beef and game is game," the applicant replied, watching him get in his car with a sly grin on his face.

"You mean cow-meat, right?" The inspector was still hoping against hope.

"Smaller but a lot smarter," he answered, nodding his head affirmatively.

He drove, trying to retrace his route along the labyrinth of dirt roads, imagining he'd die of food poisoning and no one would ever know the exact reason why. He thought about writing the episode down on his pad of paper, but thought that a call to his hospital back home would be the better choice, since his trust in the local population was now nonexistent. When telling them of what he'd eaten, the nurse in the emergency room told him to drink milk or try to throw-up. Thanking her, he pulled to the side of the road and did the latter. Never again did he accept an applicant's offer of food. And he now has a different vision of rats.

There are a few more anecdotes I could include, but the inane quotes that we'll now look at are just as zany. From hurricane Katrina, many instances of foot-in-mouth disease emanated from that disaster-within-a-disaster. As every major declaration brings out the best and worst in people, these following quotes are prime examples of the best of the worst. I was going to comment after each one, but I don't think there's a need because the words say it all.

"Louisiana is a city that is largely underwater."(Homeland Security

www.femasbest.com

Secretary Michael Chertoff at a September 1, 2005 news conference)

"I understand that there are ten thousand people dead. It's terrible. It's tragic. But in a democracy of three-hundred-million people, over years and years, these things happen." (GOP strategist Jack Burkman, on MSNBC's "Connected," September 7, 2005)

"Bureaucracy is not going to stand in the way of getting the job done for these people." (President G.W. Bush, September 6, 2005)

"I also want to encourage anybody that was affected by hurricane Corina to make sure their children are in school." (First Lady Laura Bush, getting the hurricane's name wrong while speaking to children and parents in South Haven, Mississippi, on September 8, 2005)

"I have not heard a report of thousands of people in the convention center who don't have food and water."(Homeland Security Secretary Michael Chertoff, on NPR's "All Things Considered" September 1, 2005)

"A young black man walks through chest-high floodwaters after *looting* a grocery store in New Orleans. Two white residents wade through chest-deep water after *finding* bread and soda from a local grocery store after hurricane Katrina battered New Orleans"(Captions at Yahoo news, August 30, 2005)

"What I'm hearing, which is sort of scary, is that they all want to stay in Texas. Everybody is so overwhelmed by the hospitality. And so many of the people in the arena here, you know, were underprivileged anyway so this (chuckle)—this is working very well for them" (Former First lady Barbara Bush, on the hurricane evacuees at the Houston Astrodome, September 5, 2005)

"Now tell me the truth boys, is this kind of fun?" (House Majority leader Tom Delay to three young hurricane evacuees from New Orleans at the Houston Astrodome on September 9, 2005)

"You simply get chills every time you see these poor individuals…..many of these people, almost all of them we see are so poor and they are so black, and this is going to raise a lot of questions for people who are watching this story unfold" (CNN's Wolf Blitzer, on New Orleans' hurricane evacuees, September 1, 2005)

"I'm going to go home and walk my dog and hug my wife, and maybe get a good Mexican meal and a stiff margarita and a full night's sleep" (FEMA Director Michael Brown on his plans after being relieved from his role managing hurricane Katrina's relief efforts, September 9, 2006)

"If you'll look at my lovely FEMA attire you'll really vomit. I am a fashion god……..anything specific I need to do or tweak? Do you know anyone who dog-sits? Can I quit now? Can I come home? I'm trapped now, please rescue me" (FEMA Director Michael Brown, in various emails to friends in the immediate aftermath of hurricane Katrina)

"We ask black people: it's time for us to come together. It's time for us to rebuild a New Orleans, the one that should be a chocolate New Orleans. And I don't care what people are saying uptown or wherever they are. This city will be chocolate at the end of the day." (New Orleans mayor Ray Nagin, January 16, 2006)

"Mayor Nagin and most Mayors in this country have a hard time getting their people to work on a sunny day, let alone getting them out of the city in front of a hurricane" (Senator Mary Landrieu (D-LA), on why New Orleans mayor Ray Nagin failed to follow the city's evacuation plan and press the buses into service, stated on "Fox News Sunday," September 11, 2005)

"We just learned of the convention center……we being the federal government-today." (FEMA Director Michael Brown, to ABC's Ted Koppel on September 1, 2006) Koppel responded: "Don't you guys watch television? Don't you guys listen to the radio? Our reporters have been reporting on it for more than just today."

"Our Nation is prepared as never before, to deal quickly and capably with the consequences of disasters and other domestic incidents." (FEMA Director Michael Brown, March 9, 2005)

"We finally cleaned up public housing in New Orleans. We couldn't do it, but God did." (Representative Richard Baker (R-LA) to lobbyists, as quoted in the Wall Street Journal)

In retrospect, the humor of those inane quotes probably drew more anger than laughter at the time of their utterances. Today, that lighter side is more palatable within the sheer stupidity and lack of compassion that caused those quotes. FEMA may be the butt of jokes, but the agency is immune to levity. They are deadpan and emotionless. They are like a dog that shakes hands only because it wants to get fed. They are not your friend and don't care to be.

But in the bigger picture, cause for concern is the *other* side of FEMA, the one that's hidden behind the common misconception that attending to natural disasters is their primary directive. We'll be dealing with that hidden side of FEMA in one of the last chapters, pertaining to FEMA's misdirected guideposts and their false projection of paternalism, evident in many ways.

22

HOW THE SYSTEM IS WORKED

"GOOD LUCK HAS ITS STORMS"

GEORGE LUCAS: 1944-. AMERICAN DIRECTOR/SCREENWRITER

We already know *how* it works, but a certain segment of applicants have used that knowledge to their own advantage, and still do. With seemingly no way to totally prevent the rampant theft that's been a hallmark of FEMA's disaster relief programs, some applicants continue to enrich themselves with virtually no repercussions. From generators to automobiles, forged home ownership documents to self-destroyed furniture, it's like Christmas when FEMA comes to town.

The generator debacle, which gained fame during the 2004 Florida hurricane season, exposed creative but premeditated acts of thievery for obtaining awards. Sometimes the oldest tricks were used and have still proved fruitful. For that generator "give-away," roughly 100,000 units were unleashed into eager hands that most times didn't even start them. A simple and common ploy was to buy one, have the inspector view it and record the unit in his pad, and it was an easy $836 — The FEMA dollar amount for a 5 KW unit — for the applicant that couldn't believe it was that easy. While in years past the emphasis on generators was almost nil, the Florida hurricanes somehow prompted them to become a priority with FEMA. Yes, they were always present on the pads on the unmet needs screen or as a line-item, but very rarely did applicants bother to buy them. However, the new game of power to the people took-on a life of its own once the word spread from town to town, city to city. For lack of a better term it was like stealing candy from a baby.

So once the generator was purchased, the inspector logged it on the pad, and all the applicant had to do was to return it to Home Depot, or wherever, and get a refund. And since that generator usually sold for about $500, the applicant's profit was a cool three hundred. If the applicant decided to actually use it, then it's a freebie to be used in the future for whatever purpose. But if that same generator *is* damaged in a future storm, FEMA will provide money to repair or replace it via dropdowns in the pad, specifically "Generator Repair" or "Generator Replace." For the Generator Replace, It equates to two for the price of one and everyone wins except FEMA. But it seems they really didn't care about winning or losing. When working the 2004 Florida hurricanes for PB in Orange County, I remember when a friend in Orlando called to ask me if he should buy a generator so as to make a few bucks. I told him the decision was his, but that I didn't approve. Since PaRR was also deployed to Florida, I'd have to think inspectors with that outfit also had similar experiences.

The generator gifting was devoid of prejudice as to who got one, spanning a wide economic demographic where it was assured that no one would be left off the early Christmas list. From rich to poor, black to white, no one was green with envy because their neighbor of friend got one and they didn't. There were those that basked in the sunshine of their greed when receiving FEMA's gift of eternal power, well-able to afford one on their own, and there were those who'd simply grasped the opportunity to obtain the unit that would serve them well in a future hurricane or flood. During my 2004 deployment, I remember more than a few homeowner applicants with insurance who had absolutely no right to apply for assistance, but did so with no remorse for taking advantage of the program. They'd say that they felt guilty for applying and that other people really needed the help more than them, but it was perfectly obvious that they only cared about getting a free generator. For the many applicants who had absolutely no storm damage, inspections were often issued as "generator only" to applicants with expensive homes in gated communities on tree-lined streets with Mercedes' in driveways.

At that time, FEMA seemed to be catching-on to the game and made some alterations pertaining to generator awards. The new dictum for inspectors was to make sure the unit was out of the box, appeared to be in use, and to write the applicant's registration number on the receipt, ostensibly to prevent that receipt from being used by someone with a good-looking older generator that's claimed to be newly purchased. But there are many uses for the product called "Whiteout," and copies can easily be made. The game of cat and mouse had its heyday but the game is never over for hearty souls with creative minds. Still, applicants have a fighting chance to get a freebie generator, albeit not as easily as before. That same scenario can also hold-true for chainsaws and de-humidifiers, though not abused in large numbers probably due to their lower price and FEMA payout. Generators may have been at the top of the Christmas list for gadgets, but bigger ticket items were also available for even bigger payouts, but only for the truly adept and bold.

As we know, a bedroom set is worth approximately $2,485 in Louisiana and other states that share their economic demographic, and a living room ensemble is roughly equal to that figure. As we're also aware, sometimes a redecoration is in order, and a hurricane or flood is the perfect excuse to effect that change. In my opinion, there's a lot of honest applicants who would never do the things I'm about to describe. However, and as said before, a disaster always brings out both the best and worst in everyone.

To most people, the thought of taking a garden hose to that old but comfortable sofa or chair would be unthinkable, the same for that well-worn bedroom set. But that very practice is more commonplace than imagined. Always a favorite on the holiday shopping list, applicants can still get away with that form of deception and collect the money derived from it. No, they probably don't have an exact figure to be received for their "damaged" furniture, but for some, a few extra bucks and a trip to The Salvation Army or to yard sales would satisfy them.

When you look at it in simplistic fashion, it's actually very easy to get the money for the bedroom, living room or bathroom with very little effort. However, enough damage to the house *has* to exist and be visible to the inspector to result in obtaining that award. For flooding, a distinct "waterline," — which is a ring around the walls showing the level of water that entered the house — must be visible. To qualify for a "furniture replace," at least one foot has to be authenticated. For "furniture repair," six to eight inches is oftentimes acceptable to FEMA. Floor covering is an easy one to collect some money, should the old rug or other type of flooring have been on its last legs anyway. But that's only for homeowners, as opposed to the furniture and appliances that that renters only basically qualify for.

Even though the inspector is instructed to view damaged items to qualify for an award, the fact remains that honest applicants often discard their mold-infested sofas and chairs and so forth because of the health hazards. For the dishonest ones, that furniture is included in their "disaster-relief kit" that's in storage in the garage or basement and ready to be displayed at the proper time. A good-hose-down doesn't hurt either, nor does a few hours in the sun in order to promote to the inspector that every effort was taken to save the treasured furniture. In a series of deft moves, the good furniture is moved to a basement or garage where it's elevated, should flooding have occurred in those areas, and they're covered with blankets or tarps. Usually, the inspector won't pry, but to be on the safe side, many who involve themselves in this type of fraud stack boxes around the covered evidence to make it difficult for the inspector to see what's there, should he/she be so inquisitive. But remember, inspectors are *not* investigators, but are simply there to record the visible damage, unmet needs, et cetera, and then continue to the next applicant. Just like Santa.

So in that scenario, the disaster-kit furniture is viewed by the inspector, a donation is made to your favorite charity — which is you, and FEMA will never be aware of the scam unless you tell a neighbor or friend and they report you to the fraud hotline. Also, and as we now know that a QC inspector may be calling, allowing that to happen would be obviously contrary to your primary directive, which is getting as much money as possible. But hey, you worked for it didn't you? Hard work moving furniture. Maybe you should have told the inspector you hurt your back while trying to elevate that sofa so it wouldn't be completely damaged?

If all the furniture is not damaged, the pad has dropdowns which enable the inspector to record that some, most, or all is affected. Basically, it's an X-Y-Z system: Clean by Pro or Repair or Replace. So even if the entire room furnishings aren't destroyed or damaged, then an award *may* still be forthcoming to both the honest and dishonest, the latter of whom maybe *did* hurt his back when carrying, pushing or shoving the good furniture to that basement or garage and vice-versa. But in the event that all those damaged items were removed to the driveway and expediently picked-up for disposal — which is a rare occurrence immediately following a major storm or flood, the damage that's evident in the house will have to qualify to the inspector that there was a significant likelihood of furnishings destroyed. In that case, inspectors in the past would make a comment in the pad, "PP=vrb/app rmvd pp sfty rsns mold"/pp-app discard." Now, the new program simply has buttons that say "Viewed" or "Verbal" in relation to the item. This tells the reviewers and FEMA that the applicant stated that the furniture was destroyed, removed from of the house and discarded. Through the past few years, and the fraud gotten out of hand, FEMA usually doesn't like to give money for something the inspector doesn't see. The chances are reasonable that an award will nevertheless be forthcoming, but it also depends, as said, on what that inspector puts in the pad.

For homeowners who have a full content rider in their insurance policy, the odds are zilch they'll receive any assistance from FEMA. For homeowners without a rider, the chances are much better. Renters are usually the biggest winners in the furniture game, most not having renters insurance that would cover contents. As the program has undergone more stringent requirements pertaining to homeowners with insurance, renters and uninsured homeowners are usually the biggest winners. But the income level of these two segments of applicants also has a bearing on getting an award or not.

Several years ago, that income level was included in the information on the inspectors pad, but no longer is. I never understood a need for this type of "big-brother" comportment, and there's absolutely no reason the inspector needs to know an applicant's income. So if and when you may have applied for disaster relief in the past, the inspector who came to your house had this information on his/her pad. In retrospect — and if you knew, it would have been interesting if you'd asked them how much *they* make, since they know how much you do. But that's not really necessary now, for you already know.

From the other side of the fence, inspectors themselves have worked the system to their own advantage in the past. During the 2004 Florida hurricanes, both prime contractors were willing to put anyone in the field that heeded the call because of the shortage of inspectors at that time, and some answered it for monumentally inventive reasons. Much like some applicants use FEMA to upgrade their living room furniture, appliances or transportation, two PaRR inspectors apparently signed-on to get better computers than they had back home. After attending a "class" they arrived at the field office, got their briefing, and were deployed to the field. No one heard from them again.

On PaRRs' broadcast line, Inspectors couldn't help but laugh at supervisors' entreaties to immediately contact them. At the beginning, only their ID numbers were mentioned. When still no response from them, their names were for everyone to hear. After that failed, they were threatened with "federal repercussions," as they were "stealing government property." In the end, this particular soap opera only culminated in those two "inspectors" going home with a Toshiba laptop computer each, with which to utilize in whatever fashion they choose. As humorous as this story was

— and still is, the serious side to it is that the names of applicants and their sensitive information was contained in those computers.

Though none of us ever found out the end to this saga, it just glaringly proves that even FEMA computers could be readily obtained with a little verve and panache. An interesting footnote to this is that FEMA computers, from time-to-time, were actually seen for sale on eBay. I had actually viewed a couple of them on that site, had a gut feeling, and had contacted Department of Homeland Security to apprise them of that.

As hurricane Francis spawned that particular story of theft, it was also an example of disasters that should never have been declared, specifically in certain counties. With a mean average of 45 mile-an-hour winds, President G.W. Bush saw fit to include Dade County, which encompasses Miami. We must remember that Bush was seeking a second term at that time, Michael Brown was FEMA's Director, and Jeb Bush was Governor of Florida. Just as James Lee Witt had said, disasters are political events. In the past, floods that seemed serious enough for a major disaster declaration were only designated for emergency, and severe storms that appeared to wreak havoc were also demoted to that designation.

When discussing preliminary damage assessments (PDA's) in a previous chapter, we're aware of the process of declaration, but hurricane Francis did not, by any stretch of the imagination, meet the criteria to be designated in the major damage category. Regardless, Miami/Dade, Broward, (which includes Ft. Lauderdale), and eleven other counties that were added to the original declaration were virtually spared even minor damage, and all became privy to the system you either love or hate, or maybe love to hate.

When Frances affected Miami/Dade, the winds were limited to gusts of 50-60 miles-an-hour. Remember, these were not sustained winds, which were about 30-35 mph. While sustained winds are self-explanatory, gusts are sporadic unequal forces of wind and don't inflict the type of damage as the former variety simply because of their ability to find weaknesses in structures over a short period of time. In Miami/Dade, there were approximately 22,446 applicants for disaster assistance with a combined payout by FEMA of just over $31 million. In Volusia County there were roughly 80,000 applicants, for a total FEMA payout of $57 million. So according to those figures, roughly one-quarter the number of the applicants in Volusia — where Francis was actually a hurricane, had about half the amount of monetary awards as the applicants in Dade. Certainly, this particular debacle gives new meaning to the term "a disaster within a disaster."

It was In Francis that some of the tricks to get money for furnishings were taken to higher levels — or lower, depending on how you look at it. There's certainly no doubt the declaration was severe enough in certain counties to warrant a major declaration, and many tales of theft and lies were relayed to me by inspector-friends deployed to Miami and environs. Without benefit of having a FEMA disaster furniture-kit available, many took it upon themselves to provide for the future. There were instances of people actually breaking their own windows and using a garden hose to soak their furniture so it would appear as if the storm was the culprit.

One inspector told me that she even saw a couple of large rocks on a living room floor while performing an inspection. Even though that inspector wanted to report that fraud, it wasn't a core-part of the job, and the risk of an angry applicant filing a lawsuit for slander superseded that compunction. Remember once again: The inspector is a subcontractor without any protection, and though that instance hasn't happened yet to my knowledge, it wouldn't surprise me to hear about an inspector being sued by an applicant for whatever charge is convenient at the time.

Older automobiles are another item in the FEMA disaster-kit. Much like the furniture, they have been utilized for obtaining about three times the amount of money than that living room or bedroom. But to be successful in obtaining this particular grant, a different type of effort is required. Let's get behind the wheel of the "FEMA-Car."

In states that offer cheap automobile liability insurance, this scam works rather well in locations that are prone to hurricanes or flooding, but especially floods. All one has to do is buy a car for a few hundred dollars, register it with minimal insurance (no comprehensive. FEMA will not award with it) and let it sit in the driveway or garage. When a storm hits, a call to FEMA may insure a big payday with no real effort. However, as FEMA will not grant an award to a family with two or more cars, the others have to disappear. This piece of the puzzle has been solved by simply re-registering the other car to another name and address, be it a relative or friend. Sometimes, folks wait to register their FEMA-Car when a storm appears likely to hit, thereby saving them a few bucks in insurance premiums, and sometimes they actually use the car as emergency transportation should their main vehicle fail them. Either way, the money that's been taken out of FEMA's pockets for this item alone reaches into the many millions, and is still a viable way to steal from your friendly folks at FEMA.

The most important part of this particular enterprise is to understand how the program works regarding automobiles, for if not, all your efforts will be wasted. Remember, inspectors are not investigators, but rather data-collectors. As such, many have been guilty of not thoroughly ascertaining if a car had actually been damaged by the storm or flood, and are not of the volition to invite a complaint from FEMA by an applicant who has all the evidence that their automobile *was* damaged or destroyed by a storm. Simply put, if it appears likely that the flood or storm was the culprit, the money will probably flow right into your pocket. The cap on this award is about $6500, and your car doesn't necessarily have to equal that value to get it. Whether it's a 2003 Chevrolet, a 1996 Ford or 68 Volkswagen, all are eligible.

An inspector-friend working a flood disaster in Puerto Rico, where many landslides occurred, told me about an applicant whose car wound-up about a hundred feet down a hill via a landslide at his house. The car was twenty years old, was registered, and because it was destroyed the applicant received $5,200 for it. A couple of weeks later when performing other inspections in the area, someone told him that the applicant with the old car had been bragging that he'd hardly driven it but had kept it registered in case a bad storm hit. The yearly cost for registering a car in Puerto Rico is $184, including basic insurance. Not a bad investment, I'd say.

FEMA determines damage to vehicles within three categories: damaged, destroyed, or cosmetic. Under these guidelines, certain items on a car that are deemed necessary to drive the vehicle safely are eligible for an award, such a side-view mirrors, taillights and headlights, broken or cracked windshields or rear windows. Side windows don't qualify, as FEMA expects you to cover them with clear plastic or whatever, and the same applies to large dents as it doesn't hamper your ability to drive it.

As an example, if the driver's door is totally smashed in and can't be opened, then the applicant is expected to enter and exit the car from the passenger side. Remember, FEMA only attends to the basic needs of an applicant. They don't care if your car is a Mercedes or Ford, but as said, floods are the easiest way to get big bucks for your jalopy. All you need is a fairly high waterline in your house or apartment, and you're on your way.

In a neighborhood that's been affected, by say three-feet of flood level, your car would also appear to be affected to FEMA reviewers and PB's or Vanguard's, specifically engine flooding and interior and electrical damage. The neighborhood has probably had many applicants with the same issues, so that portends well for you in your quest. The inspector *may* ask you to turn the ignition, but that's easily circumvented by simply loosening a couple of spark plug wires or whatever. I used the word *may* because very rarely will an inspector ask you to go to that length because of his/her fears of a complaint to FEMA that "the inspector was rude and accused me of lying." Remember, FEMA is all about customer service. A happy customer will spread the good word. An applicant not satisfied is the agency's worst enemy. And we must also remember that if not for their *satisfied* customers, FEMA would cease to exist.

The FEMA-Car scam has been used so successfully, and the same method could be applied to the "FEMA-wheelchairs" that I wouldn't be surprised hearing more about after this book's information becomes public knowledge. One could simply buy a used unit, powered or not but dilapidated, and plant a member of the family in it to play the game of "Invalid for a day." The person in the chair states that he/she didn't have medical insurance or even enough money to see a doctor for medical care and had bought it from a friend. The wheelchair, looking like it was sitting in the bottom of a swimming pool for a few weeks and obviously is on its last legs, was "like new" when the person bought it. The inspector, maybe a newbie and maybe not, lists the "Wheelchair Replace" or Repair" on the pad. It's always hilarious to see how some folks have fun with the system, but there's always a faction that takes that fun to an extreme.

For the heartiest of souls, the "FEMA-House" has also been utilized for rewards up to the cap amount as prescribed by the Stafford Act, successfully more times than FEMA would care to admit. Yes, some have been caught in this particular scam, but many others have gotten away with it. Simply, one owns a house or trailer with old furniture, the kitchen has dishes and accoutrements, and the bathroom has towels and so forth. There's a deed or current tax bill to prove ownership, an electric bill or merchant statement to authenticate occupancy, but in fact, no one actually lives there. There's damage to the structure, its roof has uplifted or missing shingles or worse. Inside, the furniture has been soaked with a garden hose through windows intentionally broken, and its floors were also generously watered-down. The applicant lives with a relative, but still receives mail at the FEMA-House. He/she maybe makes appearances there from time to time, just to maintain the perception to neighbors that they are an actual resident. He/she maybe cuts the grass or hires it out. If the relative he or she lives with also applies to FFMA, then the FEMA-House person will not be added to the HH residence list, for that would be noted by FEMA as obvious fraud. The plan is set. The fun begins.

Everything is prepared so as to make it appear that the disaster caused damage and someone lives there full-time, but pilfering the award is totally dependent on both the inspector's acumen and the applicant who's astute in the ways of FEMA. Should the inspector not have the knowledge to disseminate previous damage (Deferred Maintenance, or PE, meaning Pre-Existing) from that which was actually caused by the event, then that applicant will receive even more money. In turn, the applicant will refuse a request for a QC inspection, thereby eliminating any discovery of the scam.

For a monthly electric bill for minimum service of maybe $20-30 or any piece of mail with his/her name and that address, a property deed or tax bill, the investment provides a return that would make a seasoned stockbroker envious and the applicant happy all the way to the bank. Attempting this too many times could be a mistake, for FEMA's eyes and ears, however suspect, could eventually be attuned to fraud whether by a jealous neighbor or an ex-husband or wife who places a call to the FEMA fraud-hotline.

The days of free generators may be in the past, but they can still be had if one is brave enough or greedy enough to follow the necessary steps for obtaining the monetary award for it. For FEMA-Cars or FEMA-Houses, those avenues are also wide open, just as most appliances in your home are 'fair-game" From microwaves to televisions to vacuum cleaners, they're all for the taking in the world of "power-surge," should one exactly understands how it works.

In the Tennessee "straight-line-wind storm" of July 2003, (DR #1482) which lasted only a few hours, FEMA inexplicably assumed the role of a charity organization when providing everyone with new appliances should they had *claimed* they were damaged via the power surges that affected most areas. To the depths of FEMA's wasteful practices and inability to gauge the applicant's greed-factor, over 34,000 applicants from Shelby County, which encompasses the city of Memphis, received assistance for a storm that was benign at best. The total number of 1482 applicants grew to almost 40,000; the greater percentage of them applied for power-surge damage only. One friend of mine inspected over 500 homes, mostly specific for appliance damages. Yes, there were also some shingles uplifted on many houses, but that was but a minor concern for most who applied. The real reason for applying was because word got out that FEMA was replacing appliances for monetary value. Once again, Christmas came early. From this disaster, power-surge guidelines changed drastically.

I used the word *claimed* because most every inspector simply had the applicant turn-on the appliance, whether television, microwave, radio, etcetera, to see if it worked. When it didn't, that particular item was recorded in the pad as "Replace" or "Repair." No one can accurately calculate how many of those appliances weren't actually affected by power surge, but FEMA's criteria at that time was that if they didn't work at the time of the inspection then it was simply awarded to the applicant.

FEMA's ability to catch a glitch in the system is usually too late, and the guidelines were better defined in the subsequent year for items professed to be damaged by power-surge. Inspectors were instructed to check fuse boxes or breaker panels, and to look for burn marks on outlets and plugs. In retort, some applicants fought back with inventive ways to beat the new procedures that were relayed like a jungle drum from neighborhood to neighborhood, and successfully so. As we already know that inspectors are not investigators and are extremely wary of receiving a complaint via the field office of an unhappy applicant, these same methods of getting money for an appliance claimed to be affected by power-surge are still currently utilized.

In subsequent disasters, inspectors were told to smell plugs for evidence of burning via surge, to check fuse boxes and breaker panels, and for the most part they did that. For the applicant, holding a lighter or match directly underneath the prongs of a plug the night before the inspector is due to arrive can still be widely successful, and slight burn marks around the outlet cover also doesn't hurt the cause. As well, a light swipe of a black Magic Marker or a thin coat of charcoal can do the trick, but both methods have to be wiped a bit to retain just a vestige of black, and done so the inspector's finger won't be smudged. But as we know, most inspectors will only perform a cursory job and base their decision on a visual in this instance.

Any type of tape over a breaker on the panel or a fuse will cause the same positive result, especially when the applicant frenetically tells the inspector that when they'd tried to reset the breaker or unscrew the fuse, sparks flew everywhere! Even if an appliance *did* work, all the applicant has to say was that it didn't function as before, the burn marks are present, and it's then up to the inspector to record it as Replace, Repair or list it as Unaffected. In the end, it is the applicant's inventiveness against FEMA in order to get money undeserved. No, not everyone will resort to this type of fraud, but as we know, a disaster exposes both the best and worst in people.

Well we should know is that much like the Public Assistance (PA) that FEMA cost-shares with local/state governments for repair of infrastructure, those governments sometimes also pay for 25% of all Individual Assistance (IA) within certain circumstances under the Stafford Act. So in effect, the ones that choose to cheat the system aren't only stealing from the Federal Government, but they're also stealing from their own states and towns. But in the world of greedy misfits, all bets are off in the casino called FEMA. Usually, unfortunately, the silver ball tends to land on their lucky number.

Hope springs eternal. Every applicant seemingly *expects* FEMA to attend to their dire needs. But the day may come when the agency that's responsible to attend to those needs might not be available to come to the rescue as we've been accustomed to and have always envisioned them to be. And that vision has been tainted by past storms, floods, and the inadequate responses suffered by populaces' adversely affected by them. Yes, history *is* the best teacher, should we choose to listen to those lessons. As this book is written, many past disaster victims are still in turmoil due to FEMA's lessons *not* learned from hurricanes Katrina and Andrew, the 500 year mid-west flood of 1993, Super-Storm Sandy, and the many other disasters most don't know about unless they'd personally experienced them.

In the days of Portsmouth, New Hampshire's 1803 disaster, prime contractors were both a nonexistent entity and terminology. There was no operation blue roof, no debris removal firms, and no trailers. Aside from the federal government's *very* basic assistance at that time, it was also expected of the affected populace to help themselves and their neighbors, for that was the mindset in our nation's history. A barn or house burned down and friends or relatives or neighbors all pitched-in to rebuild. If a farmer's crops were obliterated by a flood or hurricane, the same effort resulted. And that's what made America great.

Times have changed within our modern era of enablement and lack of personal fortitude. We should entertain the possibility that our past history could become the present, in full-circle, but to a degree we can't imagine, and may only ponder in our wildest dreams.

www.femasbest.com

23

PAFI

"THERE'S CRACKS IN EVERYTHING. THAT'S HOW THE LIGHT GETS IN"

LEONARD COHEN: 1934-2016, WRITER/POET

We now have a concise perspective of an inspector's job and the varied personnel who perform that particular work. Some may opine that the pay is relevant to the task, but if one believes it's a pleasurable vocation and monetarily rewarding they would be mistaken. Such is the opinion held by virtually every inspector past or present, including mine. And it is that opinion which spawned the birth of an organization that would protect basic human rights for those who constantly place their lives at risk to assist others, and who also put their own lives on hold by permitting themselves to be away from their homes and family when deployed to a disaster. Some of these inspectors are heroes and many are malcontents, but we don't live in a perfect world.

In 2006 I filed a request to the IRS, asking them to make a determination as to whether inspectors actually were employees or subcontractors. Per their determination after careful examination of PB's and Dewberry's corporate regulations, they submitted that inspectors were in fact employees. However, they refused to tell me whether they were intent on enforcing that determination. At the time of this writing, they still have not done so.

I then applied to the IRS for a reward under their whistleblower program, specifically based on two distinct findings. One was related to the theft of hundreds of FEMA computers that went missing in the field, and which held sensitive information of applicants that could be used for identity theft. As previously mentioned, some of these computers were found on ebay. The other was the fact that PB and Dewberry were gaining huge tax profits pertaining to their erroneous classification of inspectors, including their failure to pay overtime wages.

During 2007 when I filed a lawsuit against Parsons Brinkerhoff and Dewberry Davis, I formed an inspectors association named PAFI, which stands for "Professional Association of FEMA Inspectors." I understood the need for equitable treatment in the workplace that others readily enjoy within similar professions, but there was no entity to address inspectors' issues. The basic objective was to assemble a contingent of inspectors who represented FEMA's best, specifically those who excelled in their job with consummate dedication and professionalism.

To bring this idea to fruition, I spent countless hours and most of my savings, only to fail, at least in my personal estimation. I'd envisioned that my membership would be in the many hundreds, but only twenty-six inspectors, at that time, had aligned themselves with me. The problem was that most inspectors were fearful of being blacklisted, even though identities are protected to this day and mandated by the guidelines of PAFI. But in retrospect I try to remind myself that I really didn't fail, for many of the changes I fought for during the lawsuit are now reality.

In 2007, and represented by the California law firm Engstrom Lipscome & Lack, the same firm that represented Erin Brockovich, myself and a two other inspectors who had joined PAFI, and who'd agreed to act as class-action representatives, filed a lawsuit against the prime inspection contractors, Parsons Brinckerhoff and Dewberry Davis. Although only those twenty-four other inspectors had joined PAFI, the objective dutifully remained: To present to FEMA only those inspectors who represent FEMA's best, specifically those who excelled in their job.

To do that job correctly, one must know their craft and perform it in a professional manner. Knowledge of housing construction was, and is, tantamount to performance when attending to the needs of disaster applicants, and PAFI's mantra is that every one of those applicants deserves the highest degree of attention.

Malcontents, such as the runners, will never be considered for inclusion to PAFI, or those others who only seek monetary reward. Though this may seem somewhat utopian, I believe that every inspector must not be apathetic when in the field. When all is said and done, it's up to each and every one of them to maintain a sense of humanity in instances of disasters.

When PAFI filed its lawsuit, PB and Dewberry held a dim view of PAFI's goals. As said, to alleviate the risk of an inspector getting blacklisted, every member's name was, and is, held in the strictest of confidence, and that alone reflects poorly on the attitude of the prime contractors who seemingly revel in the fear-based environment they create for inspectors. Those two inspectors who were brave enough to place their names on the suit risked their livelihoods for the betterment of all.

The lawsuit, filed to attain benefits such as health insurance, workman's compensation, overtime pay, access to safety equipment per OSHA guidelines, and cost-of-living raises, posed a serious threat to both prime-contractors. PAFI's ultimate mission was to ensure that those changes became enforceable by virtue of almost every inspectors membership, a force to be reckoned with. PB and Dewberry didn't want to change a thing. I still recall an attorney saying to me in regard to PB: "These guys play rough. It's a good thing you're living in Canada." Suffice to say, I felt uneasy to say the least, but persevered no matter the depth of repercussions directed toward me.

The multi-million dollar misclassification lawsuit, heard in a Virginia court, had sought proper tenure as actual employees rather than subcontractors, overtime wages to be paid, and retroactive IRS taxes paid due to that misclassification. In the end, the case was resolved out of court. Within the three years of litigation, I experienced possibly collusion between attorneys, intentional delays designed to minimize monetary damages, and the failure of the court to recognize the IRS ruling that, in fact, all inspectors should be classified as employees and not subcontractors.

Much to my dismay, and although many inspectors received some back pay, the court decided that it would not include wages earned before and for hurricane Katrina, which is significant as there were not many disasters after Katrina as opposed to before. If wages earned before and for Katrina *were* considered by the court, many inspectors would have received checks up to $200,000, depending on how long they'd worked. As it was, most inspectors received checks of less than a thousand dollars.

Nevertheless, and causing me much frustration, inspectors still had to perform their duties as subcontractors rather than as employees. After the out of court settlement, some inspectors refused to work again. However, that number paled in comparison to those who chose to continue their livelihoods, whether good guys or bad.

Added to my frustration was the fact that I'd financed this endeavor with my own personal funds, but I did not relay this to any of the inspectors who'd received a check. To this day I do not regret working tirelessly on behalf of inspectors, even though I ended up on the verge of bankruptcy at that time. But when saying that I somewhat failed within my attempts to markedly correct the system, I did gain some moral victories. In 2013, upon winning the new contract together with Vanguard, PB changed its inspector classification to an employer/employee relationship. PB inspectors receive overtime, they get W-2's instead of 1099's, and they have health insurance. Added to those perks, they also receive a debit card when deployed, get a per diem, and no longer have to spend their own funds for cars and hotels. The basic pay remains about the same, roughly about $45 per inspection. It's a great improvement, but the pay is still short of insurance industry standards. In my opinion, as well as that of many current inspectors, $75 per inspection is reasonable. Vanguard, as mentioned, still maintains the subcontractor status for its inspectors. It's my hope that this status changes, should they win the next contract.

In the past, stories of inspectors sitting in crappy hotel/motel rooms without making money to even cover their expenses abounded. And that's unimaginable in a flood, for instance, that caused so much devastation. Many were the times when we'd only get downloaded one to three applications per day, which often represented an average loss of $1500 + per week. According to the rules and regulations governing "down-time," each inspector was *supposed* to be paid $400 per day of work, the equivalent of roughly eight daily inspections. However, the decision to not abide by that rule wasn't surprising and not really astounding when we remember the enormous profits the corporate prime contractors enjoy. "Use them and lose them" is and always was their mindset.

As we discussed in an earlier chapter, both PB and PaRR were astutely aware that many long-term inspectors were burning out and had essentially outlived their usefulness. Within the classes for new inspectors that we've also learned about, there are many others available to take their place.

Included within my moral victories was the decision by the new contractor, Vanguard Emergency Management, to add perks for their inspectors, many of whom gravitated to them after PaRR lost the most recent contract. Although their inspectors are still classified as subcontractors, they are reimbursed for their hotel, cars, gasoline, and receive a per diem, which, like PB's, differs from state to state and is usually in the $50-75 range.

Vanguard's inspectors do not receive any insurance, and their inspectors still have to support themselves for the first ten days in the field before receiving their initial reimbursement.

Subsequent reimbursements are paid in the same time-frame, but if you start performing inspections on, say a Saturday to Tuesday, and you've done eight per day, you can only invoice twenty inspections by the Tuesday midnight deadline, which would between $1120 and $1440, depending on your experience. If you start on a Tuesday, then that's better because you'll be able to invoice a full weeks work at that eight per day, which would be $1960 to $2520. It's a matter of timing, when you get to the field.

Vanguard's inspectors are paid according to experience, from $35-45 per inspection. But just like PB's inspectors, not many of them can tell the difference between a joist and a rafter. In that respect, I find it still laughable that FEMA, on its website, continues to state that all inspectors are knowledgeable about construction. That is a lie. Always was. Another moral victory was to alert FEMA to the hundreds of computers that went missing in the disaster fields, which contained the sensitive information of innocent applicants. If you remember in a previous chapter, I relayed the story of two new inspectors who got a computer and were never heard from again, and about the computers on ebay. That's only the tip of the iceberg. Currently, if an inspector allows anyone access to his or hers computer, that inspector is fired, badge taken, end of story. Currently, it appears that applicant's information is safer, but time will tell. Yet another moral victory was when I received a call from the Department of Homeland Security, thanking me for alerting them that both PB and PaRR had not reported to them that computers *were* missing. "Thanks for being a pain in the ass," The DHS guy said.

No one, including me, could accurately predict the outcome of the misclassification lawsuit. It seemed that a change was in the air, and many in the business are still of the opinion that both current prime contractors are extremely concerned about their longevity in the business of housing inspection services. There is always another outfit waiting in the wings to win the contract, willing and able to reap the windfall of government money that flows from a leaking spigot. For FEMA, the presence of PAFI and its lawsuit provided impetus to those particular changes. But what hasn't changed is FEMA's dim view of subcontracted inspectors. I hope that also changes. Nevertheless, and in the end, my moral victory apparently prompted those prime contractors to alter, to a degree, their stance on my basic issues.

PAFI had a slight heart attack because of the court ruling, but it still continues to beat. Its website is femasbest.com and I hope you visit it. Becoming a certified union is within the realm of possibility. Voices of reason are finally being heard where before they were silenced with distain and apathy borne of greed. As a long-term inspector myself, it is my hope that more positive changes are to come.

24

ANDREW, KATRINA AND LESSONS TO BE LEARNED

"DEEP INTO THAT DARKNESS PEERING, LONG I STOOD THERE, WONDERING, FEARING, DOUBTING, DREAMING DREAMS NO MORTAL DARED TO DREAM BEFORE".

Edgar Allen Poe. 1809-1849. American poet/writer

Similarities between the two most destructive hurricanes in modern history abound, but are often forgotten as time passes and memories fade. For conspiracy theorists and disaster victims alike, the repeated inability of FEMA to adequately respond to these two major storms, and according to its mission, is incomprehensible at best. Yet here we are as this book is written, on the cusp of yet another hurricane season. And for many who have experienced a major storm and had endured its aftermath, those memories may wallow or vacillate within a sense of denial in the credo of "it can't happen here again."

But it can. Probably will. It's never a question of *if* but more a question of *when*. Fear: it can sometimes become the greatest motivator to enact change.

History is said to be the best teacher, and now is the time to pay heed to that adage in order to be utilized as lessons before the next catastrophic hurricane, flood or earthquake strikes. Yes, similarities abound as we look further into these two most destructive storms that left nothing but confusion, destitution and anger for hundreds-of-thousands of disaster victims negatively affected by either the inability or predilection of our nation's preeminent disaster-response mechanism to expediently respond.

I was deployed to both of these events, and for anyone who's never lived through a major storm of that magnitude and endured their aftermaths, the most apt description would be to exist in a war-zone. In lieu, it must be remembered that during both Andrew and Katrina, a different type of war-zone was being administered by FEMA, but in a more resolute fashion to the very citizens that ultimately depended on them to provide all components of disaster relief within the Stafford Act. Terrorism remains the number one priority. It will remain this way---and has been especially fortified, since FEMA fell under the shadow of The Department of Homeland Security.

In 1992, George Bush Sr. was president of the United States, but had lost the election to Bill Clinton in November of that year. In 1990, Bush appointed Wallace Stickney, a protégé of former White house Chief-of-Staff, John Sununu, Stickney's former next-door neighbor in New Hampshire, to be FEMA's Director. Essentially, Mr. Stickney's previous experience in disaster management was equal to one wanting to open an Italian restaurant with no prior knowledge of the difference between lasagna and spaghetti.

Previous to his appointment with the agency, he'd served as Salem, New Hampshire's town engineer, was Commissioner of southern Rockingham's regional planning board, and was a special assistant for environmental affairs to that states' then Governor John Sununu. Additionally, he'd served as Commissioner for the New Hampshire Department of Transportation. All these job descriptions are the prerequisites for assuming the Directorship of FEMA, for them, anyway. His last employment was at Lebanon Municipal Airport in New Hampshire, running the operation on an interim capacity.

In shades of Brown, meaning Michael, the fortitude of FEMA's diligence when appointing directors to lead them beggar's belief that this same agency is entrusted to guide and provide all those requirements within the Stafford Act that one day may more resemble a mystery novel. In lieu of any further insights of Wallace Stickney's appointment, that might as well have been awarded to your favorite cartoon character, we can defer to the fact that he knew his capabilities were limited, and most likely put forth his best effort to assimilate himself into the complicated world of FEMA via many briefings within that intent. Nevertheless, it's still difficult to comprehend his statement regarding Michael Brown in a Nashua telegraph newspaper interview, in which he'd stated: "At this point, it might work best for FEMA to have the director return to the helm of the agencies emergency center."

In deference to Mr. Stickney, he at least refrained from any further predilection to be involved in disaster relief programs. The same can't be said for Mr. Brown, however, whom in 1995 started a new business venture in Boulder, Colorado called "Michael D. Brown LLC." It was a disaster preparedness consulting firm, oddly enough. Though I'm not certain where his client-base emanated from, I surmise that they'd all suffered from short-term memory loss. Conversely, our collective memories should be razor-sharp for what the future may hold.

We all must remember that the end of the Cold War did not alter FEMA's resolve to redirect most of their budget towards threats of terrorism instead of disaster relief programs. Much like Michael Brown, Stickney's tenure existed when geopolitical maelstroms were un-folding. When Andrew decimated south Florida, Iraq was invading Kuwait. When Katrina obliterated Louisiana, the war in Iraq was peaking. As we'll be exploring in further detail in the next chapter titled FEMA's "black budget," of which has been written about by both conspiracy theorists and mainstream reporters, that budget may in fact effectually *prevent* appropriate funding for consummate disaster relief purposes. As well, ineffective and ill-equipped directors appointed to that post pose an equally dire end-result when an Andrew or Katrina strike a population center that has no idea why it takes so long for FEMA to mobilize.

Equally so, within these two storm's lineage of similarities, is the fact that both were responsible for many deaths, victims unaccounted for, and most importantly, a lax response time-frame from FEMA. Without rehashing the many media reports you've probably read since Katrina's landfall, the facts state that it took three days for FEMA to "gear-up" for a hurricane that was dead-on target for New Orleans. As in that "war-zone" previously mentioned, all the pieces were in place to facilitate that inevitability. But still, the mayhem continued unabated for weeks upon weeks.

In Florida, Andrew's 1992 landfall resulted in a similar three day initial response from FEMA, evacuation plans went horribly awry, just as in Katrina, and lawlessness prevailed virtually unabated until order was finally restored by the National Guard, who'd arrived two weeks after landfall. Before the Guard's intervention, local and state law enforcements were left to their own devices to quell the rampant crime, which always culminates within a society's breakdown.

Both hurricanes created points and counterpoints in a blame-game that resulted in no significant changes to FEMA's system. New Orleans Mayor Ray Nagin and Governor Blanco lashed out at FEMA for their inadequate response, and FEMA defended those accusations by blaming Louisiana's sorry excuse for an evacuation plan and failure to formally request to cede complete authority to oversee relief efforts. The levee system became the prime focus of attention; FEMA accused the State of misdirecting funding that was provided to strengthen them, and the State deflected those impunities with any verbiage at hand.

In Andrew, Florida's Governor, Lawton Chiles, also delayed requesting full federal assistance, citing that the initial need seemed "silly" and rebuking Bush's contention that Chiles hadn't eventually asked for it, and as the world's televisions were channeled to images of flattened homes as far as the eye could see. As Former FEMA director James lee Witt had said in testimony to a 1996 Congressional panel that "Disasters are very political events," all of us might carefully heed those words.

However applicable the levee and evacuation debacle impacted the course of events of Katrina, the most poignant aspect Andrew and Katrina shared was the total collapse of a modern population that became mired in a sort of wild-west environment until law and order was finally restored. Forgotten somewhat as the years have passed, to the ones that didn't live in the hurricanes path, are the terror and rampant confusion equivalent to what may transpire during a missile attack. That complete breakdown in itself is something that will also happen again when the next devastating hurricane, earthquake or flood occurs in a major population center, for in a major disaster, the best and worst are always displayed by those affected by it.

Alternatively, the storms that ravaged Florida in 2004 produced little negativity in comparison. Hurricanes Charley, Francis and Jeanne were devastating events, Ivan less so, and this may be because both Andrew and Katrina impacted heavily populated cities, whereas the Florida hurricanes landfall areas were of a smaller scope. As an example, Hurricane Francis did *not* devastate Miami and Lauderdale, and in fact, shouldn't have even *been* declared. But it was, just because it was an election year for the Bush's. Conversely, hurricanes Jeanne and Charlie did produce much damage to Volusia County and environs. Very possibly, however, FEMA's more expedient response may be due to the fact that another Bush was in the Governor's seat, making certain that response was decisive. Either-or, Director Michael Brown drew very little criticism during the Florida storms, but was forced out of his office when Katrina proved far beyond his capabilities, even though President Bush had lauded his efforts. Gushed might be a better word.

The fact that Andrew and Katrina happened under the watch of two Presidents named Bush would normally be fodder for rigid conspiracy theorists or followers of Nostradamus quatrains. The fact also remains that both Bush presidents made the wrong choice in their selection of FEMA Directors. It's purely conjecture to state that if James lee Witt was in charge events would have been more positive, but that wouldn't have been a negative. The lesson is obvious, but dubious as to if this practice will ever change.

In a strange parallel to hurricane Katrina, Wallace Stickney was removed by the elder Bush when criticism regarding the federal response to hurricane Andrew became extremely heightened, and he was removed from the responsibilities of coordinating relief efforts. That replacement was Andrew Card, Bush Senior's Transportation Secretary, who in later years became White House Chief of Staff for George W. Bush. If but for nothing else, Andrew Card will forever be remembered as the one who whispered into George W's ear on September 11nth, 2001 that "America was under attack," when the President was reading a pet goat story to schoolchildren in a Florida classroom.

Under almost exact conditions as Stickney, Michael Brown was hastily removed for directing relief efforts in Louisiana, but maybe not for the correct reasons. Politically, they both became liabilities to their respective administrations, and for Brown, that spelled doom to the then up-coming 2004 elections. In true newspeak, the blame-game again became prominent as no one tried to reach the core of the problems associated with Katrina, but seemingly rather chose to save face in any venue available for the mere sake of protecting votes in the state of Florida, which eventually decided the presidential election.

Both Bush presidents were proponents of "big business," and although corporations flourished under both of their administrations, as well as others in the past, it was under George W's administration that prime contractors, such as Bechtel and all the others we've un-covered, enjoyed immense and uncontested profits. Much like using the FEMA budget as their personal ATM, no-bid contracts became the norm when FEMA's emergency response mechanisms evolved from utilizing small user-friendly housing inspection service firms, like Vulcan and the other mom and pops, to corporate entities such as Vanguard and Parsons Brinckerhoff and, in the past, Dewberry Davis. They all devour fat contracts with insatiable appetites.

A different type of eating machine also existed in both Andrew and Katrina, one that hasn't received much press but is hauntingly similar in nature to both storms. In Florida, the devastation spanned to the outer-reaches of the Everglades National Park that buffers heavily populated areas. In Louisiana, the Bayou Sauvage National Wildlife refuge borders or is within

New Orleans' city limits. Even though alligator population numbers aren't entirely accurate, a multi-year study to discover an approximate number was implemented by The US Geological Survey (USGS) in 2004, and it's been estimated that at least one-million are in the Everglades. In Bayou Sauvage, that population count is similar. Within those estimations, it is also known that many migrant workers were located in or near these wild expanses of swamp and hungry predators.

Totals of deaths directly attributed to Katrina are nebulous, but are even more speculative as those of Andrew. For the former, approximately 1300 fatalities were reported. For the latter, fifteen died as a direct result of the hurricane, and another 25 "Indirectly" per figures from NOAA. Other sources have placed that number at a bit less or a bit more, fluctuating in the effort to define fatalities directly attributed to the storm, as opposed to indirect. But the numbers of those *missing* in both hurricanes *could* to be much greater and almost similar. According to The National Center for Missing and Exploited Children, approximately 1300 Katrina children were still unaccounted for as of December 2005 and those numbers have currently not been significantly altered. Accordingly, The National Center for Missing Adults, and reports by USA Today, estimated, at that same date, that 6600 people remained missing.

For Andrew, the numbers officially reported as deaths attributed to the storm pale in comparison to the 5000 + reported in various blog-sites and alternative news-sites. Knowing other housing inspectors who were also deployed to Andrew, stories and rumors of bodies stuffed into body-bags and disposed of were commonplace. From one inspector, I learned that bodies of three Jamaicans were swept to Florida's shores by the winds and surge of Andrew, but am not sure if those deaths were included in the vacillating account of *actual* deaths. I also saw bodies in various states of dismemberment and decomposition, and also saw a very large military presence that oftentimes made me feel I was the enemy because of their eerie comportment.

In the book by K.T Frankovitch, titled *Where Heavens Meet*, an exact number *was* reported by one Roy Howard, who'd introduced himself to her as a Chief Petty Officer when she was conducting a lecture in Clearwater, Florida in 1999. Mr. Howard claimed that the death figures reported were totally inaccurate, and that via his sources in the National Guard, "the actual count was "5,280........something," he had said. Additionally, he also stated that another 1500 bodies were retrieved by the Coast Guard from the lakes and surrounding waters, all quietly disposed of in incinerators by both the Guard and FEMA.

This number of deaths may seem like a plausible estimate in a hurricane of Andrew's magnitude, but one might also wonder why so many have not been reported as missing by either relatives or friends. Part of that may be attributed to FEMA's recalcitrance in providing information to those relatives or friends, as its stated policy is to not give any information of that type. That's same situation also occurred in Katrina.

If the approximate total of 9000 trailers destroyed by Andrew are taken into consideration, either a miracle of sorts transpired or that body-count of 5280 may harbor *some* semblance of accuracy. As most everyone knows, whether by virtue of living in them or not, trailers are the most susceptible structure in a storm of magnitude.

Home is where you hang your heart. There are always a significant number of people who refuse to abandon their property, either by sheer stubbornness or in the hope that a hurricane will suddenly veer-off course or diminish in strength before landfall. But should we take those 9000 trailers and assume that many people did just that, a heightened death-count for Andrew may reflect it. We must also remember that entire neighborhoods were totally demolished and virtually unrecognizable to even its former inhabitants, some of whom had no relatives or friends who would actually report them missing. Additionally, and especially in the mayhem of Andrew's aftermath, people lose track of others, sometimes simply assuming that this person or that have quickly re-located. In theory, this scenario would make sense. In reality, it may also prompt sensible guidance regarding reconsideration of the actual number of deaths.

Dade County, Florida, had a sizeable population of migrant workers on farms and otherwise, and it's plausible that many of them decided to weather the storm instead of seeking public shelter. Makeshift camps were commonplace, far-removed from prying eyes but close enough to make a day's meager pay. Many of them probably had families either abroad or state-side, and one can only imagine the frustration of a wife, brother or other relative seeking information about that person when they became among the missing. Some of these family members may have been illegal immigrants themselves, had maybe barely spoken English, and would obviously find themselves totally lost in any attempt to locate a loved one.

A name is given to the police. That name becomes just another number in the netherworld of the missing. The same could hold true for a concerned neighbor who reports that a certain someone hasn't been seen and their house or trailer is demolished. In Louisiana, the same scenario could hold true, Katrina swallowing victims and disposing them in an abyss of non-existence as if they'd never inhabited the planet. But if there *are* many missing---including the ones *not* missed by anyone in either storm via lack of follow-up information, than one would correctly surmise that bodies existed somewhere. Then again, maybe not.....

When deployed to Hurricane Katrina, I had heard stories that had initially sounded irrational, but which were relayed to me by rational inspectors in and around New Orleans. Reports of alligators swimming up and down flooded streets eating corpses or the injured unable to defend themselves, sounded more like a script in a horror movie than reality. But when one considers that not only humans were adversely affected by Katrina and Andrew, then we may consider that an unknown number of people *were* indirect casualties. In New Orleans' Ninth Ward, National Guard troops shot and killed a twenty-two-foot alligator weighing an estimated four tons. Too old to catch game, it fed on humans either already dead or close to it. For Andrew, it may be possible that many others met that same fate, but will never be authenticated for many reasons. In Louisiana's St. Bernard Parish, locals told some inspectors that some bodies will never be found because alligators had taken them away.

On some days I can still smell the stench of death when deployed to Katrina and Andrew. I remember walking up the stairs to a house and smelling that smell. It's something that you can never forget. It's something that's somehow ingrained into your senses.

In parallel, both Andrew and Katrina were pockmarked with media reporters' frustrations that FEMA had refused to let them accompany any search and rescue teams deployed to water-ways or flooded urban areas. Whether that directive, probable or not, had existed in other instances of media black-outs when transitioning from FEMA to the local police and National Guard, there apparently *was* a concerted effort to prevent violent episodes from appearing in the mainstream media.

Pictures of "sensitive" situations were not allowed to be taken. In one instance "Reporters without Borders" told of a Times-Picayune photographer's camera being destroyed by police after he was observed filming a lengthy exchange of gunfire between the police and supposed rioters. In another case, a photographer from the Toronto Star was detained by police and his film taken when he was observed taking pictures of a clash between them and citizens, who the police claimed were looters. In a blog by NBC anchorman Brian Williams, he'd reported that police officers were seen aiming their weapons at media crews, that reporters were no longer allowed into either the Convention Center or the Superdome, and that that no one was allowed to photograph dead bodies. In other reports, circulated in blogs, National Guard troops were under orders to turn-away all journalists, effectively preventing them from photographing anything that was not meant to be seen by anyone but them. Apparently, Bush, FEMA and everyone down-the-line was successful in their predilection to obliterate the First Amendment when censoring reporting from the war-zone of Katrina.

In a type of hurricane gallows humor, both of these storms were open to incalculable pratfalls both on the part of FEMA and state governments. Three days after Andrew's landfall, Miami/Dade County Emergency management Director Kate Hale had asked "Where is the cavalry on this one?" Bush and FEMA sprang into action, sending the Army in to provide mobile kitchens and tent cities. In Katrina, Mayor Ray Nagin and Governor Blanco somewhat echoed that same refrain, and with similar results. Disaster relief should certainly not be susceptible to political differences within Democratic or the Republican Parties, but it will, unfortunately, remain both an obstacle and forbearer of things to come.

And maybe history has been attempting to teach us that, as mammoth hurricanes strike our shores with indifference. The lesson we must learn is to somehow limit our dependence on FEMA in the future, just as they are heightening their predilection to more attend to terrorism issues than to disaster relief. It's not a question of if, but when. The likelihood of more catastrophic storms, floods or earthquakes demands that we must prepare for them. And that preparation should emanate from the knowledge gained through the painful experiences of repeated failures, such as in Andrew and Katrina.

In an article by Miami Herald staff writers Martin Merzer and Tom Fiedler, they'd asked the same question many of us have asked ourselves, but one that may never be fully answered:

www.femasbest.com

"If we can do it for Bangladesh, the Philippines, for the Kurds in Iraq, why in God's name can't we deliver basic necessities of life to the ravaged population of our own Gulf Coast?"

25

THE DARK SIDE OF FEMA

"Don't tell them---then it will not exist"

Joseph Paul Goebbells: German World War Two Information Minister

Called the "Shadow Government" or "Secret Government" in the circles of conspiracy theorists who attempt to investigate FEMA's vaults of secrets and hidden agendas, the word *Theory* could transpose to *claim*. In itself, the term conspiracy theory is ambiguous, for a theory is not one in actuality if it's proven to be true. As said in this book's introduction, most notions without basis of fact would not be addressed, but there are certain and *factual* anomalies within FEMA's apparent hidden agendas that do hold enough plausibility for us to intelligently explore further.

During the horrendous days of hurricane Andrew and Katrina's aftermath, examples of totalitarian rule gave new rise to conspiracy theorists' beliefs that FEMA is but a wolf in sheep's clothing. People were left to fend for themselves without food or water for many days, or housed in shelters guarded by soldiers. It was an indelible image that one could more easily understand if transpiring in a third-world country.

In British media reports, most notably those of *Mirror UK*, tons of food, NATO Ration-Packs, were inexplicably withheld from distribution to Katrina victims. In Canada, *CTV* reported that food, medical supplies and personnel were denied permission to assist by Department of Homeland Security, but that the Canadian Red Cross was eventually admitted to the disaster warzone. During the aftermath of the two most publicized and powerful hurricanes in modern history that lashed sections of the United States into submission, lessons have apparently not been learned from either storm.

The classroom remains open for those with open minds and long memories. Once again, we must remember that FEMA's primary mission is *not* relegated to disaster relief, but to administering its many forms of authority when a situation warrants it, and maybe even if it doesn't. Armed with powers from the Executive Orders outlined in this book, the reality of a catastrophic event — that any hurricane or flood would pale in comparison to — may trigger FEMA's clandestine mechanisms that would prove to be a nightmare scenario unimaginable to anyone, except to those who have delved into facts within or beyond this book's information.

Originally, FEMA's charter defined its role for planning and training activities, specifically concerning natural disasters, nuclear war, the event of an enemy attack on the United States or on its territory's soil, and incidents of domestic civil unrest. However, the latter seems to be the only item of that charter that both politicians and conspiracy buffs currently tend to focus, and maybe rightfully so. FEMA's mission is both secretive and rigid to the general public, information leaking out in drips from a faucet of denials against frustrating attempts to uncover the truth behind the well-stitched layers of its inherent ability to maintain and extend an aura of paternalism to its citizens who may eventually become victims of natural disasters. They are verbal thoroughbreds.

But that invincibility may be somewhat waning due to the efforts of those who adamantly demand the truth and are not willing to simply abide by irrational conspiracy notions. For us, we're simply dealing with the facts. And within that, opinions will most certainly foster in whichever fashion is personally suitable.

In our chapter lineage that explained the birth of current FEMA, which sprung from the Federal Emergency Preparedness Agency, President Gerald Ford ordered that agency to implement plans to establish absolute government control of the mechanisms that control distribution of energy sources and the flow of money within America's financial institutions. In his ensuing Executive Order # 11921, this dictated that when a State of

Emergency was declared by the President of the United States, Congress was not to be privy to review the implementation of it for a period of six months.

In those poignant three words that nebulously describes a "State of Emergency," we may ask ourselves why it was inserted to begin with. Whether a hidden agenda or not, the fact remains that the enactment of that EO effectively allows the President of the United States to become a dictator. However that may sound, the fact remains that the structure of the EO expressly and quintessentially provides for that occurrence.

We know that President Jimmy Carter created the agency via an Executive Order, but it was during the administration of Ronald Reagan that FEMA's true purpose became evident to those in control but remained clouded in mystery to those outside that confined sphere. During his term, FEMA was elevated to intelligence-level status. A senior-level board of varied departments was also created that became the "Emergency Mobilization Preparedness Board" (EMPB), which was a precursor to the current Cabinet-level office of Homeland Security.

During Reagan's term, a series of national "training" exercises was created in preparation for prognosticated or conceptual domestic events, such as mass riots in multiple cities, nuclear war, biological infestation, or any form of violent upheaval that would necessitate the suspension of the Constitution *and* an ensuing declaration of martial law. Through the powers given to FEMA, they alone would be directing these operations. Garden Plot and Cable Splicer and REX 84 are but three of these training exercises we'll look further into, but for now, we'll concentrate on the architects of FEMA's possible hidden agendas, and within doing so, I'll maintain my credo of only addressing plausibility's, borne of pertinent facts.

As we may remember the name Louis Giuffrida from our list of FEMA directors, Reagan's Deputy at that time, John Brinkerhoff, was equally resolved to employ every avenue available in order to culminate the directive of attaining a plan that would completely deal with any form of massive civil unrest. FEMA was —and still is, continuing their efforts started in 1987 and in a paranoid-style reminiscent of the cold war days.

Many are familiar with the name, Oliver North, but some may not be acquainted with his involvement with FEMA in the early nineteen-eighties. Though his involvement was short-lived, it was both impacting and disturbing, given his lineage in illegalities of the highest order. Assigned by National Security advisor Robert McFarlane, North joined Giuffrida, (also a former Colonel in the US Army) to oversee and complete the formulation of the EMPB. Reagan's implementation of the EMPB created not only that board, but it also gave a small group of people the opportunity to enjoy enormous powers via the twenty-seven Senior Interdepartmental Groups, (SIG's) in one of which North was a Deputy Director of political and military affairs, as well as being a National Security Council liaison.

It must be noted the both North and McFarlane, as some may well remember, were co-conspirators in the Iran-Contra scandal. Consequently, they utilized their executive authority awarded by Reagan to alter civil defense planning to a level of consummate domestic control directives with both the police and military as the vanguards. The precursors were domestic insurrection or nuclear war, but both would result in massive military mobilization to quell it.

Giuffrida was astutely aware of the Posse Commitatus Act of 1878, but was quoted as saying that "it was misinterpreted," all the while being a staunch proponent of its limitations that he sought to change for the purpose of its dissolution. For those who don't know about the Posse Commitatus Act, it forbids the military's involvement in domestic affairs, and prevents it from arresting American citizens. Passed on June 14th in the latter phase of the Civil War's reconstruction period, it was designed to prevent a repeat of the atrocities directed at the citizens of conquered Confederate states, where acts of unmitigated aggression were inflicted upon those American citizens at the hands of federal troops entrusted to uphold the law. Additionally, thousands of profit-seeking individuals that we may now refer to as "entrepreneurs," traveled to the southern states seeking easy profits by purchasing real estate and businesses' for pennies on the dollar, and then became the protagonists of many anti-government disturbances. In those days, they were called "carpetbaggers," the term derived from suitcases they'd travelled with and which contained wares to sell for inflated prices or cash to buy whatever they desired. Turmoil was created from greed and apathy. Riots burgeoned from the growing discontent and mistrust of the very government looked upon as a protector.

In this modern era — and should the event occur that requires intervention of local and state authorities who prove powerless to handle it, the military may simply have to be "deputized" by FEMA to successfully circumvent the Commitatus Act. In lieu of that, however, Public Law # 109-364, also known as the "John Warner Defense Authorization Act" of 2007, *was* designed to amend/circumvent Posse Commitatus and the Insurrection Act of 1807, thereby allowing the federal government to take control over any states' National Guard and deploy federal troops anywhere in the country during a public emergency. The Insurrection Act clearly states that local and state governments should be entirely responsible for enacting initial responses to contain domestic disturbances, and was designed to *limit* Presidential power as much as possible. Unfortunately, this may not be the case today.

The only instance's in American history of the implementation of *Federal* martial law was in Hawaii from 1941 to 1945 and President Lincoln's imposition of it two times. In 1864 Kentucky, its purpose was to quell anti-union riots. In 1862 it was declared in wide-spread fashion, whereas its declaration was aimed at *any* citizen in the United States deemed as being disloyal to the Union. Under its exact functioning, curfews are established and enforced, military courts/tribunals are utilized for trials, arrests are conducted by military personnel, and they assume *total* control over a population.

The closest instance to that example in modern times was during the Los Angeles riots of 1992, when units of the Army's 7nth division and Marines from Camp Pendleton were deployed to that city. Law and order was somewhat established before those troops arrived, and thus, martial law was not enacted. By issuing Proclamation # 6247 on May 1, President Bush commanded all persons to cease and desist from any and all acts of violence. That same day, he issued EO # 12804, which authorized the use of armed forces to restore order. However, martial law was never declared.

Deployment of federal troops to quell civil disturbances has occurred many times in the past and were all affected via Presidential Proclamation, but sans a formal declaration of martial law. As examples, during the labor-related violence in the coalfields of 1914 Colorado, President Woodrow Wilson ordered infantry units to disarm all persons, sheriffs and deputies, police, and even members of that states' National Guard. In Idaho, federal troops were deployed by President McKinley, and that state's governor declared martial law on May 3rd, 1889. During that period, prisoners were held for several months, mostly miners who were committing acts of violence during the heated labor-related mining issues.

During the days of post-Civil War reconstruction, President Grant commanded residents, under the Enforcement Acts of 1871, to deliver to the military all guns and ammunition, and he suspended Habeas Corpus in nine of one state's counties, whose African-American citizens were being murdered and terrorized by the Ku Klux Klan. Basically, Habeas Corpus is a legal action through which a person can seek relief from unlawful detention. By denying it, one is at the mercy of their captors.

A point to consider would be that under the exact guidelines of martial law, it *can* be implemented by the local "commander," should immediate action be required, and should communications thwart the relay of that information to the president. As we know, that would seem impossible in this day and age of cellphones, computers and the like, but one can never prognosticate or discount the occurrence of that conceptual anomaly.

What, for instance, would transpire if the power grid failed? In the event of massive civil unrest or a well-planned attack on our mainland that could hamper or destroy communications capabilities, martial law could be declared by the one highest in authority in a demographic area of the event.

As an example, in past history, General Andrew Jackson issued the order for martial law in New Orleans during the war of 1812, after capturing that city from the British and being unable to confer with President James Madison in expedient manner. In these modern times, this same scenario could transpire in that the *Regional* Director of FEMA could be visiting anywhere within the confines of a demographic, communications could be rendered useless, and effectually, he/she could issue that declaration with full authority, suspend the Constitution, and impose virtual dictatorial power.

The same would apply for *any* instance of the above, be it a state's governor, a city's mayor, or the General of an areas National Guard. Well we might recall the infamous quote of General Alexander Haig when saying, "I'm in charge now," after President Reagan was shot in an assassination attempt and Vice President George W. Bush was "in the air" and out of direct contact.

Even though a natural disaster has yet to result in martial law in the history of the United States, Mayor Ray Nagin *verbally* declared it by instructing local and state law-enforcement authorities to not pay attention to Miranda or civil rights in the aftermath of hurricane Katrina, but he didn't hold the legal power to do so. Instead, the Governor of Louisiana issued a State of Emergency, which culminated in the deployment of troops to assist in quelling the mayhem. In the recent past, and to clarify, the only instance that *almost* brought the scenario of *federal* martial law to full fruition was those 1992 Los Angeles riots. As that particular "civil disturbance" didn't gravitate to other cities in similar magnitude, wide-spread martial law was *not* declared, and as such, mechanisms were never

www.femasbest.com

emplaced via Executive Orders that *could* have taken hold.

We'll never know what could have transpired if St. Louis or Miami or Detroit rivaled or superseded the gravity of Los Angeles' insurgency. And we can only imagine the consequences should we not be vigilant regarding FEMA's omnipresent and dictatorial powers, which are validated by the facts outlined.

In some articles I've read through the years by conspiracy theorists, I personally find some faults, borne by the apparent penchant to instill a sense of fear. Yes, those writers are certainly attuned to the *possibilities* of domestic Armageddon, but they seem to be more aligned to offering a type of mass hysteria that intelligent folks would instantly recognize as irrational. Nevertheless, factual information offered by media reports or Senate hearings on the subject of FEMA is often pondered momentarily by those who are too busy with the daily doldrums of life to take the time to study the truths that lay before their eyes. Americans seem to be totally confident in their perceived ability to conquer any obstacle, and maybe rightfully so when remembering D-Day and Iwo Jima. But those locations are very far removed from our present form of government and current distant wars, and we may consider that instead of an enemy invading our shores, an enemy from within may foment equal but dissimilar damage and devastation. With no recourse other than to reflect on our decisions at the time when a resolution could have possibly been found, no action becomes inaction, destined to be a fault that lies within us all.

In the same vein, it would have better-served the Florida Sun-Sentinel's purpose to simply plant a reporter into either a PB or PaRR class back in the 2004 hurricane season and *become* a housing inspector, which would have enabled an actual first-hand and irrefutable look into the facets of that particular program. Per that analogy, it's up to each of us to intelligently dissect information, to reach the conclusion between possibility and probability.

The *probability* of underground facilities operating for undefined reasons under FEMA's direction is extremely high. The likelihood of detention camps existing for an unspecified purpose is to that degree also. But what we'll need to do, as the words in this chapter flow, is to not only make a firm decision between fact and fiction, but to take a stance where irrefutable information can lead to only one resolute opinion.

For example, we know that George Bush Sr. was Vice President under Ronald Reagan, but some folks still don't know that his lineage in the oil business is very deep. He'd once owned a company named Zapata Oil. Zapata acquired Pennsylvania Oil and it became Pennzoil. His son, George W, was also heavily invested in the oil business and has proven to be a friend of corporations via the fat contracts awarded to the firms outlined in previous chapters. And that is irrefutable. Important for us to also remember is that the President in office holds the key to FEMA's disaster-relief funding, and which could augment appropriations beyond its original directives. Every single declaration stems from his signature alone. If The President of the United States doesn't sign, the buck stops there.

For all we know, Reagan could have been suffering from the illness that eventually overcame him while in office, and George Bush Sr. was actually steering the rudder of the good ship government. During his term as Vice President, Bush had started the Task-Force on Combating Terrorism, and named himself head of the Terrorist Incident Working group from 1984 to 1985, long before Osama Bin Laden became a household name. These events *may* be linked to what we've all experienced after his tenure, but we'll never know for sure. But what we *do* know is that whatever information is offered in this chapter *can* be assimilated and brought to finite conclusion, whether you are motivated by fear, anger, or the penchant to seriously question the fodder that mainstream news purveys. And with that thought, the FEMA Detention Camps are a good venue in continuance of our journey.

Yes, "facilities" *are* embedded throughout our entire Country, but for what exact purpose? For us, now at the latter-stage of this book, we'll segment this elongated chapter for ease of consumption. Following will be explorations to the underground bunkers of FEMA, their contracted security personnel, the black projects, additional insights into FEMA's funding and the links between them all, so we can compare the pertinent facts to the mainstream fodder and conspiracy theories. Per this book's compendium, the intention remains to be concise, but to also be thought-provoking.

DETENTION CAMPS

In virtually every state, facilities exist that would defy, in these modern times, a sane reason or purpose. But in the past, prisoner-of war (POW) detention camps *were* scattered around the country during World War 11. The inhabitants of these camps were Japanese, German and Italian prisoners of war, and also Japanese-Americans civilians who were obviously not enemy soldiers. As paranoia usually strikes deep in the bowels of government, this was diabolically evident during that particular time.

When President Roosevelt signed December 1941's Executive Order # 3066, which effectively sent over 110,000 mostly United States citizens to relocation camps, entire families were forced from their homes and jobs due to nothing less than the assumption that any one of them could be a spy or a close friend of "Tokyo Rose." In their absence, homes were looted, personal possessions lost forever, and lives were totally disrupted in the name of freedom. But that freedom didn't exist for those detainees who were in fact prisoners of war, and whom had never donned an enemy uniform nor had ever spoken against the United States Government. And in fact, they were mostly patriotic American's, whether naturalized or native-born.

They'd embraced their country with arms and hearts opened wide, but their eyes were closed to the unthinkable possibility that they'd be held captive for no just reason or pertinent charges.

The definition of a "detainee" is that of one kept in custody and not allowed freedom for an unspecified period of time. The definition of "incarcerate" means to be imprisoned. Somewhere between these two interpretations, the semantics, the specific result is to be denied freedom of liberty.

In Guantanamo Bay, Cuba, captives are still currently held without benefit of trial. They were, and maybe still are, systematically tortured sans any assistance or intervention from the United Nations that's supposed to uphold all facets of the Geneva Convention pertaining to the treatment of POW's. And we could assume, with an open mind, that some are innocent. The very location that current prisoners of war are held in the Caribbean basin is an irony itself, as it was part of the spoils ceded via "leasehold" to the United States at the end of the Spanish-American War.

In conspiracy theories at that time, some believed that the United States actually blew-up the battleship USS Maine to instigate the war that eventually enabled the United States to appropriate Puerto Rico, the Northern Mariana Islands and the Philippines — which eventually re-attained their sovereignty — and that little slice of Cuba affectionately known as "Gitmo." In light of Guantanamo Bay's current status, we may ask: "Why do so many facilities with razor-wire and guard towers currently exist within our own nation's boundaries?"

For a moment, let's place ourselves in the mindset of a WW 11 Japanese family that's just been visited by armed soldiers at their home in San Francisco. You are told to quickly pack-up your basic necessities and are ordered to enter a bus or a military vehicle. You ask why but you get no definitive answer. Your wife and children are crying, but no emotions are exhibited by the ones that came to take you away to somewhere that's also not specified, but that's only said to be a "safe-place." In the bus or vehicle are others just like you, all Japanese and all bewildered. Deep inside you know this is a mistake, but you also know, as the bus pulls away from the home in your adopted country, that life will never be the same.

In a demographic that may afford one the opportunity to discover where the truth may lay or to ascertain the void between a theory and claim and a fact, the following locations of camps are for sheer perusal, possible insight and maybe some self-discovery. There are purportedly 600-800 of these facilities.

The readers of this book, who are within reasonable proximity to the ones listed, have the opportunity for a weekend excursion to either a dead-end road or a glimpse into the future. It must be noted that you *may* encounter individuals assigned to guard some of these facilities. Caution should be exercised.

Most of these facilities are reported to be similar in design, with razor-wire fences surrounding an inner-structure of numerous buildings and staffed by armed guards, military or contracted personnel from the private sector. As well, there have been reports of soldiers not of United States origin present at these camps. Some have speculated that they are United Nations troops. Additionally, most all of these facilities are reported to be either renovated or constructed near railway heads, major highway systems, rivers or airports. With that alone, the question may be asked as to why they are near transportation points. To begin, we'll focus on some of these homes away from home for WW 11 detainees, and for whoever may inhabit them in the future.

1: In Arizona, there are two former WW 11 detention camps currently renovated or in process thereof, according to reports via the "Patriot Movement" and from various other sources. In Florence, there is a fully-operational and renovated facility currently holding 400 "prisoners," but which can accommodate 3500. In Pinal County on the Gila River, a former Japanese detention camp may be in the process of renovation or upgrading. In Alabama, the former WW 11 German POW camp at Aliceville purportedly has a capacity of 15,000.

2: At Indiantown Gap Military Reservation, north of Harrisburg, Pennsylvania, a WW 11 POW facility is said to have been renovated by former President Jimmy Carter, and is an active station previously used to hold Cubans during the Mariel Boatlift. In Crossville, Tennessee, there is a former WW 11 German/Italian POW Camp that's been renovated, and training facilities supposedly exist that include ropes over a rappelling deck. At Fort Douglas in Utah, a previously inactive military reservation has been renovated to its former status as a WW 11 POW camp. In West Virginia, at Beckley, Alderson and Lewisburg, former POW camps have been reportedly converted into prison complexes capable of interning several times their current populations, which includes the women's reformatory on that site.

3: Central Utah's Millard County is purportedly the location of another WW 11 camp being renovated. At Camp Lejeune in North Carolina, at New River Marine Airfield, another WW 11 Camp exists, this one with a "mock city" that could resemble many towns in America. In that same state, yet another renovated detention camp is at Fort Bragg, and is said to be located at the Special Warfare Training Center. In Scottsbluff, Nebraska, a former German POW camp is either renovated or in the planning stages, and at Camp Perry in Ohio, a former German/Italian POW camp has been renovated.

There are many more WW 11 camps reportedly scattered around the country in either functioning condition or in-process thereof, and their purpose is as mystifying as it is disturbing. To augment those particular camps listed, many hundreds more either sit idle or are currently being used by small numbers of prisoners that pale in comparison to the actual populations these centers can actually accommodate. One could ask that, if so, then the information received about our overcrowded prison facilities is either faulty or misleading, at the least.

4: Should you be in Nevada at Pine, a camp may be about ten miles south.

www.femasbest.com

In the town of Wells, one could be in the "O'Niel Basin," some 40 miles north past Thousand Springs and off of Highway 93 west. In Pershing County, you might want to travel I-80 to mile-marker112, where on the south-side is a country road that you'll go down about a mile. Three-quarters of a mile off that road is something that's either there or not. If you're in Ohio, near Lima, there's a facility said to be a FEMA detention camp near the old Stone Quarry in the area of Interstate 95 that has fences and a railway line leading to it. In Allenwood, Pennsylvania, a federal prison located south of Williamsport, on the Susquehanna River, is said to have a current population of a few hundred, but has the capacity to hold 50 times that number.

5: California may have its own share of camps, such as in Pearblossom, at the intersection of Avenue 116 and the Pearblossom Highway. In Filmore, one may possibly be found on highway # 126. In Valencia, another may be at the intersection of the 5 and 405 freeways. Still another could be in Glendale. For that one, the adventurer would have to take I-5 to Western Avenue, then proceed North up the hill until the park is reached, where one would walk up to a reservoir to see what may be seen.

5: For the *very* adventurous, and last but not least for those near Marion County Indiana at Indianapolis, a controversial site at the closed Amtrak facility is supported by photographic and video evidence that it contains helicopter landing pads, barracks, towers, and high fences with razor-wire. For this particular site, the most disturbing reports pertain to its red/blue/green designated zones that are near one-way turn-styles, and its large furnaces that are a mystery in itself. Once again, should you find one of these camps listed in this chapter, caution should be used as interactions with unfavorable results have been reported by those who've reported to have come in contact with armed guards devoid of a sense of humor. Equally without levity, may also be the fact that Halliburton subsidiary Kellogg-Brown and Root (KBR) announced in January 2006 that it had been awarded an "indefinite delivery/indefinite quantity" contract, with a maximum value of $385 million from DHS, to construct detention facilities over a period of five years.

Per our lax immigration policy and porous borders, the federal government may explain that "facilities" exist due to the future necessity of detaining illegal immigrants should a mass-exodus emanate from either Mexico or Central America, much like the Mariel, Cuba event. Regardless, their existence is, for some reason, not yet fully explained for palatable consumption. In the relative sense, these facilities may be of benign nature or not. In the end, only time will tell.

Via a US Army memorandum of July 1994, filed as "1994 ATKO-KM/ Draft Army Regulations on Civilian Inmate Labor Program," it established procedural guidelines for the creation of civilian prison sites on military installations. For that, our personal guidelines for the future may be reconsidered within the prospect of an Orwellian scenario.

Interestingly, FEMA, as of 2013, began to ship massive numbers of caskets to many areas of the U.S. and its territories. These charcoal-colored caskets, appearing as such with a triangular shape at their tops, are actually a cross between a body-bag and casket due to their composite materials, lightweight construction, and ability to be stacked. All of these units were shipped and stored to locations near detention camps or to those camps. As an example, 30,000 of them were shipped to the FEMA camp in Puerto Rico. As far as I know, FEMA has not been officially queried as to the reason for those caskets, but to those with inquiring minds, the answer may be perfectly obvious.

As ground-level camps are apparently ready and waiting for no defined detainees, incarcerates, or whatever as yet, FEMA's underground facilities pose a different type of authentication, for they can't completely viewed unless you've been allowed to fully inspect one. The indicators prove that they *are* there, but their actual purpose continually remains highly suspect. Even if someone who'd worked in one of them divulged some classified information, the multi-layered governmental compartmentalized system usually disallows a complete profile by any one employee. Nevertheless, some reports have described its inner-workings, and it's with those also that we continue on---but down — to the netherworld of FEMA, where shadow meets substance and sustenance.

UNDERGROUND FACILITIES

Similar to the camps regarding their wide-ranging demographics, subterranean facilities are not as numerous. The word subterranean is a misnomer of sorts, as many are *within* a mountain. But as they are *below* a summit of an existing natural geographical structure, the term would be apropos. Fifty or-so are said to exist, most of them holdovers from the Cold-War days, and staffed by varied military personnel, such as Navy, Army and Air Force. The North American Air Defense Command (NORAD) in Cheyenne Mountain in Colorado Springs, Colorado, is the one most heard of, but others are still cloaked in secrecy, especially those under FEMA's absolute control. In this subchapter, we'll refer to them as sites, installations, facilities and bunkers and fortresses, since they encompass all those definitions.

In the heated days of the Cold War, 1950's America was an obsessed and paranoid population that had built fall-out shelters in their backyards, stocked with canned goods and other necessities. Children were instructed by school teachers, during "drills," on the best ways to survive a nuclear attack by the Russians. We were told to not look at the flash and cover our heads. I can still taste the fear when recalling that emotion as I write this, for I was one of those schoolchildren, maybe like many of you reading this book. Little did we know about the depth of that Cold War, the actual truth that lay behind it, or the mechanisms that were being firmly entrenched in Washington to continue *their* way of life should the bomb fall.

As children, the word paranoia was not in our vocabulary, but it was the byword of adults in Washington D.C. whose fears reached epic proportions, and to the extent of fortifying their salvation. "Continuity of Government" (COG) was the prime directive, for a government disabled of its leaders becomes a totally vanquished adversary. Anyway, that's what they thought.

The National Broadcast System was the early form of alerting the general public to the *probability* of a Russian nuclear attack, much like today's sirens in communities exist to warn residents of an impending tornado or tsunami. Often, television programs were interrupted for a test of that system, and I well-remember covering my ears at the harsh-wailing-electric-noise that abruptly displaced the friendly voice of Bugs Bunny or Daffy Duck. Many miles south of my home, and unbeknownst to me, children in business suits were enacting a more resolute solution regarding the threat of complete annihilation. They started to build underground fortresses.

And the building never stopped, even as the Russian empire disintegrated to the shadow of their former self. Most everyone on the planet was aware that the button would never be pushed, but for Ronald Reagan, Oliver North, Louis Guiffrida and everyone in-between, the Cold War's tap was simply clogged with refuse from the mistaken opinion that a major threat to America was not completely eradicated. No, it wasn't the Russians that remained that threat — which they knew, for the real enemy was to strike from within our own shores, at any time or place. Today, the National Broadcast System is still in place, but has been consolidated into FEMA's control. I have yet to hear a test, or that harsh wail from a television or radio in my adult life.

In a book, titled *Underground Bases and Tunnels* by Dr. Richard Sauder, he authenticated the existence of hundreds of installations of varying scope and size that lay under the United States. In a type of hidden world, they exist in way that the Antarctic explorer Admiral Richard Byrd would never have imagined when he envisioned "The Hollow Earth Theory." In Byrd's view, and from others that followed, civilizations existed below us, an opaque mirror image of life on ground level. For FEMA, that view is limited, for the secrecy in which they operate and exist is one that's borne from the "need to not know." But the *need* to know has been somewhat achieved in relation to FEMA's prioritized secrecy regarding their subterranean bunkers; some information has filtered through the many layers of filtered glass by suspicious and inquisitive minds that had sought the truth.

It may seem a gargantuan and almost impossible task to construct mammoth facilities underground, but the technology to build them has existed since post-Cold War days, and developed by the scientific laboratories at Los Alamos, New Mexico. Specifically, this was a boring machine named the "Subterre." Utilized to burrow through the hardest of rocks and powered through a nuclear reactor, it heats the surrounding surfaces to a molten substance, leaving in its path a smooth-glazed lining that appears as a finished surface. The question of how they were built may be answered, but the question of why remains wide open for debate. Obviously, it would require a lot of money to build machines such as the Subterre, not to speak of the cost of the actual construction of the hidden facilities that this machine was but the beginnings of. The next subchapter will touch on that.

FEMA's information about its below ground ventures is sketchy at best and, purportedly, only a handful of Congressman and Senators have pertinent information about them. In the movie *Independence Day*, I found it laughable that the President of the United States wasn't aware of certain programs and expenditures when finding out about the alien experiments. But in reality, every president knows exactly what's transpiring on his watch. Although this may sound strange that others who *should* be privy to functions of sensitivity in government are not, we should consider that even former FEMA Director Wallace Stickney stated that "I was aware funding was being passed through, but didn't know where it was going, nor did Congress, which demanded to know."

Yes, the *need* to know seems to be only conveyed to those of a selected circle. The need *to not* know is apparently more prevalent within FEMA's penchant for secrecy. And that mantra holds true for everything the agency does, including its programs that created their underground fortresses. And now we'll see where some of them are.

The most infamous of FEMA's underground enclaves is Mt. Weather, a subject of intense dialogue and frustrating Congressional investigations pertaining to what actually transpires there. From tantalizing but limited reports, this facility resembles more of an underground city, replete with a hospital, offices and other buildings, a power plant, water-purification system and a mass-transit system that runs on rechargeable batteries. Varied reports calculate that Mt. Weather is staffed by anywhere from a few hundred to double that.

In this multi-faceted enigma located in Bluemont, Virginia, satellite tracking systems to keep tabs American citizens are purportedly part of its functions. As an example of that particular function, some FEMA subcontracted housing inspectors who couldn't hit the field to perform inspections because most of New Orleans' inhabitants weren't even there, were instead deployed to Dallas, Texas, to disburse $2000 subsidies to displaced Louisiana's Katrina applicants. The inspectors had a direct link to staff at Mt. Weather. In a matter of *seconds*, that person at Mt. Weather had precisely authenticated who was qualified to receive the subsidy, or not.

Data-collection on millions of Americans is said to be a large part of its directives, and as revealed from Senate Subcommittee hearings in 1975. During those hearings, Senator John Tunney had alleged that Mt. Weather's databases operate with few, if any, safeguards or guidelines. Information, contained on the facilities computers, are files of military installations, medical and educational institutions, transportation, agriculture, wholesale and retail services, population demographics and stockpiles. Additionally, nine federal departments are delegated to Mt. Weather's oversight responsibility, as is also five federal agencies that include the Federal Communication Commission, Selective Service, the Federal Power Commission, Civil Service Commission, and the Veterans Administration.

"War games" are said to also be played there, by those children in business-suits previously mentioned. But those particular exercises are of a domestic nature, as opposed to games being directed to a foreign enemy's assault on our shores. Infinitely beyond Pac-man and Grand Theft Auto, these games are, most likely, *not* attuned to a nuclear attack because no one on Earth wants to push that button.

The possibility exists, however, that a suitcase bomb of Russian heritage — via that country's inability to locate many of those nuclear devices — has fallen into the hands of a terrorist group that's simply waiting for the opportune time to utilize it. Thankfully nothing has happened since 9/11, and for some, that may be indicative of our nation's ability to thwart plans in process. For others, it could appear to be a concerted effort by FEMA, and everyone below and around them, to choose fear as the ultimate weapon against American citizens. Within that fear-based dogma, a "crib" of sorts has to exist with which to direct that powerful weapon. Places, such as Mt. Weather, may be the backbone of the systematic placement of installations in order to foment its mysterious but apparent function.

For the workers that staff this and other similar installations, compartmentalization is a key ingredient to alleviate the occurrence of any information being passed between departments. As an example, lunch in the cafeteria isn't a social event, and it's common knowledge to not discuss activities from one department to another. Most don't even know how many exact floors lie within the structure, but some are of a restricted nature in the complex that's estimated to have about ten levels. As a mere FEMA-contracted housing inspector currently has to pass an FBI fingerprint and DHS background check, the ones who work in their underground environments are subjected to even more extreme incursions into their personal lives.

Purportedly, the Echelon Surveillance Network, operated by the U.S. Government from Menwith Hill in Yorkshire, England, may be linked with Mt. Weathers' computers, thereby providing minute details of virtually every American citizen. Echelon can track and monitor voicemails, emails, faxes, financial transactions, travel information and telephone calls. Essentially, every worker in any FEMA facility is a character in a Sci-Fi movie, predicating the future that we may now be entering. But more than that, we may all be on the cusp of that Orwellian-type world, should the probabilities of this chapter prove to be reality.

Besides the functions so-far described, Mt. Weather and its clones are also designed to house the upper-echelons of government for extended periods of time should the event transpire that above-ground situations warrant it, whether due to massive civil unrest or any peripheral need to relocate them to a failsafe environment.

Mt. Weather is said to be a self-sustaining command center for FEMA. It is a formidable spoke of the wheel in the Continuity of Government Program, and it's the core reason of its existence. Should a declaration of martial law be enacted via a nuclear event or massive civil disturbance that would constitute a national emergency, the President of the United States, his cabinet and remaining executive branch would be relocated there. From that facility, government would continue functioning. Should the president and his executive branch not survive to enter the confines of Mt. Weather, a parallel government is purportedly is in place, staffed by one person who heads each individual executive branch.

FEMA would then be the one to enact the COG. However, a Presidential appointee is in place to assume that former above-ground role. But should the director of FEMA be the one to survive the president, vice president, the speaker of the house and that appointee, he, or she, would be the one in total control. Thankfully, that scenario has yet to be played-out. For the life of me, I couldn't begin to imagine the quality of life under the leadership of Michael Brown.

www.femasbest.com

During the senate subcommittee hearings on Constitutional Rights of 1975, it was realized that Congress had little knowledge or oversight, in the budgetary sense or otherwise, pertaining to expenditures of the Office of Emergency Preparedness, and augmented by the testimony of retired Air Force General Leslie Bray. In that testimony, General Bray had said that he was not at liberty to describe precisely what Mt. Weather's role, mission and capabilities were, and the same held true for any other location of facilities. In the thirty-three years since those hearings, any relevant insights can only be further identified through the actual information of well-placed individuals willing to divulge it. The secrets that remain may very well be hidden for quite some time.

Much like the attempts to discover the true purpose of Area 51 in Nevada, it would seem that more than a few would be prone to reveal certain aspects of Mt. Weather. That information continues to be sparse. In Nevada, a plane leaves every morning from the far end of McCarron airport, its passengers ferried to Area 51 and back again at the end of the workday. The reason why none of those passengers are willing to speak about their work may be due to either the "Oath of Secrecy" that they are required to take or the fear of reprisal should they make the fatal mistake of compromising it. And such it also may be with the staff and workers of Mt. Weather and its counterparts. Numerous in numbers, their purpose is relative to Mt. Weather's, all operating within the dark side of FEMA.

Raven Rock is purportedly one of the earliest constructed facilities of its type, circa 1950. Located about 50-plus miles north of Washington DC, this mountain was perceived as an ideal site because of its composition of greenstone, one of the hardest rock substances on earth. This FEMA underground/in-ground bastion, which reaches approximately 650 feet below the mountains 1529 foot summit, is said to contain a fitness center, medical facilities, convenience store and a barbershop. But aside from these creature-comforts afforded to those that staff this complex, its purpose only conjectured, it may also be a mirror image of Mt. Weather pertaining to its functions. Expansion is said to be still ongoing, and if so, the nuclear energy that's driving the Subterre(s) may have been better-served in an effort to attain low-cost power in order to heat and cool our homes, etcetera.

Besides Georgia's Regional facility in Atlanta, there's another FEMA site to that city's north at Kennesaw Mountain, and which is said to be connected to Dubbins Air Force Base. Another is south of Atlanta at Forest Park, and one at the FEMA regional Center in Thomasville. In Olney, Maryland, near Laytonsville, a FEMA/National Security Agency (NSA) supposedly exists on Riggs road off-of route #108. In Klamath Falls, Oregon, a facility, manned by FEMA, CIA and FBI staffers, is said to be an underground detention camp and monitoring station. Further west in near Oakville Grade in Napa County, California, is a site that's reputed to be an essential component for the COG Program, and it has been reported by residents of the area that they've observed helicopter activity, both coming and going.

In Maynard, Massachusetts, another FEMA facility is reported to be partly staffed with Wackenhut-type security personnel. In Battle Creek, Michigan, a facility is said to be fully operational. Once again, we'll save the best for the last, as the site at the Greenbrier Resort in West Virginia defies all semblance of explanation. Actually, this facility is totally *under* it.

Located in White Sulphur Springs, about 250 miles from Washington DC., its secrets may be even more closely guarded than any other site, including Mt. Weather. With approximated living-space for 700-800 people, this massive bunker-type facility is said to be the housing for the members of the Senate and Congress should an event of proportions necessitate it. However, the *exact* location of this particular enigma is purportedly only known to several of the nation's highest-ranking officials. I'm guessing that the President is one of them.

But even as we're attempting to ascend to a different type of surface, we must understand that we'll probably never know the actual reason for underground facilities, camps and everything else said in this long chapter, until the mechanisms that control them are switched on because of an event — whether internally manufactured or not — becomes reality. In that respect, it may be like a light bulb in your home that you know you should have replaced days ago because you noticed it flickering but had elected to think it would repair itself, or that you'll simply install a new one when it completely died. But when reading a good book under that bulb that suddenly failed to emit light, the store was discovered to be closed when going there to purchase a new one. Such is the same series of events we may experience in the brighter aspect of life as we know it to be, but that may grow dimmer as time marches on and the world changes before our eyes in rapid fashion.

As we know, light bulbs are cheap in price. Conversely, disaster relief is a costly venture. We read about money spent on floods or hurricanes, but we never know exactly where the excess goes. We also know that Mt. Weather, Raven Rock and the rest were not funded by an anonymous philanthropist, so where does all that money come from? In part, it comes from the taxes each of us pay. But it may also emanate from sources never imagined. As the information gleaned from this book will testify, If there's nothing to hide, than why hide it? Akin to a child hiding a precious marble from a schoolmate, FEMA's predilection to mask the *probabilities* of detention camps insults the intelligence of astute individuals. FEMA's recalcitrance to admit the actual function of underground facilities compounds that insult.

And so, albeit more briefly than the last two segments of this chapter, we'll now briefly explore the funding of FEMA's possible aspirations, which we can only conjecture. Beyond their irresponsibility regarding adherence to Stafford Act regulations, which dictate exact disaster relief mandates, the secretive nature of the agency continues-on to the hallowed halls of government, and its "safeguards" of accountability.

FEMA'S FUNDING

On the road to accountability, FEMA and Congress have an annual fender-bender at the intersection of tolerance and confusion. In the bizarre world of federal funding, the sheer lunacy of this continual accident rivals that of someone giving money to a crack addict every day to look for a job. This subchapter could be a book in itself, but in the confines of simplicity we'll make this a short one.

All expenditures for disaster relief are drawn-down from the Federal Treasury, where all of our tax dollars eventually wind-up, such as the money procured from taxes on food, clothing, gasoline, and virtually everything you purchase. Individual states allocate their portion of taxes to their own demographic programs, the federal government takes a portion of those proceeds from road tolls and cigarettes, and that can of beer you probably think you might need if you've so-far read this book in one sitting.

The Treasury Department isn't a bank as we know it, but it *is* where all the money is allocated from for disaster relief. When congress appropriates funds to FEMA via that "Presidential Request," borrowing from various other programs is the norm, for the federal budget exists only as figures and not as actual dollars existing. For instance, should you have received a letter from FEMA asking for money back like the two women captioned in a previous chapter, you will also have received a letter from the Treasury Department in unison with that original correspondence. Our printed money, with pictures of dead presidents who could be turning over in their graves, isn't worth its face value, compliments of a twenty-trillion dollar debt. But to the federal government, those dollars are as good as gold. Go figure.

In 1991, FEMA's budget, appropriated by Congress, was in the vicinity of $2.4 billion. In 2008, that budget was approximately $8.2 billion. In 2015 it was even more. But those are only *initial* budgetary figures; the federal government and Congress can't know exactly how much funding disaster-relief may be needed in any particular year. Accordingly, "Emergency Supplemental Appropriations" are afforded by Congress. For Hurricane Katrina, $10 Billion was appropriated within the first four days, and an additional $50 Billion in the next two days. $88 billion was appropriated to the disaster-relief fund for Katrina, Rita and Wilma through June of 2006, but that is only a part of the multi-faceted sources of FEMA funding. In total, $125 billion is what Congress had appropriated to the gulf coast states for actual disaster relief funding.

To put this in perspective, the greatest expenditure in United States history before Katrina was the 9/11 event, which totaled $20 billion. After that, California's Northridge earthquake of 1994 totaled approximately $8 billion, Florida's 1992 hurricane Andrew 26.5 billion. As the years pass, so does the cost of attending to disasters, it seems.

The three areas of FEMA's funding channels are directed to its Disaster Relief Fund (DRF), Disaster Support Activity (DSA), and the payment of its full and part-time workforce. As you may remember in a previous chapter, DSA is also an acronym for Disaster Survivors Assistance, specifically the "door-knocker" cadre. The greater part of the net amount for actual disaster-relief tasks is ferreted through the DRF, and next would be the DSA, which is the entity that "ensures" timely disaster response, responsive customer service, and cost-effective program management.

The majority of FEMA's workforce is comprised of "non-permanent" employees, which are those of 120 days to 4 years tenure, and they are paid from the DRF. Permanent employees, however, are paid from the non-disaster-relief fund, such as its Director, who's paid approximately $150,000 per year. Within all this, though, is the GAO September 2006 report, stating that FEMA was unable to produce accurate information on the exact number of staffing positions it had in the years 2001-05, and where they were located within the agency. What's to hide?

When President Bill Clinton elevated the FEMA Directorship to a cabinet-level position in 1996, its purpose was to provide a direct line of communication with those two individuals for the end-result of more effectively tasking-out the duties of other federal agencies, but it hasn't attained the desired result within the existing myriad steps taken to procure direct funding. The Office of Management and Budget (OBM), formed in 1970, is the largest Cabinet-level office within the Executive Branch, and it is responsible for overseeing activities of other federal agencies, including FEMA.

The bulk of OBM's 500 employees are career and politically appointed, and all are tasked with the monitoring the adherence of assigned presidential policies. In addition, positions within the OBM, including its director and deputy director, are either presidentially appointed or senatorial confirmed positions. Added to that confusion are even other entities, such as the Office of Information and Regulatory Affairs, the Office of Federal Procurement Policy, and the Office of Federal Financial Management. If you're drinking that well-deserved beer, try to take slow sips so you can absorb the rest of the mayhem, which deals with accountability or lack thereof.

In 2006, Congress required FEMA to provide weekly reports on its spending. Previously, the first supplemental appropriation didn't contain *any* reporting requirements for Katrina's initial $10 billion. In a clear message, Congress rescinded $23.4 billion from FEMA's DRF, and directly appropriated those funds to the twenty-three various agencies under FEMA's umbrella that were eligible for them, such as the US Forest Service, Coast Guard, department of Agriculture, et cetera. As this held true for the other two supplemental appropriations, it would seem that Congress may be on the correct side of Accountability Road. But still, only a handful of top-level individuals know *exactly where* the money emanates to construct underground facilities and the camps and whatever else lurks in the dark world of FEMA's ultimate goals.

It may sound converse that Congress readily appropriates disaster relief funds to FEMA and still requires/demands accountability, but the fact remains that money *must* be given, for Congress couldn't ever hope to find a reason for denying those funds to victims of disasters. Given that, the only avenue intersecting the road to accountability is monitoring *where* it goes, and that is a gargantuan task as we now understand about the complexities of federal funding.

Between 1982 and 1992, Congress appropriated to FEMA approximately $240 million for purposes of disaster-relief and $2.9 billion for non-disaster purposes. In 2008, President Bush's budget proposal to Congress, for $553 billion, was dedicated to defense, homeland security and international affairs, and it represented a 10% increase from 2007. Ambiguous at best, appalling would rather suffice.

FEMA is designated to be an Intelligence-level agency, and as such, requests for ancillary funds are submitted without full explanation for expenditures. They are appropriated under reasons of "National Security" or the invoking of secrecy under the COG. Even if members of Congress attempt to become fully informed regarding a certain funding program, this *may* be denied. The Secretary of Defense can waive his right to disclose any and all information, except to *senior* Congressmen. On the Presidential level, that can be waived by simply invoking "Executive Privilege."

Claims had been made, in 1982 to 1984, that FEMA was partially funded through covert operations during its early years through drug-running operations in Central America, directed by Marine Lieutenant Colonel Oliver North and others within the Reagan administration, such as Edwin Meese and Robert McFarland. This was the basis of the Iran-Contra scandal, wherein arms for drugs were exchanged in lieu of actual cash for those arms. Oliver North, in his position at the National Security Council, was simply a part of the continuous planning for Continuity of Government that was held as a high priority in the Reagan Administration, and also for administrations dating back to President Truman.

These covert operations by FEMA, DOD and the CIA, of which will be explored in the next segment, were planned for the prognosticated mass-exodus of people from Nicaragua and its neighboring countries, possibly affected by the overthrow of a Sandinista government not friendly to America. FEMA was *not* "funded" in the true sense, but rather, its peripheral agendas, in coordination with its high-level agency status in government, allowed FEMA to be a decisive factor in the penchant of protecting the mandate of COG.

Drug profits were *not* and never were the monetary source of disaster-relief funding, for to do that would entail the equivalent of a vast fleet of 747's loaded to the brim with cocaine. But cocaine was, and maybe still is, the drug that converts to the cash necessary to fund FEMA's *peripheral* agendas.

During the early-to-mid 1980's, kilos of cocaine in bulk quantities of 500 to 1000 could be purchased in Colombia for roughly $2000 per. After trans-shipment to Central American countries, that value rose to two to three times that amount. But once those kilos landed on US soil, each one had a wholesale value of approximately $30,000 and upwards to $40,000 each for bulk sales of one to five units. If we do the math, that would come to about a $50 million profit, which could easily fund programs/exercises such as REX 84, Garden Plot, Cable Splicer, Night Train, Watchtower and Orwell. Multiply that by ten transactions and a half-billion dollars would suffice to fund other projects that, at this time, only a few may have known of.

Out of the Iran-Contra affair came dark overtones of its diabolical nature; seven mysterious deaths occurred, two of which were individuals who had threatened to reveal the truth. One of them was outspoken Mississippi Congressman Larkin Smith, who'd co-sponsored legislation to strengthen drug enforcement laws.

When a lawsuit was filed by former Green Beret William Tyree during the time of Iran-Contra, and in an effort to expose the drugs for funding operation, no definitive result has yet occurred. Tyree still sits in jail with a life sentence for the murder of his wife, which he still insists was planned and performed by the CIA. Mr. Tyree remains adamant that the CIA murdered her because she'd held a diary that held pertinent and incriminating evidence that would expose Operation Watchtower, the name of the covert plan that was the precursor to the scandal known commonly as Iran-Contra. This funding, if true, was for the development of contingency plans for domestic civil unrest and *not* for FEMA disaster related purposes. The next segment of this chapter will explore that further.

The thought of black operations/exercises being funded through drug profits at this juncture in time would not be seriously considered by most, but we must also remember that the wars in Vietnam, Iraq and Afghanistan were and are fought on soil that either produces or are conduits for them. In the latter country, Poppy production is at an all-time high, and Iraq is a trans-shipment point for the heroin that's manufactured from that Poppy. In Viet Nam, the "Golden Triangle" was the counterpart of the cartels in South America.

Those instances are not meant to be construed as the actual reason we'd gone to war with those countries, for that would be more in tune to a conspiracy theory. Instead, the point to ponder is *where* the money *not* appropriated from Congress may come from. And if FEMA *did* garner funds in the past from forays into the drug trade, then no one can attest if that habit has abated. Yes, reality is far removed from conjecture or theories, but the parameters of FEMA's funding remains cause for concern and requires dedicated accountability.

In 1992, a GAO report had concluded that less than 10% of FEMA's funding was actually directed to natural disasters. Until pressured by politicians and various media outlets, the agency didn't divulge the existence of its "Mobile Emergency Response Fleet" (MERS) that has the capability of supplying power to entire communities, and which possesses state-of-the-art communications systems. Their exact numbers aren't really known, but estimates are from 30 to 300. Apparently, FEMA didn't have the predilection to utilize them during Katrina, which would have revealed another secret.

In the world of black projects, and those called "Deep Black," which are also known as Unacknowledged Special Access Programs (USAP), secret, top-secret and confidential projects by FEMA, DOD and CIA are all on a need to know basis and circumvent standard reporting requirements to Congress. In lieu of conspiracy theories or claims, the fact remains that the dollar requirements to fund such massive undertakings are not open to full examination and never were. In the next and final segment of this chapter, we'll try to arrive at some possibilities, and we'll explore some secret projects that aren't so secret any more.

BLACK OPERATIONS/EXERCISES

Commonly known as "Black-Ops," they extend far from the Delta Force's Black Helicopters that seem to instill fear in those that maintain their existence. Beyond that image of dark purposes hovering in the skies, exercises conducted by FEMA, or in liaison with various other agencies, may prove to be equally chilling. For our purposes, we can include them in this chapter's color of choice, for their purpose can't be compared to anything of a positive nature, but rather that of something sinister.

Even as the existence of clandestine maneuvers were only discovered in the early to mid-1980's, the cloak of secrecy that once surrounded these exercises — these operations — has only culminated in continued denials (known as "plausible deniability") of their existence by FEMA, more questions from politicians and citizens as to why they were planned, and what event or events may trigger them to become reality.

The precursor to exercises, such as REX 84 and its counterparts, can be traced back to Ronald Reagan's tenure as Governor, specifically, to the

www.femasbest.com

California Specialized Training Institute (CSTI). When installing Louis Giuffrida as FEMA's director in 1971, his personal views on civil disturbance became the basis for future programs such as REX.

Thousands of police from every state, and some even from foreign countries, attended a week-long intensive training regimen consisting of civil disorder management, intelligence gathering, and mass-arrest tactics. An avowed proponent of martial law, Giuffrida believed that legitimate violence is integral to our form of government, and from that source would be the remedy to purge weaknesses. Security obsessed, it's said that he advocated martial law in anticipation of widespread uprising by black militants, and proposed the incarceration of millions of African-Americans in relocation camps.

Reagan's footprint on FEMA is very pronounced when we take into consideration his attention to the Vietnam War's unpopularity, which caused mass demonstrations in the early 1970's and as we back-track to his tenure when Iran Contra came to-be. In retrospect, one could say that it was he who was responsible for FEMA's evolvement from a primarily disaster-relief agency to its current duality. When installing Louis Giuffrida as Director of FEMA, that decision markedly altered FEMA's previous mission, and thusly had embedded its future history through the exercises conducted in 1984 that were possibly a precursor for things to come.

As well, FEMA's former acting Associate Director, John Brinckerhoff (not related to the contractor PB), was of the same mindset, working closely with Giuffrida in the planning of the exercises we'll now explore.

We've already delved into Oliver North's and his cohorts' escapades, but Operation Watchtower was the name given to the drug-trafficking enterprise in Central America that became the pivotal focus on the Iran-Contra debacle. Its counterpart at that time, "Operation Orwell," was administered by the US Army Special Forces, and its objective was intelligence-gathering of politicians, judicial members, and state law-enforcement personnel. Purportedly, Orwell's prime purpose was to collect sensitive or embarrassing information, should anyone discover the existence of Watchtower, and use it to thwart any investigations that might emanate upon that discovery.

Between these two operations, similar funding enterprises were utilized, specifically the drug profits that were purportedly ferreted through the major New York crime families. In the realistic sense, that conduit is certainly with merit; to sell the vast amount of cocaine that was required to fund Watchtower and Orwell, they couldn't just be sold to a neighborhood wholesaler. Equally with merit are other operations, possibly intended to alter life in our own neighborhoods.

As a precursor to the Urban Warrior exercises of 1999 in Oakland and Monterey, California, which we'll also cover, REX 84, Garden Plot and Cable Splicer are said to be the culmination of the planning by North, Guiffrida, Brinkerhoff and many others, possibly including President Reagan, who'd adamantly disavowed any knowledge of them.

As the Vietnam War protests *were* firmly entrenched in Reagan's psyche when serving as Governor of California, the conceptual necessity of containing hundreds of thousands of protesters for prognosticated future incidents of greater magnitude ultimately resulted in REX 84 and its companions. For Operation Cable-Splicer, the mundane and inexplicable scenario of hundreds-of-thousands of Nicaraguans assaulting the borders of the United States in a mass exodus defies sensible logic. If one looks at a map of Central America, they'll find that in the way of that approach would be the very large country of Mexico, which would most certainly prevent any mass incursion into their domain. Secondarily, that sheer number couldn't be supported in the detention camps existing along the borders of Texas, Arizona or New Mexico. Yes, they could be transported to other camps, but that would present logistical problems.

In Garden-Plot, or "Civil Disturbance Plan 55-2" by its codename, its particular poignancy in relation to its counterparts may be either disturbing or promote a serious cause for reflection. All of the above operations were of circa 1981 to 1984, and I personally can't shake the stigma of George Orwell's novel of 1948 entitled "1984." That novel was written in 1948, and Orwell's real name was Eric Arthur Blair. Simply, he reversed the last two digits of the novels title from the actual year of writing, envisioning that by 1984 his prognostications would reach fulfillment. In shades of Stanley Kubrick's epic movie, 2001, which was based on a short story titled "The Sentinel" by the late Arthur C. Clark, that future did not *fully* eclipse the intended target era. Interesting to note, however, would be the *actual* link to Blair and Clark. Blair was born in Bengal, India and Clark made his home in Sri Lanka, previously known as the former British possession of Ceylon. In 1948, Clark wrote "The Sentinel." That same year Eric Blair wrote 1984. Both were British subjects and resided in former British territories. Coincidence or not, the fact remains that writers, much like other artists, often shared ideas.

Since the exercises such as REX culminated in the year 1984, one can either deflect the coincidence as a mere twist of fate or deem it a harbinger of things to come. Even though Jack Anderson broke the story about REX 84 *in* 1984, it's a non sequitur because the operation itself was code-named to that year. But as history is always the best teacher, as said several times in this book, it's always up to the individual to ascertain the consequences of those lessons not learned.

For each and every operation produced from FEMA to CIA to DOD, they all project a dire and dystopian future, should they be designed for purposes beyond our imaginations or comprehension.

"REX-84 Alpha Explan" is an acronym for Readiness Exercise 1984 Exercise Plan, a civil disturbance portfolio that encompassed the *possibility* of futuristic riots or civil disturbances of magnitude in America's streets that would pale in comparison to the 1864 Kentucky riots, 1914 Colorado, and maybe beyond to 1992 Los Angeles. In simple form, this was a plan implemented and coordinated via facilities such as Mt. Weather to test, in *theory,* the armed forces ability to contain and detain large numbers of American's in cases of civil unrest or natural emergencies. For instance, what if gasoline was $7.00 a gallon? What if food prices doubled from their current high levels? What if more banks fail? Would a domino effect occur? No one can predict the strike-point of a nation's tolerance, for unrest can be caused by varied predicators. These things may never happen, and hopefully not, but what if they did?

The interesting element of Rex 84 is that although some conspiracy theorists continue to state that exercises were "conducted" from April 5 to 13nth, no one has yet, to my knowledge, isolated the exact location of those initial exercises. Rumors were that they were conducted in the Coridellera Entre Rios region of Honduras, near the meeting-point of the Bocay and Amaka rivers in northwestern Nicaragua. The participants were said to be over a thousand Army troops, flown clandestinely from Texas in C-130's. These aircraft were one of the trigger-mechanisms that vaulted the Iran-Contra scandal to public consumption when those cargo planes were discovered to have been outfitted for transporting personnel instead of cargo.

In truth, REX and its appendages were initially war-games, drawn on a map in the dark confines of underground facilities operated by FEMA, DOD, CIA, and their brethren.

However, facets of these operations *were* conducted many years later during Operation Urban Warrior, and in full-view. Some conspiracy writers have said that REX was a Continuity of Government plan, and they would be correct, for every Black Operation *is* designed within COG's mantra. But the prognosticated detainment of hundreds of thousands, to even millions of people, would *not* directly interfere with COG, as those designated members of government would be previously and totally insulated from the effects of it within those underground facilities we've previously visited.

In short, REX 84 was more of a detainment-readiness exercise, wherein large numbers of a civilian population would be relocated to pre-designated locations for processing, interrogation and containment. This scenario would *only* take place when *Federal* Martial Law was declared, and Habeas Corpus was denied. As history attests, when martial law was declared, Constitutional rights *are* suspended, but not necessarily so for the ultimate purpose of totalitarian rule. FEMA, CIA, DOD and everyone in-between are keenly aware of a growing population within the United States, the lax and archaic immigration policies that augment that population to ever-growing numbers, and the distinct possibilities of domestic or civil unrest due to economic reasons, to natural catastrophes, or to threats of terrorism. In turn, lessons were learned by the United States Government in the 1950's when the threat of Communist infiltration was the precursor Russia's nuclear capability, which resulted in those backyard bomb-shelters in towns and cities across the country.

One only has to reflect on the McCarron/Walter Act of 1950, wherein loyalty-clearance programs were instituted to separate loyal American citizens from Communist-leaning individuals and subversives, resulting in lives ruined by being inserted on the "Black-List." It would seem converse to say that REX was conceived in benign attitude by those planning for a certain scenario, but the fact remains that anything is conceivable, as history attests. Paternalism seems to be our mode of perception when envisioning our government's supposed purpose of being responsible to uphold our liberties and way of life. Unfortunately, we may all pay the price for that utopian vision, should the scenario unfold that elevates exercises such as REX to reality. In that vein, parental lineage also existed in 1984, specifically the next Black Operation on the menu of this chapter.

Operation Garden Plot was/is an augmentation of REX's formula, but more diversified in some aspects. Operated and conceived by the DOD, Army, Marines, Air Force and Navy, among others, its focused intent was to control all areas of communication and allow, under a certain appendix in a subsection, to excise total power over a population, should local and state law-enforcement officials not possess the ability to quell projected types of civil disturbances.

The demographic social structure pertaining to those who may be likely to instigate a civil disturbance is far-reaching, from resistance groups to religious organizations to racial profiling, and to any person deemed to be "nonconformist." The latter might seem to be ambiguous, but the fact remains that the power to judge who is and who isn't a threat can be administered, under certain circumstances — such as the failure of the power grid, as previously mentioned — by the authority of the person in command of an affected area, whether it be a General, a governor of a state, a regional FEMA director, or even a city's mayor.

Under a subsection of Garden Plot, the social demographic expands still, defining tax-protesters, militia groups, and general anti-government dissenters as "disruptive elements." For everyone, under all the above classifications, the use of deadly force is to be used against any extremist or dissident who perpetrates any and all forms of civil disorder.

Operation Cable-Splicer is yet another subprogram of REX, and is basically centered on the conceptual event of a mass exodus crossing the Mexican/United Sates border. For this, initial containment of those people would be expediently administered, and they would then be transferred to detention camps before being deported. Additionally, Cable-Splicer calls for the federal government to affect an orderly take-over of local and State governments, its police forces, and so forth.

Within the frame-work of the three operations thus far captioned, "Night-Train 84" is another sub-program that incorporates similarities to the others, but is more attuned to REX. For Night Train, FEMA was the lead agency in its direction and formatting, utilizing several other agencies for its intended purpose. Essentially, it was a duplicate of REX, developed by FEMA as a parallel for comparisons sake. Within them all appears to be somewhat of a redundancy and duplication; aspects of one overlapped another. Whether that anomaly is attributed to fail-safe mechanisms or not, we can only conjecture. But we must keep in mind that exercises/drills are conducted many times in a given year on military bases throughout the country.

For Rex and Night Train, they were factual and real-time field exercises far from the safe haven of the United States, utilizing that purposeful geographic locale to ultimately test and observe the personnel involved with them. And we may also keep in mind that Rex and its companions were basically *conceptual* plans. They remain as such, until conception may transpose to reality.

The culmination of the "paper-plans" we've so-far discussed *became* reality for four eventful days in March 1999. Code-named "Urban Warrior" and developed in part by the Marine Corps war-fighting laboratory in the mid 1990's, it transformed two California cities into virtual war-zones. In Monterey, where the operation was sub-coded to "Operation Sea-Dragon" for communication reasons, it and counterpart UW in Oakland provided a glimpse of what may actually transpire should the right pieces of the puzzle fit in place.

From ships in the bays and helicopters in the skies, 6,000 Marines, 700 Navy personnel and a contingent of British Royal Marines arrived faster than one could say "Martial Law." From REX 84 to Garden Plot to Cable-Splicer, their individual intents were tested, reviewed, and dissected in underground facilities, within the possibility of triggering their actual necessity. War-games, as it were. Fun stuff.

The greater part of the testing centered on the conditioning of the street-level military units to assume the role of authoritarian figures. The lesser part was the "acceptance" of the population. It was a dress-rehearsal of sorts. Everyone became, for those three days, an actor or actress on a stage of presumptive events.

Urban Warrior's directive was to also field-test a scenario called, "3-block war in 3 dimensions," which is somewhat of a variation of SWAT teams' training technique developed from Reagan's/Giuffrida's CSTI. 3-blocks is the defined area that's easily controlled with correct numbers of troops, wherein the population, within city-blocks, have escalated from demanding humanitarian relief to fomenting civil unrest, resulting in troops performing riot-suppression techniques to urban combat.

3 dimensions are defined by tall buildings, street-levels, and underground tunnels/sewers, all areas to be contained and populations removed to peripheral locations. Locals were hired to play reporters, angry civilians, police and everyone in-between to provide a precise dichotomy of such an event occurring in the future, and to also provide improvements to a real-time scenario.

Marines herded "refugees" into buses, barking orders to "Keep your heads down and keep your hands up!" At checkpoints ringing the cities perimeter, civilians were stopped, searched, and their identification authenticated. All persons deemed to be "suspects" were taken to processing centers, interrogated, then transported to "migrant shelters." Troops practiced "crowd control" when citizens demanded food and answers to simple questions.

New technology was also tested, such as the "Mobile Counter-Fire System" that's housed on an armor-plated truck. Equipped with cameras and audio sensors, those two devices work in tandem and can isolate the exact location where gunshots are coming from, and will automatically return fire to that target within two seconds.

Another field test was accomplished via the deployment of a remote-controlled vehicle dubbed "SARGE," which stands for Surveillance Reconnaissance Ground Equipment. Resembling an off-road one-passenger vehicle, it's dropped from a helicopter to survey a "hot area" without incurring loss of life to initially reconnoiter with personnel. Also tested was a state-of-the-art communications system that would link one soldier to another in combat situations, and is monitored by satellite so as to ascertain the exact location of an individual without error.

But mistakes were made regarding the acceptance of troops invading, as protests against Urban Warrior transpired, resulting in arrests and convictions for the ones who'd resisted against their local government's decision to allow the exercise to be conducted.

The folks who did participate in Monterey and Oakland were just actors and actresses on a stage, getting paid as an "extra" on a Hollywood movie set and reveling in the excitement. For the Marines, Navy personnel and British troops, it was a classroom of lessons learned that may be applied for something in the future we all don't want to experience. But the fact is that these operations/exercises are most likely a product of wasteful spending, whether black-budget or not, for they portend to serve a purpose yet unfulfilled and hopefully so. Within the color of choice, those Delta-Force helicopters, previously mentioned, descended to the streets of Kingsville and San Antonio Texas, for an "exercise." They also made their presence felt in Swanboro, North Carolina, much to the chagrin of the local population.

In this very long chapter we've become attuned to both possibilities and probabilities, monetary sources, and an underground network that Jules Verne couldn't have imagined. We've learned about camps that exist, but can only ponder what their existence may actually be for. After reading this book thus-far, we may, as well, harbor thoughts as to what could happen if FEMA is not there for us in the future, in time of natural disasters. Though not a probability, it remains a possibility.

We've learned the hard way from hurricanes Andrew and Katrina, and we've also learned that FEMA's depth of perception is suspect at best, as is their interpretation of critical thinking. In the future, lessons not learned could equate to a virtual death-knell in our personal lives should we persistently choose to to rely on a FEMA that continually projects false paternalism and continually enables those who've been accustomed to monetary benefits. Life is cyclical. Changes are a constant. Nothing stays the same.

In this next chapter, the central character may be you, or maybe a close relative affected by a major storm, suffering the consequence of a catastrophic hurricane that will *probably* come to fruition in the future. It's never a question of if. It's a question of when.

www.femasbest.com

26

HURRICANE OTTO/9/24/2032

"WE SHALL DRAW FROM THE HEART OF SUFFERING ITSELF THE MEANS OF INSPIRATION AND SURVIVAL".

SIR WINSTON CHURCHILL. 1874-1965. BRITISH POLITICIAN/STATESMAN

Just as that name conjures an image of a lumbering obese simpleton, the most devastating hurricane to ever reach the shores of America seemingly stood still for two days as it raked Florida's eastern coast and its midlands with unrelenting 180 mile-per-hour winds and unceasing bands of rain. In Miami, ten feet of sewage-inundated water flowed relentlessly but slowly through the streets of Hialeah and Coconut Grove, to Coral Gables and beyond.

Further north in St. Lucie, you've heard news reports on the radio and television that houses were swept into either the sea or the Indian River by the over twenty-foot storm surge that may have well been a tsunami.

In some news reports, it was said that a hurricane Otto had hit Central America in 2016, but that the name was never retired by the National Hurricane center. But you didn't care about the past, only that he arose from the dead.

You imagined the fury of Otto as he struck your home in New Smyrna Beach, the walls probably buckling under the weight of a fat man not giving a damn about anything except causing misery, frustration and anger.

And that anger breeds deep within like a mosquito on water as you and your family venture outside of your bug-infested motel room in Macon, Georgia, compliments of a long drive necessitated by the mandatory evacuations. At times, it seemed that you were outrunning a ghost. Your wife tries her best to assure the kids that everything will be okay, but deep inside you both know that life will never be the same, much like the one's who'd suffered during 2029's hurricane season. For a moment, you reflect on the memory of the two category five storms in successive weeks that had hit eastern Texas and Louisiana and into portions of west-coast Florida, causing monumental damage and spawning riots from Galveston to New Orleans to Tampa.

Martial law had been declared, thousands of people were killed by Guardsmen or police, and tens of thousands are still homeless, according to a recent news report you'd read.

FEMA had delivered on their promises of providing relief, but had instead elected to randomly dole-out $1,000 to $10,000 checks to storm victims. Instead of housing inspectors performing the inspections, as they had for many years, FEMA deputized the National Guard — just as they'd deputized them during the riots — to canvass neighborhoods and perform them after aerial damage assessments were done.

They called it the XYZ System, meaning some, most or all in relation to their damage. Guardsmen, in teams of two and usually accompanied by a drone flying overhead, would ascertain how much damage had occurred and have the homeowner or renter sign a document that would enable funds to be sent to them. But, In effect, they were simply reality checks, for it seemed that everyone expected FEMA to come to the rescue in the manner they'd always had in the past.

There were some books written which you didn't read, but there were online news articles and television reports that you did read and hear, all saying that the agency's funding had continually experienced drastic cutbacks in its budget during the last several years, and that the ongoing war on terrorism necessitated that funds be directed to that more important issue. There was something called the Stafford Act that was

www.femasbest.com

suspended by a Presidential Executive Order, and there were other things that were also changed.

It was hard to understand what was really happening between the lines. It was said in one news article that maybe they simply realized that the system was too complicated with the corporations they'd historically contracted with, and the unceasing fraud from applicants had finally been the straw that broke their backs.

 As it came to pass, FEMA's new rules dictated that everyone has to pay for their own choice to live near or on the ocean, and the days of big money given to people would be over. And for you, while managing a slight smile to your wife, that particular decision may now be equal to hiring the captain of the Exxon Valdes for sailing lessons or seeking financial advice from a bankrupt professional sports star.

Those thoughts are interrupted by little voices soft, as your three little girls keep repeating that they want to go to home to the bird-house, the name they gave it because of the screened room on the rooftop. But there's no way to tell them that there's probably no home left to go to, no words to convey that there will be no more watching the space-shuttle launches and no more Saturday afternoon barbeques.

For a moment, you blame yourself for not heeding the advice of those who'd said Florida's coasts were a target for hurricanes. In the next, you blame the ones — particularly your real estate agent — who had convinced you to believe that New Smyrna Beach was in a naturally protected area, and that's why the Kennedy Space center was built near there. Right now, you'd trade this nightmare for a simple house in the middle of a forest where hurricanes never tread.

Relenting to the children's wishes and your own angst, the decision is made to leave the safe confines of Macon and drive back to whatever may lie ahead. Your 2024 Jeep Cherokee is loaded with all the possessions deemed important, and you know that everything else left behind either lies at the bottom of the ocean or floating on its froth, maybe to someday land on a distant shore like a note in a bottle.

Your real estate files are tucked on top of your wife's business documents, the unspoken thought occurring to you both within a quick glance that there will be no one willing to buy any property that may have survived, or anyone wanting to purchase a meal at the restaurant she'd opened last year. Well remembered are the stories of small seaside towns on Florida's west coast that were washed away like someone had erased them off the chalkboard of existence, the vast plains of wetlands replacing thriving communities where only scant wildlife and rugged fisherman now dare inhabit.

$212 remains in your wallet from the $500 taken out of the ATM machine after leaving the house, the daily limit allowed. Three attempts yesterday to extract money from your account that held just over seven-thousand-dollars proved fruitless; most likely it was the result of communication lines destroyed. Calls to the local bank in New Smyrna only resulted in static and added frustration.

Your name is David Montague but you may as well be John Smith, lost among the other refugees equally destitute as you. Maureen is your wife and your three children, age's four to nine, depend on you to relieve their suffering. Jill, June and Jennifer always relied on you as both parents and teacher, but now it's not certain that aura can be empowered any longer.

At forty-four years old, you feel like the weight of the world has fallen on your shoulders. You've always believed in God, but your faith is slipping to an abyss of unknown depth. Prayers were offered last night in this motel room of gloom and doom, while stoically playing the part of a strong man whose wisdom is now suspect within your questionable decisions that brought your family to this point of turmoil.

With the children's toys and games loaded, the doors are shut at ten-fifteen in the morning. Silence cuts the air like a knife to a heart as you drive slow but thoughtfully on the way to route 75 south. Memories of the past few days play in your mind like a montage. There was the three days before Otto struck, everyone glued to the television and praying he would veer-off-course or lose steam. There was the next day, when all of those hopes faded like a promise never kept. Then, there was the order for evacuations thirty-six hours before projected landfall, the roads caked in gridlock like a scene from a disaster movie.

You remember that it took almost four hours to reach the city limits of New Smyrna Beach, a drive that usually took about twenty minutes. You can still visualize the first drops of rain on the windshield from Otto's outer bands that rapidly turned to sheets that seemed to challenge windshield wipers to eradicate, and you can still hear honking horns and angry yells from the cars that surrounded you. An indescribable feeling in the pit in your stomach causes you to wince when remembering a particular event of yesterday.

The phone call, which took five attempts to connect, was made to the insurance company, but the effort was possibly a moot point since the house had wind coverage but not for flood, and all the damage might be attributed to that same cause. The agent explained that since the house was built on concrete columns — and if the surge destroyed those columns and collapsed the upper wooden structure, then the cause of damage would be attributed to flood via storm surge. However, should the columns have survived and no surge entered the house — but the wind damaged or destroyed the upper structure, then the wind policy would be valid. You'd argued that the rain and wind would cause the surge, but your opinion was quickly rebuffed by the agent with a voice devoid of any discernable emotion.

"Storm surge causes flooding," Mr. Montague, he'd said. "Try to keep in mind that there's many thousands of policyholders just like you. And also try to understand that we're doing the best we can for all of our valued customers."

Maybe as a placebo, he then said that since no one could verify what damage the house had actually incurred at this point, an agent will be coming as soon as possible to perform an adjustment. At the end of that conversation, you recalled the reports from the news media and the National Hurricane Center you'd accessed on the motels computer, that the surge reached over twenty feet on central Florida's east coast. That was more than enough to swallow any structure that stood in its path.

As route 75 is reached and the ramp taken, you now recall the reasoning for not bothering to get flood insurance. Trying to shield yourself from blame, you force yourself to remember that mistakes are a part of life, that no one is immune to them.

The Bethune Beach section of New Smyrna was like an east coast version of Malibu; Virtually every house was on either concrete or wooden columns, all with wooden upper-structures on the roughly six-hundred foot wide spit of land that separated the ocean from the Indian River. Most houses utilized the lower level for parking or maybe a laundry area, but there were a few that had actual living spaces on that level.

Though every house was only a few feet above sea-level, the high elevation of the upper-structures provided a sense of safety in the unlikely event of a storm ever striking the area. The thought of a hurricane striking here wasn't a real concern because of the shallow waters and the perceived safety-net of the space center's location, and you were always sure that the government always knew something you didn't. But if a storm did hit, the house's fifteen-foot elevation would simply allow any water to flow harmlessly underneath, and after it receded everything would return to normal.

There was no need to pay the $8,000 yearly premium for flood insurance. If any insurance was needed it would be for wind, and that was expensive enough at over $5,000 per year. But in retrospect, that decision was

www.femasbest.com

flawed, just like the one that led you to believe Bethune was located in an oasis of protection from any forces daring to intrude.

You wish the house had a mortgage, for the bank would have required a flood insurance policy. You regret buying the house with the $240,000 left to you in Uncle Peters' will, and wish that you'd never left New Hampshire to move to Florida for the good weather and a well-paying job as a graphic designer. You wish and wish and wish as route 75 rapidly resembles a parking lot, filled with people who are maybe are sharing similar thoughts.

After almost twenty-two hours of driving, sometimes at ten miles an hour on 75 to route 40, checkpoints and roadblocks in Ocala manned by National Guardsmen and State Police are redirecting everyone to locations of shelters as they walk along the road between the lines of cars. They say that no vehicle traffic is allowed any further due to debris-filled roads and standing water ten miles ahead on the mostly two-lane road, and that everyone had to cross the medium-strip to proceed back towards route 75, whether north or south.

You tell a young Guardsman that you needed to get as close to New Smyrna as possible and he shakes his head, telling you while looking at a list in his hand that it would be days before anyone is allowed there and that the closest possible shelter is in Deland. You ask if any motels or hotels are open, and he replies that every hotel has folks sleeping in their lobbies and parking lots. Your heart sinks because the reality of your situation becomes a nightmare. Maureen writes down the directions to the shelter with shaking hands. The girls start to cry. The Jeep is maneuvered across the road. You feel like you've just entered a war-zone.

75 South takes you to route 4 east, where only one lane is cleared for traffic. All along the drive, heavy machinery was clearing away fallen trees and limbs, packing them into fleets of dump trucks driven by men with the same look of shock on their face as you. For the next five hours the same scene is repeated: fallen trees and forests laid bare, dump trucks and

bulldozers and horns honking. Along the streets of Deland, the damage seemed minimal; most houses had missing roof shingles, but all had tree branches littering front yards. For some unknown reason---whether by divine intervention or not, Otto had chosen not to fully incur his wrath here. Either-or, an oasis has been found.

The sign with an arrow directs you to the shelter so near yet so far away from home. A parking space is found. The children cry and they want to go home. Maureen tells them that this is an adventure, and she reaches into the console for the high-power binoculars always kept there when going to the beach with the girls to keep close tabs on them. They take turns looking through them and start to act like little girls again. You both manage to smile. A cabin in the woods fills your thoughts.

Like the scenes you remember from television when the hurricane of a few years ago shredded lives and hopes and dreams, crowds of people gather at the high school's entrance, refugees carrying blankets and children's toys. After about two hours, the clan of Montague that may as well be Smith arrives at the head of the line and registers. There are some still cots available, the older woman with strain on her face and a voice hoarse said. The crinkles of her white shirt intersecting the Red Cross on its pocket verified the organization still had some life left in it. The relief effort was augmented by volunteers from the community, she added, when seeing the look of relief on your face.

While holding hands like the blind leading the blind, you, Maureen and the children meander through groups of people clustered together. Murmurs fill the hall like a thousand extras on a Hollywood movie set, but no discernable words are heard as the gymnasiums doors are reached. As your eyes canvass the unimaginable that's now your reality, several cots on the right-hand back wall appear to be empty. Stepping carefully between people sleeping or sitting or crying on their cots, the thought occurs that there will be no privacy and little rest, judging from the snoring and coughing that rises above the low chatter from maybe five-hundred conscripted movie extras living their own movie nightmare.

In the distance, at the other end of the shelter, a man and woman wave to you and call your name. You recognize them immediately. Don and Barbara, the nice retired couple you'd met last year while walking on the beach and who'd bought a house a couple of blocks down the road , are maybe reflecting on their own mistakes as they meander through the sea of cots on their way to you. With hands shaken and hugs shared, they relay a similar story as your own, in wavering voices on the edge of fear.

They'd wound-up in Valdosta, Georgia, the lucky recipients of a motel room where cockroaches roamed freely and mice nibbled their food. Don relays a story he's heard from a friend in Virginia that FEMA is going to use satellite imagery to ascertain the damage and distribute checks to disaster victims, the amount of which will depend on the level of damage observed. You tell him that it's the same system employed during the 2029 hurricane, and he didn't remember that. You change the subject because it's useless to fight the system, and instead converse about the media reports that said most coastal communities have been obliterated, that some are still under water.

As the conversation continues with subjects only spoken by those on the cusp of losing everything, the loudspeaker jumps to life, its droning voice alerting that the Salvation Army and National Guard are distributing food at the shelters entrance. Realizing that food wasn't a priority until now, you, your family, and the neighbors that used to be, assemble at the rear of a human wave that slowly makes its way to the shelters entrance.

The thought enters your mind that this may be repeated for many days. You silently pray for a miracle to allow extrication from this place of sorrow and destitution.

* * * *

The last three days passed slowly, the routine becoming unbearable within the bland packaged meals served and insatiable need to see if your house is truly gone. But that will soon be reality, for the announcement over the loudspeakers two hours ago reported that roads have been cleared and residents of New Smyrna are being allowed back to view their damage. Your belongings were quickly loaded into the Jeep, and you're on route 44 with Don and Barbara following in their red pickup truck, a blue tarp covering its bed piled high with the remnants of their life. Traffic is slow and tedious, the frustration building within you while stopping at checkpoints manned by National Guardsmen asking for proof of residency every two miles or so. A Guardsman tells you that the roadblocks are to prevent looters from plying their craft. He also says that parts of Bethune beach are inaccessible, when asking about that.

Along the way, as your stomach churns from stress and fatigue, landmarks once familiar are now almost unrecognizable. Continuing on Route 44, it appears as if a bomb was dropped on the shopping mall to your right where the Walmart used to be. Further on, where the road becomes 3rd Avenue, the Publix supermarket at the next mall has suffered the same fate, as does every single store on its flanks that once served a vibrant community. And still further on, and as Bethune is now drawing near, Maureen's art gallery, on the left hand side of the road, has been reduced to scatterings of wood and shingles.

She closes her eyes as if wishing to wake up from a nightmare. You rub the back of her neck and don't say a word, for no words could comfort that type of pain. You wonder how many of these businesses will rebuild, but you know deep inside that the chances of this happening again are better than good, because Florida is a sitting duck for Otto's companions who will be visiting in the future.

As you drive slowly, Maureen remains silent within her own thoughts and the kids stare out the windows at the massive destruction with tear-filled eyes, not uttering a word as their faces press against the glass and the binoculars sit idle on the seat. You're glad they don't ask any questions because there's no answers to submit, but your own eyes well with tears as you look at them through the rearview mirror with only memories in the distance.

Virtually every structure has been flattened, the only remnant being piles of wood, glass and concrete where once stood the heart and soul of New Smyrna. Favorite restaurants and nightspots are passed with fond recollections. The local hardware store that was a throwback to the old days with its wooden floors and friendly service are already missed. Since the company you work for is located in Daytona, directly across from the beach, you assume that it has also been destroyed. But even if it hasn't been, there's little chance for any business for quite a while, since graphic arts will be relegated to little importance in the aftermath of a storm such as this.

      Approaching the next checkpoint, where Atlantic Avenue intersects with Turtle Mound Road, your eyes gravitate to the left, observing blank spaces where both old and new houses once stood along the one-way narrow road that separated them from the enemy ocean. Small waves of no importance lap the formerly landscaped triangle separating the two roads, the relentless ocean seeming to still stake a claim on territory with the authority vested within it. You remember when some had said that one day the sea will fight back from overdevelopment and uncaring attitudes that transformed its beaches from peaceful enclaves filled with birds and wildlife to gaudy condominiums that catered to inhabitants without knowledge of fragile shorelines and dunes.

Staring ahead through the windshield, while stopping to once again show identification, those condos that had once hugged the shore have been leveled, as were the dunes when construction had begun on them many-many years ago. The old adage about not fooling with Mother Nature has never been more poignant than now, and in a way, you're thankful that the concrete monstrosities have been obliterated. In the next, you feel sorrow for all the retirees who lost their dreams when Otto came to town. And then, symbiotically, you wonder how the people in Central America felt in 2016, when Otto had come to their town.

As he checks your papers, the Guardsman tells you there's one more checkpoint about a quarter-mile up the road, and also advises that no one is allowed past that barrier. Behind are Don and Barbara. Behind them are several other cars, all of their occupants most likely experiencing gut-wrenching emotions in this caravan of broken dreams.

In silence, the kids stop looking out the windows and Maureen covers her eyes as you drive slowly and pray silently for divine intervention. On the right and left of the four-lane road named 3rd Avenue that becomes two-lane Turtle Mound Road, virtually every home is destroyed. A few have sections of their first floors remaining, resembling more a construction site that was left unattended for better things to do.

The last checkpoint looms in the distance. You breathe in and out deeply, and feel like the end of the world has been reached.

Ten cars or more are parked alongside the road at the barricades. Don and the remaining vehicles behind them pull over also. Together, you walk towards the crowd of twenty people or more, all gathered to the side of the yellow barricades with black letters emblazoned on them spelling NO ENTRY. Some folks you recognize and some not, but hugs are shared and tears are shed, for all are in the same dire predicament with no exit in sig;08 pm ht.

Beyond the check-point, the sea has virtually taken-over the land that once supported a busy road. Above unknown feet of still churning seawater, chunks of asphalt point to the sky as if an unknown force had pushed them to escape their watery grave. Neighbors that had only offered a wave on the road or idle conversation on the beach tell you in rapid-fire words shot out of the cannon of emotion that Guardsmen surveying the area by boat and helicopter two days ago reported that only three houses are still standing. You ask which ones, but nothing is known except for that.

The girls keep repeating that they want to go home to the bird-house and their voices grow loud within the frustration and confusion they're not able to fully convey. Within the ear-shot of those cries for absolution, a young soldier moves forward and motions for you and your wife to step over to him. In a soft and comforting tone, he tells you that a house that looks like it has a bird-nest on top of it is one of the structures still standing. Not knowing whether to scream in ecstasy or cry in gratitude, it's quickly decided that both of those emotional exhibits have no place within the grief that surrounds you. Instead, you run back to retrieve the binoculars, hoping you can see for yourself the miracle never thought probable.

As Maureen, the children and the crowd, wonder what you're doing when climbing to the roof of the Jeep, that miracle becomes apparent through the eyepiece of wonderment and awe. Before you, one-quarter mile away, the birdhouse sits proudly on a roof still intact. Unmistakable, somehow it survived.

The smile on your face that spoke a thousand words and the affirmative nod of your head is greeted with clapping hands and pats on the back after descending from the vantage-point that may have a few dents from the weight of anticipation. But it matters not, for all that does is that somehow the worst has never happened. The girls shout loud that the birdhouse is okay and your wife hugs them tight in a circle of joy. The crowd filters back to their stations of disbelief, huddled together and hoping that the remaining two houses is one of theirs.

Voices filter to your ears, questions about if you'd seen any other houses still standing. But yours was the only one observed to have survived, and so you meekly tell them that no other roofs were visible because the binoculars aren't powerful enough to view the remaining miles of road after your house. Even though you did see that Don's house wasn't there anymore, you don't have it in you to let him know.

Don and Barbara point their thumbs up to the blue sky, the expression on their faces epitomizing hope that they too will be the recipients of salvation. Pulling his emotions together in the tight knot of his own inner turmoil, Don pulls you aside with a gentle grip on your left arm, telling you in realistic but soothing words that he remembers a similar incident in the past where a few houses in a large lakefront community had amazingly survived a tornado, and that the federal government bought every single from the owners at thirty cents on the dollar. You pat his hand that still grips your forearm and manage a smile, and then approach the guardsman who'd seemed compassionate.

You ask him if you could take your family home by boat, the thought entering your mind that one could be borrowed. In retort, he patiently explains that the helicopters have observed two wide channels cut between the ocean and river and that most likely the entire Bethune area will be deemed unfit and unsafe for any further habitation, but he couldn't tell you if the government would wind up buying the properties.

When asking when you'd be able to gather the personal possessions from the house, he opined that in two or three days that would be allowed. After shaking his hand and thanking him for his kindness, you walk back towards your family, observing the overhead electric lines and poles that are destroyed, and reasoning that potable water is not possible due to underground lines probably also destroyed.

Stopping several feet from Maureen and the kids, your cellphone is extracted from its cradle on a belt holding up pants long overdue for a wash, and digits are pressed. Your insurance agent answers in the same monotone voice after three dialing attempts. Questions are asked that you really don't want to hear the answer to.

Yes, there will most likely be a federal buyout at some point in time. Yes, he was happy that your house survived the maelstrom. No, if the house is either fully intact or damaged, then the windstorm policy might be superseded by the buyout. Yes, if the upper structure of the house incurred wall or roof damage that can be attributed by wind, then the wind policy will attend to that.

After absorbing that monumental information akin to a wealthy vegetarian family hiring a chef who specializes in the various ways to grill meat, you ask what they can do for you now. In reply, he explains that there's no additional living expense clause in your policy, so there's probably nothing that can be done for you. In anger, your voice reaches the crescendo of frustration when demanding to know that if a federal buyout doesn't occur, what will happen to the house.

"Have no idea," he replies. "Maybe they'll turn it into a lighthouse."

"I can't believe you just said that! You're a jerk!"

"You're essentially uninsured," Mr. Montague, and I'm sorry for the gallows humor. Please accept my apologies. We value all of our policyholders. Have a good day." The phone is tucked back in its cradle as the weight of the world rests precariously on shoulders that weaken with each passing minute. In the distance, a birdhouse sits proudly that will never hear the laughter of children or smell the smoke of Saturday barbeques. The children tug at your pants and insist on going home. Maureen shakes her head in disbelief after over-hearing the telephone conversation.

With her cell phone pressed to an ear, her mother and father in Arkansas, whom she's kept apprised of events, are asked if she and the family can come home to them. And then you call your parents in New Hampshire, telling them that all is lost. As the children see the tears flowing from the face of authority and strength, they gather around you in a circled embrace, saying that another birdhouse can be built and everything will be okay. Though not sure if one ever will be, the only hope for the future is to leave the past behind and continue on.

Parting words are shared with former neighbors now disbursing to their vehicles to travel their own lonely roads. As every beginning has and end and every end has a new beginning, everyone that lived in Bethune, and beyond to other enclaves utterly destroyed, will need to summon the strength to both forget and dream again.

The children climb into the back-seat and the doors are closed on the life once known that will never be retrieved. A U-turn is made and a wave to the National Guardsman is mustered. Memories are recalled while looking in the rearview mirror that also captures the children staring in the distance in silence but with sniffled tears. A place to stay and a rental truck must be located. You hope that access to Bethune will be granted in the next few days.

In Little Rock, jobs will have to be found and, eventually, another house built or purchased. As you drive past the triangle and onward to that new life, a promise is made to the children that another birdhouse is in their future. Importantly also, are silent promises to never again live near the ocean or to ever again visit this place that only harbors regrets and sorrow.

Maureen holds your hand and squeezes it tightly. In turn, you grasp her fingers and stare straight ahead. With only the money left in the bank and no help from insurance or FEMA to depend on, but maybe a federal buyout that might be around $70,000, survival is dependent on inner strength and fortitude, all carried on the shoulders of a family now more closely knit because of a man named Otto who saved the birdhouse, but didn't permit any entrance to it.

27

SOLUTIONS TO THE QUANDARY?

"SINCE WE CANNOT CHANGE REALITY, LET US CHANGE THE EYES THAT SEE REALITY".

NIKOS KAZENTZAKIS: 1883-1957. GREEK WRITER

We can all agree that FEMA requires a drastic overhaul, but remedies to repair the dysfunction remains elusive. As evident in chapter eighteen, the ease of garnering money is as rampant as it is outrageous, for no finite solutions to circumvent fraud and waste appear on the horizon. At the core of the system, the no-bid or preferential contracts to corporations such as AshBritt, Fluor, Shaw, CH2M Hill, Parsons Brinkerhoff and the rest of the gang beg for change, but reality states that business will proceed as usual unless politicians with power and fortitude come forth to alter the manner in which FEMA comports itself pertaining to those fat contracts. Laws can be changed and accountability can be improved.

Fair business practices of including local and state firms in disaster areas need to be addressed. And this, as we may remember, is specified in the Stafford Act. All it takes is courage to begin those changes, and Congress and the Senate should be pressed to attend to them. At the higher level, President Trump will hopefully initiate amendments to disaster-relief appropriations, and to take a firm look at the waste, the nepotism and the greed displayed by all the prime contractors from inspection services to debris removal, et cetera.

As PAFI had endorsed Donald Trump for President, it's my hope that, as an astute businessman and a vanguard of truth, he does exactly that. Should he mount a full investigation into FEMA's wasteful and apathetic business practices, he merely has to peruse GAO reports and senate subcommittee hearings in order to arrive at a crossroad that has only held four detour signs.

The ultimate solution within the quagmire FEMA has created and been imbedded in, particularly regarding the housing inspection program, is to divest itself of prime contractors for inspection services and to mandate that the agency administer a hands-on approach.

As we remember from a chapter in this book, FEMA personnel were once tasked with performing inspections, but they'd failed to process sufficient numbers of inspections because they had a hefty salary and, in fact, really didn't care about the applicant. Call it lazy or call it whatever comes to mind, but that system will also not work again. In lieu, in this chapter I've outlined similar changes regarding other prime contractors, all who have no viable place in the disaster-relief mechanism — or system, if you will.

With utter contempt, mega-corporations enjoy a free ride on the FEMA gravy train, disaster- after-disaster-after-disaster. With sheer disregard for victims of those disasters, all of them utilize other's misfortune to enrich themselves. But as we've learned about the extent of those profits via the actual cost of trailers, tarps and cubic yards of debris, that would be a likely place to begin the process of change. Caps can be put on contracts, and firm mandates of local hiring and contract awards can become reality. Yes, it sounds easy. And well it should be. But like the jigsaw puzzle that remains unsolved, FEMA steadfastly maintains autonomy in its world of over-complications and under-achievement.

The pivotal question never answered is why FEMA chooses to continually align themselves with corporate entities far removed from the demographic of where a disaster event actually originates. As we all know from our knowledge of the intricacies of martial law declared when southern states defied intrusions to their liberties, we can also surmise that a modern day version of those carpetbaggers spoken about in chapter twenty-one continues to exist today.

As the motivations of people of apathetic nature and suspect motives seems to never change no matter the time in history they exist, we can also

www.femasbest.com

surmise that corporations of magnitude, devoid of human emotion, are continuing that practice. Essentially, the bottom-line of profits has replaced the predilection to truly assist others in time of dire need. Disaster-relief has morphed to disaster capitalism.

We know that communities affected by major disaster events become eligible to receive federal assistance, it incorporates cost-sharing, and results in a negative financial situation felt both locally and statewide. But the core aspect of recovery should be, in fact, directed towards those communities whose economies are affected and oftentimes destroyed via the federal government's own mandates that prevent those economies from attaining positive results. To that end, local and state contractors, whether for debris-removal, temporary roofing or delivery/site-preparation for alternative housing, must become the vanguard of disaster-relief efforts.

Stimulation of those local and state economies can only be successfully attained by a hands-on approach at a demographic level, rather than be subjected to FEMA's predilection to doing business as usual with those that are of no positive consequence to an affected economy's recovery. As outlined in each of the following sections of this chapter, this will be the relevant issue as we peruse through possible solutions to the task at hand. As history is the best teacher, we should all realize that the carpetbaggers of today still walk among us with disdain for victims of natural disasters, but with similar inherent fortitude and focus for the bottom-line that supplants their survival.

Equitable resolutions need not be difficult to attain, and I think that readers' of this book might have suggestions that would be intelligent and inspiring. But as said many times, FEMA is not of that particular mindset, instead opting to maintain their business as usual comportment that testifies the ongoing spoils-system — their nepotism, is still alive and well.

Like one wearing a blindfold seeking exit from a labyrinth, it will be up to each and every one of us to utilize our instincts in the best possible fashion to understand that change is inevitable and corrections are necessary to extricate ourselves from the confines of entrapment.

Yes, solutions are available to repair the engine that was once a disaster-relief machine. No, this will not be an easy task, for FEMA's paternalistic mantra has seemingly transposed to one of a different nature, and as outlined in chapter twenty-one. To that effort, some of those solutions will now be offered. For some, each state government will act as an ad hoc prime contractor. To clarify, although these are rudimentary suggestions, they may prove to be the catalyst for significant changes.

ALTERNATIVE HOUSING

Trailers, mobile/manufactured structures (units) will obviously be needed in the future to house disaster victims who've lost their homes, but the likelihood of these units being over safe levels of formaldehyde is great unless stringent testing is done at the point of manufacture. As we've seen, apathy is the mode of operation for every single prime contractor associated with this venue; proper testing is merely an afterthought in the quest to attain profits and stature within FEMA's list of preferred prime contractors. Consequently, that selfish comportment caused harm to many individuals who'd lived in one.

Solutions:

1: Manufacturers will be required to construct every unit with "grade-one" plywood that limits the resin and adhesives found in "chipboard" utilized previously for cost-cutting measures. Additionally, all resins attributed to formaldehyde vapors will be substituted for standard fastening techniques such as screw-shank nails or neoprene screws for exterior applications. Interior plywood walls will be ½ inch. Exterior will be ¾ inch.

2: No unit destined for use by an individual affected by a declared disaster will be issued unless independent testing is enacted by local/state officials before shipment to their designated areas.

3: FEMA's purchase of any alternative housing description will be limited to manufacturers of those units who abide by the construction guidelines set forth. If not, their contracts will be revoked without recourse. Further, second-tier vendors will be disallowed from entering into agreements of purchase with prime contractors for the sale of units.

4: Housing areas (FEMA-Villes) supported by infrastructure, such as water and electricity service, will be facilitated by FEMA and be located in adjoining or nearby unaffected counties that are in close proximity to railway lines within a disaster-declared state. This might somewhat negate the hardship for individuals already displaced, but who can still travel to places of employment not affected by the event. As well, this will vastly reduce the cost-prohibitive aspect of unnecessary staging/storage areas previously utilized. Instead, delivery to site is managed without unnecessary middlemen clogging the system.

5: Unloading from rail and placement of all units shall be performed by state certified local contractors. Should no local contractors have the means to perform this, contractors available throughout that State will be employed for that purpose. Additionally, security for housing areas will be administered by the police departments servicing that location.

6: Housing areas leased by FEMA will be located in areas not designated as a flood-plane. Infrastructure such as water/electricity/sewage systems will be constructed by local/county contractors approved by those governments. All units shall be set with pressure-treated piers on concrete footings that meet State building codes.

7: Manufacturers will work in liaison with FEMA for projected units delivered at wholesale monetary value, and will provide mass-transportation by railway at FEMA's cost. Noted, is that most manufacturers locate their sites near railways.

8: Amend laws pertaining to the existing duration of habitation of designated units by disaster victims, wherein those individuals be allowed to purchase those alternative housing units at the site of their choice, and afforded by SBA loans,

9: Enable each individual residing in a unit to view a report of formaldehyde levels, completed by a local or State official.

10: Create an occupation date of eighteen months from initial "move-in," wherein every habitant of units will then be required to either purchase it or pay to FEMA a just rental sum that reflects an individual's income.

OPERATION BLUE ROOF

We know what the basic material actually costs, but it's simply another system to ensure that the top-tier prime contractors are afforded huge but unnecessary profits. Inane it is to produce a product so important to disaster-relief efforts and complicate it further by contractually inserting unnecessary steps in the process of manufacturing to delivery. Like taking a lollipop from a baby, once again they make suckers of us all. But simple solutions *can* be realized and change affected to minimize charlatan profits gifted to prophets of greed. In the end, it's tax dollars gone to waste. And to that end, it's the corporations who enjoy tax breaks for simply being in the right place at the right time.

For the tarps that provide a respite from the elements and temporary peace of mind in the aftermath of a major storm, a more simplified plan could be easily enacted should those in power care to consider alternatives at hand.

Solutions:

1: State governments in hurricane prone areas such as Texas, Louisiana, Alabama, Mississippi, North and South Carolina, and Florida, should set-aside funds for purchase of tarp material whether from All-American Poly or another vendor. As every state can somewhat prognosticate the amount of temporary roofing required, using past major storms as examples, that material should be procured and held in storage until needed. Per the cost-sharing formula, FEMA will provide funds to assist in that purchase. Additionally, strapping and fastening material for tarps will also be provided and stored as well.

2: Contractors registered with local and state governments will be assigned the task of transporting tarp material from warehouse to secondary storage facilities, the cost of which will be the responsibility of that contractor—and included in his bid for services. Each county will have a minimum of five such contractors to insure expedient delivery and installation of temporary roofing, and to also insure acceptable performances within that task. Each contractor will have the latitude to hire local subcontractors to assist in installation, and who are also certified by local and state officials. Should an approved contractor not be licensed in a particular county that's not serviced by another, that contractor(s) will be expediently and appropriately licensed to assist in the endeavor of attending to disaster victims requirements for temporary roofing to the best of his ability. Any contractor not performing a minimum of seventy roofs per week will subject themselves to review and possible termination of their contract with both local and State officials. Additionally, "set-aside" contractors listed by those local and State governments will be employed to perform that work under the same conditions.

3: Through FEMA's registration and inspection system, applicants for temporary roofing will be identified by means of a drop-down ("temporary roof required") item on inspectors' pads. In turn, FEMA will relay that information to appropriate county and local officials who will then transmit it to contractors. Subcontractors will then receive assignments from their contractor who will inspect that work via their particular employee(s) designated for that purpose.

4: Ceilings for installation fees for temporary roofing will be adhered to so as to prevent price-gouging. Square-footage pricing should be regulated, less than $1.00 for example, and profits are to be disbursed between contractors and subcontractors within that square-foot value. Included in that price-structure, contractors and sub-contractors are also obligated to remove temporary roofing when applicable for no added fees, and at the applicant's request.

DEBRIS REMOVAL

For this particular and most essential task in a storms aftermath, its labor-intensive nature and requirement for machinery and fleets of trucks, the Stafford Act dictates that State and local firms must be coordinated to affect the desired result. As we know, prime contractors such as AshBritt doesn't even own trucks, and even if they did, to transport them many miles to a disaster area is not cost effective.

As we also know, each county within a state has trucks, bulldozers, loaders and the like to facilitate the task of clearing debris. Utilized in conjunction with private firms, the amount of vehicles would suffice in that effort. All the prime-contractors outlined in chapter nine are simply middle-men, making a profit from benign efforts. In the end, it's the local workforce that's relegated to taking a backseat in the relief efforts conducted in their own communities.

As we may remember, in a previous chapter about debris-removal prime contractors, the Stafford Act specifically states that local firms should be tasked with this. Once again, I'll quote Section # 307, Item #1 in the Stafford Act: *In general, in the expenditure of federal funds for debris clearance, distribution of supplies, reconstruction, and other major disaster or emergency assistance activities which may be carried out by contract or agreement with private organizations, firms or individuals, preference shall be given, to the extent feasible and practical, to those organizations residing or doing business primarily in the area affected by each major disaster or emergency.*

This common theme of greed and apathy, that infects each entity of disaster-relief, begs for change. Each community should be afforded the right to enable their own recovery, and debris- removal is the primary focus to attend in the aftermath of a storm. Yes, the cost is abnormally high, but only because of the insertion of those prime-contractors into the dysfunctional system that readily allocates those profits. Should local and state governments take a firm approach, the same result of removing debris will be realized, but with more expedience and cost-effectiveness. Again, the focal point is to stimulate stricken economies; not to enrich corporations with no motive other than profit.

Per the solutions below, the State becomes the Ad Hoc prime contractor for this particular and important task.

1: An office will be created at the state level that controls funds allocated by FEMA for debris removal. Arbitrarily, the initial sum might be $10 million, those funds acting as a startup mechanism for work required and transferred to that state office when an event of magnitude appears imminent. In turn, that office will act as conduit to local and county governments that will allocate funds to local contractors who are properly licensed and certified.

2: A minimum of five contractors per county will perform the work, and in liaison with local town/city workers utilizing existing fleets of trucks and heavy equipment. Each town/city/municipality will ensure that its fleet of trucks and heavy equipment are available and in excellent working condition.

3: A ceiling price of $17 per cubic yard will be adhered to by all contractors. Additionally, FEMA will allocate such funding necessary to enable an efficient system of expediently transferring funds from the State office to counties/towns/cities requiring those funds for work completed on a weekly basis by said workers.

4: FEMA personnel, in liaison with local officials/inspectors, will be posted at landfill or burn sites to document amounts of actual cubic yards removed by each contractor. This will prevent false reporting of cubic yards and ascertain the performance level of those contractors.

5: Each contractor or subcontractor shall be paid weekly and according to amounts of cubic yards delivered to disposal sites. Should any contractor or subcontractor not deliver an acceptable weekly cubic yard total that will be designated by county/city/local authorities, that contract will be open for review and possible termination. This will insure rapid removal of debris and consequently expedite relief efforts.

HOUSING INSPECTION SERVICES

The same type of problem exists in this program, but can also be easily corrected. As we know from the short chapter about PAFI and what we've also learned in chapter thirteen, experienced inspectors are unsatisfied and most newbies are either poorly trained or unable to grasp the concept. Compared to the wage scale of counterparts in the insurance industry, FEMA's subcontracted housing inspectors are essentially paid a minimum wage.

Within the FEMA inspection program we also know that the spoils system is in-place, but *has* no place in it. We're also aware, from the chapters dealing with housing inspectors, that although only PB inspectors are protected by insurance, they still have no safety equipment and have no real job security.

For comparison's sake, picture yourself working in that factory job mentioned in chapter eleven for fifteen to sixteen hours per day without any benefits or job security. Queries to a supervisor about a pay raise is construed as a complaint; explanations pertaining to faulty adherence to the factory's daily output are met with apathy and indifference---even though that factory fully realizes that a human being is capable of only so much. Finally, the threat of termination supersedes your better judgment, for bills have to be paid and life must be supported by income. That would, in my mind, be equal to being employed in a sweat-shop located in a foreign country, but controlled by a United States corporation. Housing inspectors fall victim to a similar treatment. Local contractors for debris removal or Blue Roof in disaster-declared areas are as well subjected to this usury.

Per my current knowledge, many long-term inspectors are electing to refuse deployment calls rather than to be subjected to loss of money from little or no work, or simply because they've finally realized the truth about the unfair system that both PB and PaRR, and now Vanguard, have utilized successfully. Yes, there *is* a severe shortage of professional inspectors currently available or *willing* to work. Should a major hurricane make a USA landfall like Katrina, or multiple hurricanes strike a particular state like Florida in 2004, the likelihood of sufficient numbers of qualified inspectors sent to the field will be *extremely unlikely.*

To ensure that adequate numbers of fully trained professional housing inspectors are available to FEMA, the only solution is to terminate the contracts of the prime contractors and hire housing inspectors as an actual cadre, much like the DSA, AKA the door-knockers. By eliminating those contracts, not only will billions of dollars be saved, but FEMA would be assured of having dedicated professionals for many years to come. For instance, let's think about the approximate $30,000 per month that PB and Vanguard supervisors make per month. Multiply that by ten to twelve supervisors each. It's just another waste of money

combined, PB and Vanguard has over 100 inspectors who maintain possession of their pads 24/7, even when not in the field. These inspectors are referred to as either *Perma-Pads* or *QRT's* — standing for Quick Response Team. Some of those inspectors are the Runners spoken of, and they should not be included in the cadre because of their past indifference to the needs of disaster-relief applicants. As it's been said, you can't change a Leopard's spots.

Like every other prime contractor's unnecessary involvement in efforts of disaster-relief, PB and Vanguard, and in the past PaRR, are simply middlemen in a head-hunting enterprise, procuring aspiring inspectors whom oftentimes have little or no knowledge of home construction. Together with the solutions below, a positive change can be attained to facilitate a well-oiled machine that James lee Witt once envisioned, and one that serves everyone to the highest degree, from FEMA to the inspector to the applicant.

In a previous chapter's information, we've learned that before the Mom and Pops — before the advent of the corporate prime contractors PaRR, PB and Vanguard — all inspections were performed by actual FEMA personnel. But it proved to be ineffective because those FEMA personal enjoyed lengthy lunches and felt secure within doing 3-6 inspections per day while enjoying a nice salary.

Subsequently, when FEMA realized that this wasn't tantamount to efficiency, the agency had the bright idea to incorporate multi-national corporations to attend to the logistics of supplying inspectors and quality control systems, setting-up field offices, hiring review staff and accountants and assigners, and the list goes on. But as life teaches that everything is cyclical, we may beg the question that maybe it's time for FEMA to once again take a hands-on approach to the disaster-relief program. And as said before, maybe it's time for FEMA to focus on one particular word in their acronym: FEMA stands for *Federal Emergency Management Agency*. Maybe it's time for them to focus on the word "Emergency."

Since we know that PB and Vanguard are simply middlemen who are in it for the money and are not really needed, it makes perfect sense to hire inspectors from PAFI's inspector list, and for FEMA to take-on the responsibilities of the prime contractors at a savings of yet more billions of dollars, since FEMA personnel would be assuming those tasks at their current salaries. For instance, when a disaster is declared, FEMA would setup the field office, have sufficient personnel to monitor inspectors' activities in the field, attend to inspector corrections that are reviewed by FEMA review staff, and so forth.

The inspector cadre, of approximately 800 veteran and mid-level experienced inspectors, will have his/her own computer (pad) 24/7, which, in a slightly below average disaster-event year, would be a sufficient number. This alleviates the unnecessary task of assigning computers at the field office, and also alleviates yet another PB or Vanguard employee leeching on the wound.

Any inspector errors are reviewed by FEMA staff, which already peruses PB and Vanguard's own review staff. By doing this, yet another unnecessary expense is alleviated. For any corrective actions for inspectors who may require in-the-field updating on procedures, then FEMA's Ride-a-Longs, who sometimes accompany PB's or Vanguard's QC personnel, can certainly be of value as they are already on salary. Assigning work could also be done by FEMA employees, and everything else that the contractors do. Inspectors would be issued a debit card, which will be used to pay hotel, car rental and gasoline expenses, and so on.

Ideally, FEMA would initially recruit its cadre of housing inspectors from PAFI's list of the top-tier inspectors, the aforementioned 800. But we must also keep in mind that another hurricane like Katrina could strike, or another 2004 hurricane season could happen again. And if those types of event occur, at least 2,000 inspectors will be needed. And that's at the least. During Katrina, about 3,000 inspectors were in the field. During Florida's 2004 hurricane season, almost 4,000 were in the field. Utilizing the hands-on approach, FEMA will themselves be responsible for the ongoing training of approximately 1200 reservist inspectors, who between PB and Vanguard, currently have one disaster under their belts. FEMA would require all those individuals to attend one seminar per year at FEMA's regional offices and hosted by FEMA housing inspection instructors.

In-the-field supervision and corrective training would be administered by FEMA personnel. Any inspector who continually can't grasp the nuances of performing an inspection will be terminated. It must be noted that many qualified inspectors can be drawn from various other professions, such as the insurance industry, but who have not shown any previous interest because of the low pay and hardships and everything else captioned in this book.

FEMA will pay for all travel and hotel and ancillary expenses for training seminars. Additionally, all inspectors are mandated to complete, to FEMA's satisfaction, monthly Online Training Modules (OTM'S) so as to keep abreast of changes pertaining to inspection guidelines. Should any inspector not adhere to this policy, that inspector will be terminated with no recourse or appeal. Expenses for travel to and from these seminars by attendees will be paid by FEMA via each inspector's debit card, issued upon satisfactory review on an individual basis, and in liaison with PAFI's observations.

Following, is a synopsis of the captioned issues and current status', when applicable.

SOLUTION # 1:

PAFI works in liaison with FEMA. FEMA hires PAFI's 800 inspectors as a cadre. The 1200 others will be reservists. Call-outs for deployment will be strictly enforced. Should any inspector refuse a deployment for any reason other than health-related or dire personal issues, that inspector will be terminated with no recourse or appeal.

Currently, inspectors who refuse three consecutive deployments are either removed from the call-out list or moved-down in its call-list. The latter is the general consensus.

SOLUTION # 2:

FEMA shall maintain a core-base of 800 top-tier inspectors with an additional 1200 as reservists. This will ensure that sufficient numbers of inspectors will be readily available should a major disaster strike. As noted previously, the ideal number of reservists is 2500. For the additional 1300 inspectors, it's just a matter of additional training classes and more supervision.

Currently, a core of roughly 400 top-tier experienced/veteran inspectors is available for deployment, supplied by PB and Vanguard en masse. Additionally, another 1200 have moderate experience. The many thousands who've only attended a class have no experience in the field. It must be noted that many top-tier inspectors who have elected to not be deployed because of disaffection in varied ways would be most willing to become active again in this new program.

SOLUTION # 3:

When deployed as a core member of the FEMA cadre, or as a reservist, each inspector shall be provided with health insurance and be afforded safety-equipment according to OSHA specifications.

Currently, PB provides health insurance, but no safety equipment. Vanguard does not provide any insurance or safety equipment.

SOLUTION # 4:

Each inspector will be compensated for work performed via a mandated $75 per inspection, and be afforded an additional overtime wage of $37.50 per hour. For days when less than 4 inspections are downloaded, that inspector shall be compensated for the value of eight inspections per-day at a rate of $60 each. Unemployment benefits will be available, should inspectors have reason to apply for them. The cadre and its reservists will be issued a DHS/FEMA debit card, which will be used for inspectors' expenses, such as hotel, car rental and so on. Daily per diems will still be afforded.

Currently, PB pays its inspectors $25 per hour, plus an additional sum for each inspection. This pay-scale has incentives, which if attained can result in roughly $45-50 per inspection. Overtime wages are available but are judiciously paid. Each inspector, when deployed, receives a GSA per diem, which varies from city to city and is usually between $50-100 per day. Inspectors can apply for unemployment benefits. Vanguard pays $35 per inspection for new inspectors and $45 for experienced. No overtime wages are available. They also provide the GSA per diem. The *average* hourly pay of $40 per inspection for Vanguard inspectors, completing eight daily inspections within a twelve-hour period is $27.00. The average hourly pay for Vanguard inspectors performing twelve daily inspections is $41.00. Those figures are before taxes. And we must also keep in mind that working twelve hours a day is lenient. Most inspectors work fourteen hours and sometimes more, including their nightly telephone calls, mapping and so-forth.

SOLUTION # 5:

Each inspector will be assigned by FEMA a precise demographic area for the expressed purpose of maximizing quality and quantity of inspections performed. Additionally, each inspector will service that certain area for the duration of his/hers deployment to facilitate patterns of applicant fraud and properly gauge damage levels within a designated area to augment the prevention of such. Further, and at FEMA's discretion per numbers of inspectors remaining in each county at the end of the disaster-application period, those certain inspectors will attend to all appeal inspections processed or in-process. As this period usually results in a minimal work-load, the rate of pay will be equal to eight inspections per day at $60 each.

Currently, both PB and Vanguard do not keep inspectors in a designated area to maximize efficiency. Many inspectors find themselves driving 100 to 200 miles per day to complete a few inspections. I have heard of some *still* driving those distances for one inspection. As well, some inspectors have driven those distances even though there was another inspector in the vicinity. Appeal inspections are still paid the normal wage, with no added incentives.

SOLUTION # 6:

Every inspector will be subject to up-to-date and rotating DHS/FBI criminal background checks to alleviate the past failures of individuals allowed access to a disaster field when recently convicted of a crime or investigated for violations that would ordinarily prevent them from being deployed. Any inspector found to have any serious offenses, such as DUI felonies, and regardless of when it occurred, will be immediately terminated with no recourse or appeal.

Currently, Department of Homeland Security does complete and very invasive background checks. Someone might be able to slip through the cracks, though. Nothing is perfect.

Should any of the proposed solutions to the current housing inspection program debacle not prove useful, an alternative model *could* be viable. Theoretically possible, it would entail a virtual restructuring of existing programs, whether by Presidential Executive Orders or Congressional empowerment. The Stafford Act is archaic in some respects, developed decades ago when the world was a much different place. But mechanisms remain in place to achieve the desired goal of attending to the basic needs of disaster victims. The word *basic* is the keyword. Though far-removed from the model we are familiar with, this solution was briefly touched-on in the somewhat dystopian Hurricane Otto chapter, but will now be explained further.

SOLUTION #7

When a major disaster is declared, wherein Individual Assistance (IA) is needed, the National Guard will be deployed to affected areas in order to evaluate damages to property and document medical needs. Two times per year, approximately 2,000 guardsmen will attend a class to maintain their knowledge of how to properly ascertain basic damages and needs. These classes could accommodate 200-300 at a time, via a power-point method. Multiple classes would be conducted simultaneously so as to be expedient. Guardsmen are now taking the place of subcontracted housing inspectors.

For many years the National Guard has been successfully deployed domestically and internationally. They are all dedicated professionals and their pay-scales pale in comparison to subcontracted inspectors. An E1 Guardsman, a Private, makes approximately $1,379 to $1,491 per month. An E5, a Sergeant, makes approximately $2,123 to $3,013 per month. An E9, a Sergeant Major and the highest designation in that cadre, makes approximately $4,709 to $7,311 per month. A Warrant Officer/Tech Specialist makes approximately $2,764 to $4,755 per month. A subcontracted inspector for PB or Vanguard makes an average of $500 per day and incurs an additional $200 per day in expenses for hotel, car and gasoline and per diem, of which FEMA foots that bill under contract. The Runners, previously spoken of in an earlier chapter, pocket approximately $1,000 to $1,200 per day. I use the word "pocket" because that's what they do.

Using these figures, and assuming that this disaster is of significant magnitude, the average daily savings using 2,000 E1 to E5 National Guardsmen instead of 2,000 subcontracted inspectors is roughly 1.4 million dollars per day. In a thirty-day deployment, the savings would be 36 million. And let's not forget that there will be no need for the PB or Vanguard supervisors and their daily $900 pay. There have been times in the past where both contractors were deployed to the same disaster. Each contractor had, as said in a previous chapter, about ten supervisors.

www.femasbest.com

Twenty supervisors making $900 per day equals $18,000 daily. Multiply that by thirty days and it grows to $640,000. Sometimes, disasters last for several months. The math speaks for itself. As well, a video camera's captured information is worth a thousand words.

Currently, a subcontracted inspector takes a required three to five interior/exterior pictures of each DD he/she inspects, and which are transmitted to FEMA review staff. Instead of oftentimes poor quality pictures, clear videos would be indisputable real-time evidence of claimed applicant damages. These approximate three-minute videos would be taken by a Guardsman. The videos would be taken via the same type of tablet used by subcontracted inspectors, but would incorporate no programs other than the video capability and one that would enable uploads to FEMA staff.

Before deployment, short refresher classes are conducted for Guardsmen, which would include refreshers for taking videos. Two Guardsmen arrive at the home. One attends to the applicant interview and the other attends to the video. Every room does not necessarily have to be videoed, as only a random sample of damages is required. Video footage is transmitted to FEMA's review personnel. Upon upload, a verification screen will validate a successful upload. The video will then be deleted to preserve data space. The Guardsman attending to the applicant will have a one or two page form, which is pre-loaded with the applicant's registration number, name and household (HH) resident list. Any medical needs will be noted, if extraordinary circumstances are present, and a Y or N — yes or no — box will be checked. Personal identification, such as a driver's license, viewed or not, will also be checked. Damage to the home will be listed as X, Y or Z, meaning minor, moderate or major. The applicant signs the form, testifying that he/she is the owner or legal renter of the home.

Homeowner applicants, upon applying to FEMA whether online or by telephone, state that they have insurance or not, have a deed or tax bill to prove ownership if no insurance. Renters state they have proof of occupancy. These are all currently asked of applicants, but FEMA necessitates that subcontracted inspectors nevertheless validate these items upon performing an inspection. Utilizing the hands-on approach, it's now up to FEMA *and* the applicant to verify all documents. There is no need for anyone else, whether guardsmen or an inspector, to perform this redundant task. The average inspection would take approximately fifteen minutes.

FEMA, upon review of the video footage and the basic report of Guardsmen, crosschecks all applicant information — which they currently do anyway.

Homeowners with insurance, but whose companies deny their claim, are eligible for an award. Homeowners, whose insurance companies accept their damage claim, either in part or full, will not receive any FEMA assistance. Renters with content insurance will be subject to those same rules. For eligible applicants, FEMA will issue appropriate awards: X will be $2,000. Y will be $5,000. Z will be $10,000. These are merely arbitrary figures, but they basically coincide with current FEMA award figures.

Under this system there is no need for contractors, such as PB or Vanguard or their subcontracted housing inspectors. The system is streamlined and uncomplicated. Billions upon billions of dollars are saved. In the oftentimes cyclical nature of life, the paper forms once employed by housing inspectors before the advent of computers is again utilized. We may also consider how other countries — Cuba and the Philippines come to mind — attend to their hurricanes or floods or other disasters. Typically, their military takes the forefront of disaster recovery. No they don't have an entity like FEMA, but somehow they rebuild.

In the future, it's not a stretch of the imagination to envision drones becoming an integral part of disaster relief programs. Drone technology is advancing at a rapid rate. A mid-range unit equipped with a video camera can be purchased for between $400 and $1,000. However battery life for most any unit currently on the market is limited to about thirty minutes. Nevertheless, military units with far-greater capabilities could be purchased, and at a reasonable bulk price. Imagine a drone taking the place of the Guardsman taking those interior and exterior videos. Imagine that unit programmed to automatically upload the video. Most certainly, technology is becoming more and more prevalent within our daily lives. The present seems to mimic the past. We must all recognize that adaptability is essential in many ways.

As said before, the time may come when each American has to take the same hands-on approach that FEMA has to also embrace. Instead of continually relying on FEMA for assistance that oftentimes becomes a cat and mouse game between the applicant and the agency, and instead of expecting excessive monetary compensation from a government twenty-trillion dollars in debt, each individual must discover and employ their own abilities to help themselves. Change is often hard to grasp. Change is the only constant in life.

Other than solution # 7, though extreme but nevertheless effective, all the above rudimentary proposals from debris removal to tarps to inspection services may be the beginning of changes necessary to ensure fairness and sensibility within programs currently and obviously dysfunctional. For applicants particularly, amendments must be enacted to insure their *basic* needs are met during times of disaster.

As we remember when speaking about the pratfalls of homeowners insurance, that particular area needs to be addressed in serious fashion. To correct that, FEMA must change existing rules to allow those homeowners access to disaster-relief funds under the Stafford Act. Since duplication of payments are prohibited under that Act, FEMA simply has to disburse those funds and be repaid by the insurance company. Although it's FEMA's policy to encourage individuals to procure insurance policies, it's obvious that many cannot afford the premiums, while others are cancelled for varied reasons. For business-owners who incur damage to their livelihoods and are referred to the SBA's Economic Injury Disaster Loan (EIDL) program, expedited avenues must be found in order to alleviate the oftentimes long process of actually obtaining those funds. Both home and business owners require that expeditious funneling of money in order to quicken the recovery process, and allow communities to function once again.

Other aspects of FEMA's programs that were addressed for change was the inclusion of chemical, biological or nuclear incidents that previously did not qualify as major disasters under the Stafford Act. As opposed to the types of events we're all attuned to such as floods and hurricanes, the twenty-first century brings with it new possibilities for catastrophic occurrences such as these, and needed to be recognized as potentially threatening as any others.

We could continue with the many other changes needed, but the ones captioned are sufficient for now. Hope for the future might be at hand regarding these changes, but we shouldn't hold our breath for any rapid deviation in their business model, specifically the labyrinth of contractors and subcontractors. In many ways, FEMA's heart pumps cold blood through arteries clogged with repetitious rules of engagement. Yes, change comes slowly, but change is inevitable. Nothing lasts forever.

www.femasbest.com

28

CLOSING THOUGHTS

Throughout portions of this book, possibilities and probabilities have been offered for rational consumption sans peripheral support of rudimentary conspiracy theories. Instead, we've dealt with claims substantiated by physical evidence that still defy rational purpose. Often in these pages, the word "system" was used, for that's essentially what the entire FEMA program is. In a way it's a Ponzi scheme, or maybe akin to a pyramid hierarchy wherein the lower levels lack the information of the higher levels with which to gauge what's actually going on. I remember that the supervisors always told us to not, under any circumstances, reveal to an applicant anything about the inspection process, and to simply tell that applicant to call the FEMA help line. In my opinion, that's like taking sailing lessons from Gilligan.

In a dictionary, the word *system* is defined as "a set or arrangement of things so related as to form a whole; a set of facts and rules arranged to show a plan; an established and orderly way of doing something." For all of those definitions, FEMA's persistent and futile attempt to enact its original mantra in orderly and expedited fashion remains converse regarding the latter definition of the word "system." For the other two, those definitions remain apropos; for a "whole" exists, as in FEMA's structure, and facts and rules *do* apply to a plan. However, the fact remains that holes in this system are never filled properly, and that the established way of doing business is no longer acceptable or conducive to progress.

We've spoken about accountability pertaining to FEMA's funding, but we know that the chances for absolute examination of that funding may never transpire. As such, the same could be said for the mysteries of detention camps, underground facilities and military exercises with apocalyptic code-names. And that lack of accountability also transcends to FEMA's predilection to align itself with multi-national corporations that have as much place in disaster-relief as a chain-smoking boy scout at a jamboree. But in a way, the entire program of recovery is a fun-filled event in itself, for everyone laughs all the way to the bank.

In the core facet of disaster-relief, the applicant who receives funds through fraudulent actions deserves as much blame for FEMA's debilitation as any prime-contractor; for theft is theft, no matter if one enacts it while wearing a business suit or dirty shorts and T-shirt. In the end, nothing is served except portions of greed to those that choose to use the system to their own advantage.

In chapter twenty-two, a catastrophic storm such as Otto would effectually expose FEMA's dysfunction in entirety, for they simply — and currently — do not have the resources to successfully attend to anything of that magnitude. As we all witnessed in the aftermath of hurricane Katrina, that eventuality wouldn't surprise us in the least. But if we do harbor any doubts, pertaining to their ability to properly respond, then it would also make perfect sense to *prepare* for that probability.

We've spoken about the housing inspector program and solutions to correct the faults within it, but it may come to pass that the most efficient way to perform that important task is to *not* have any housing inspectors. Instead, the "XYZ" alternative may be employed, utilizing the manpower of the military such as National Guard who don't require monetary compensation, and would thereby eliminate fraud, waste and the over-complications that FEMA is famous for. It would be the end of disaster relief as we know it, and maybe rightfully so.

Disaster-relief has transposed to rampant disaster capitalism, equitable only to those who use the system for monetary rewards. Inexplicably, in the humanistic sense, FEMA has somehow absolved themselves of their true purpose. FEMA stands for The Federal Emergency Management Agency, but maybe, as said before, it's time to focus on the word

Emergency. FEMA needs and ferret-out applicants who feel enabled to get monetary awards from automobiles that were never affected by a flood or hurricane or a microwave that was faulty before a disaster, simply because they're of the mistaken belief that they're "owed" from the taxes they've paid. But many don't even pay taxes, becoming still a greater part of the problem of an already stressed economy that shows no definitive signs of cure. In turn, corporations deem themselves impervious to examination by virtue of political contributions, relying on both past and current favors with which to embed themselves further, to greater heights within the system called FEMA.

In chapter twenty-three, we'd explored solutions that effectually placed the state and local governments as *Ad Hoc* prime-contractors, thereby transferring that responsibility on their able shoulders so as to enact disaster recovery more effectively and allow their communities to markedly improve those economies in better fashion.

As we know when the first disaster declaration was enacted in Portsmouth, New Hampshire, an agency such as FEMA didn't exist, but that city *was* rebuilt, sans the "assistance" of prime-contractors and housing inspectors and everything in-between. Yes, that was then and this is now; modern times versus post-revolutionary war United States. However, and as history is the best teacher, methods of attending to recovery efforts may lie in the affected states and communities that finally elect to take control of their own destinies rather than to allocate those duties to those with no allegiance or compassion to areas affected by storms, floods, etc. Well we might remember that the Red Cross had to resort to affecting a $40 million loan with which to continue their good work during the mid-west floods of 2008. Certainly, that alone should cause concern for us all. But other facts should also spur us to personally examine why we persistently elect to take hand-outs under the auspices of "disaster-relief" from a government not willing to divulge the true existence of camps, underground facilities and mysterious exercises that are never fully explained pertaining to their actual purpose.

The series of executive orders that propelled FEMA to its current status as the vanguard of domestic security are mired in conjecture, and they require our deep concern as to why these EO's were created to begin with. We must remember that the civil unrest from Vietnam War protests, racial riots, the beginning of the "Patriot" movement and archaic immigration policies that propagated too many people per square-inch, had all transpired from Presidents Kennedy to Johnson, Carter to Reagan, to Clinton and beyond.

As the world becomes more complex, and with an increasing population as each year passes, twentieth century threats will morph to modern incidents of more serious magnitude that twenty-first century solutions have yet to offer satisfactory resolutions to. Truly, we can trace the evolvement of FEMA to its present form via the administration of Ronald Reagan and cohorts thereof. However, every successor to his lineage has continued to enable that evolvement with no apparent thought of consequences, and that no Pentagon war-room could ever accurately prognosticate.

Conspiracy theorists have alarmed us to the degree that we fear the unknown, yet most can't begin to calculate the steps to a *possible* takeover by FEMA. Logistically, though not *impossible*, that occurrence would certainly entail massive numbers of military personnel, coordination to the finite degree, and *depend* on acceptance by those that become victims to that scenario. But we must remember that every American soldier--- whether National Guard, Delta-Force, Army Rangers or Special Forces — has a mother, father, brothers, sisters and long-term friends who could also be subject to that apocalyptic prognostication. No matter how someone in the military has been conditioned to follow orders, genetic and personal loyalties will often supersede those orders. Within that alone, we may ask ourselves if enough soldiers would be actually *willing* to perform FEMA's dirty-work.

America has, obviously and sadly, lost much of its sense of nationality, but there still remains enough to prevent FEMA and its subordinates, such as DOD, to successfully place citizens in camps that apparently *do* exist. Remember, FEMA is an Agency that *coordinates* efforts. By themselves — sans Executive Orders — FEMA *cannot* enforce measures such as martial law and Habeas-Corpus, but *would* depend on those EO's that allows them that ultimate empowerment. Essentially, the many variables that no 'war-game" scenario planned in any underground facility would become readily apparent when American lives and liberty are most seriously threatened.

As said in this book's introduction, many more pages devoted to FEMA could be written. But in my estimation, enough pertinent information has been provided in order to ask questions and ponder inner-solutions. In that effort, it's up to each and every one of you to assimilate that information and attain satisfactory answers. To that end, the importance of personal beliefs, when presented with factual knowledge, can only improve a system so-far unacceptable.

The days of free-flowing government money are almost gone but will never be forgotten. For the diehards, such as applicants willing to push their luck, or corporations still ensconced in a spoils-system, history is just another seven-letter word.

I've thought about writing a follow-up to this book, which would document the lawsuit I'd filed against the housing inspection prime-contractors Parsons Brinkerhoff and Dewberry Davis, and may do so. Right now, I'm trying to catch my breath from writing this one.

For now, the storefront is still open, but the backroom's door of hidden agendas is ajar.

FEMA

Bibliography for FEMA (THE STOREFRONT FOR DISASTER RELIEF A BACK ROOM OF HIDDEN AGENDAS)

(Disclaimer) Note; Many of these sources may be outdated, as research was mainly conducted between 2007 -2010

FEMA Concentration Camps/ FEMA Funding/ Dark side

http://utah.indymedia.org/news/2003/07/5561_comment.PHP

http://www.geopoloticalmonitor.com/content/bankgrounders/2007-09-20/US-FEMA-Camps

http://www.bibliotecapleyades.net/sociopolitica/esp.sociopol_fema01.htm

http://Stewwebb.com/legal%20lawsuitalleges%205funded20%by%20laundered%20drug%20%profits.

http:// www.ratical.org/ratville/cah/aopof911p10.html

http://www.federalobserver.com/archive.php?aid=541

http:// maritimes.indymedia.org/news/2001/12/759.php?thene=2

http://www.publiceye.org/liberty/fema/fema_2.html

http://en.wikipedia.org/wikinsurrection_act

http://www.lawandfreedom.com/site/constitutional/hemopres.html

http://en.wikipedia.org/wiki/habeas_corpus

http://en.wikipedia.org/wiki/martial_law

http://en.wikipedia.org/wiki/conspiracy_theory

http://en.wikipedia.org/wiki/united.states_treasury

http://en.wikipedia.org/wiki/rex_84

http:// www.sourcewatch.org/index.php?title-operation_cable_splicer

Project for the Exposure of Hidden Institutions

http:// www.pehi.eu/organizations/usaps.htm

http:// www.bibliotecaplyades.net/sociopolitica/esp-sociopol_fema01.html

ACLU Testimony

http:// www.aclu.org/natsec/emergpowers/14499le620040804.html

http:// www.historycommons.org/entity.jsp?entity=oliver_north

FEMA

FEMA History

http://100777.com/node/136/print

http:// www.100777.com/plan.htm

http:// www.100777.com/30.htm

http:// www.sourcewatch.org/index.ph?title=operation_cable_splicer&redirect=no

http:// www.fema.gov/about/regions/redionii/index.shtm

http:// www.wikipedia.org/wiki/fema

http:// www.fema.gov/about/history.shtm

http://www.washingtonpast.com/wp/dyn/content/article/2005/08/29apr2005082901445.html

http:// www.miamiherald.com/mld/miamihearld/news/opinion/12569332.htm

Quotes

http://politcalhumor.about.com/od/currentevents/a/katrinaquotes_2.htm

http://politcalhumor.about.com/od/currentevents/a/katrinaquotes_4.htm

http://politcalhumor.about.com/od/currentevents/a/katrinaquotes_3.htm

http://politcalhumor.about.com/od/currentevents/a/katrinaquotes.htm

Andrew

http://www.everglades.national_park.com/bird.htm

http:// www.perc.php?subsection=58id=371

http://www.nexusmagazine.com

Sourcing Executive Orders

http:// www.archives.gov/federal-register/codification/executive.orc

http://www.halexardria.org/dward287.htm

http:// www.archives.gov/federal-register/executive-orders/disposition.html

http:// www.rumormillnews.com/cgi/bin/archive.cgi.?noframes;read

http:// www.uhuh.com/laws/list_laws.htm

www.femasbest.com

http:// www.rumormillnews.com/cgi-bin/archive.cgi/noframes;read

http:// www.fas.org/irp/offdocs/d/indes.html

http:// www.gpoacess.gov/fr/index.html

http:// www.acess.gpo.gov/cgi-bin/locate.cgi?headline=federal%2

http:// www.loc.gov/rr/news/directives.html

http:// www.fas.org/irp/offdocs/eo/index.html

http:// www.archives.gov/federal-register/executive-orders

http:// www.fas.org/irp/offdocs/pd/pd57.pdf

http:// www.fas.org-irp-offdocs-pd-pd57.pdf

http:// www.archives.gov/federal/register/codification/executive.orc

http:// www.fas.org/irp/offdocs/eo/eo-12127.htm

http:// www.khouse.org/article/1999/235/

http:// www.gpoacess.gov/fr/about.html

http:// www.orgin.www.gpoaccess.gov/fr/

FEMA Regions/Disaster types

http:// www.fema.gov/news/newsrelease_fema?id=38811

http:// www.fema.gov/about/regions/regioniv/index.shtm

http:// www.fema.gov/about/contact/regions.sltm

http://www.fema.gov/about/structure/shtm

http:// www.fema.gov/news/newsrelease.fema?id=43043

http:// www.fema.gov/news/newsrelease.fema?published=1&id=43019

http:// www.fema.gov/news/diaster_totals_anual.fema

Assorted News Articles /Local& Federal

http:// www.sunsentinel.com/new/local/florida/sfl-fema24apr24,0,5679997.story

http:// www.sltrib.com/utah/ci_3004197

http:// www.insurancejournal.com/news/southeast/2006/01/06/63811.htm

http:// www.historycommons.org/entity.jsp?entity=oliver_north

http:// www.federalobserver.com/archive.php?aid=541

http:// www.subtopia.blogspot.com/2007/03/state-of-fema.html

http:// www.en.wikipedia.org/wiki/king_alfred_plan

http:// www.pulitzer.org/year/2006/public-service/works/neworleansps19.html

http:// www.florida-cracker.org/archives/002594.html

http:// www.pogo.org/contracts/katrina/co-katrinacontractingb.html

http:// www.democracynow.org/article.p1?sid=05/08/09/1411231

http:// www.www.guardian.co.uk/wtccrash/story/0,1300,583869,00.html

http:// www.sunsential.com/news/sfl-fema-coverage,0,6697347-sto

http:// www.bloggersblog.com/hurricanekatrina

http:// www.time.com/time/nation/article0,8599,1103003,00.html

http:// www.ipsnews.net/news.asp?idnews=30234

http:// www.Fema.gov/news/newsrelease_fema?id=20355

http:// www.risingfromruin.msnbc.com/2005/12/your-tax-dollars_1_.html

http:// www.nbc6.net/hurricanes/5321185/detail.html

Katrina

http:// www.chron.com/cs/cda/ssistory.mpl/editorial/3375918

http:// www.reuters.myway.com/article/20050907/2005-09-07t202716z_01_sp1773106_rtr.dst_0-news-censorship-dc.html

http:// www.foxnews.com/story/0,2933,173759,00.html

http:// www.usatoday.com/tech/science/2005-12-11-katrina-mystery-deaths_x.htm

http:// www.ctv.ca/servlet/articlenews/story/ctvnews/1125978665424_119

http:// www.msnbc.msn.com/id/131535520

http:// www.bioneers.org/whoweare/quant.php

http:// www.laseagrant.org/hurricane/fisheries.htm

www.femasbest.com

http:// www.freepress.org/departments/display/19/2005/1460

http:// www.bayousauvage.fws.gov

http:// www.buildneworleans/blog.com/200602/trash-talk.html

http:// www.msnbc.msn.com/id/1315320

http://www.wwltv.com/topstories/stories/wwlblog092350.85d62b32.html

GAO & Reports

Senate Reports/ OBM / Fed Observer /POGO

http://cache.search.yahoo-ht2.akadns.net/search/cache?e1=utf-8&P=femas+funding=throu

The Center for Catastrophe Preparedness & Response

http://hsgac.senate.gov/index.cfm?fuseaction=pressreleases.print&pressrelease_id=104

http:// oversight.house.gov/story.asp?id=1420

http:// www.gao.gov/htext/do3926.html

http:// www.federalobvserver.com /archive.php?aid=541

http://cache.search.yahoo-ht2.akadns.net/search/cache?e1=utf-8&p=femas+funding

http://oversight.house.gov/story.asp?id=1420

http://en.wikipedia.org/wiki/united_states_office_of_management_and_budget

http:// www.federalobserver.com/archive.php?aid=541

http://pogo.org/p/contracts/katrina/co-katrinacontractingb.html

http://news.yahoo.com/s/ap/20080331/apongocastpe/fedoverhaul

Parsons Brinkerhoff / Dewberry Davis

http:// www.publicpurpose.com/ut-pblie.htm

http:// www.foxnews.com/story/0,2933,205422,00.html

http:// www.answers.com/topic./dewberry?cat=biz-fin

Executive-orders (continued)

http:// www.archives.gov/federal-register/executiveorders/1989-bush.html-22

http:// www.fas.org/irp/offdocs/eo/index.html

http:// www.rumormillnews.comchi-bin/archive.chi?.noframes:read

http:// www.fema.gov/txt/library/fpc65_0604.txt

FEMA Directors

http://www.washingtonmonthly.com/archives/individual/2005_09/007104.php

http://en.wikipedia.org/wiki/james_lee_witt

http://en.wikipedia.org/wiki/louis_o_giuffrida

http://www.time.com/time/nation/article/0,8599,1103003,00html

http://en.wikipedia.org/wiki/fema#list_of_fema_heads

http://en.wikipedia.org/wiki/michael-d-brown

http:// www.cnn.com2005/politics/09/09/katrina.washington/index.html

http://www.nashuatelegraph.com/apps/pbcs.dll/article?aid=/20050911/news02/1091100

http://en.wikipedia.org/wiki/wallace.stickney

http://en.wikipedia.org/wiki/posse-comitatus_act

FEMA Contracts

http:// www.washingtonpost.com/wp-dyn/content/article/2006/08/08/ar20060808015881-2

http:// www.msnbc.msn.com/id/11995762/from/rss/

http:// www.fema.gov/news/newsrelease.fema?id=19576

http:// www.usaspending.gov/fpds/fpds.php?psc_cat=r&parent_id=256810&sortby=f&det

http://www.mysanantonio.com/news/metro/stories/mysa101705.5a.shelter.contracrts.865

http:// www.en.wikipedia.org/wiki/ashbritt

http://www.washingtonpost.com/wp.dyn/content/article/2006/08/08/ar2006080801581_

http:// www.dodig.osd.mil/audit/reports/fy07/07-038.txt

http:// www.taxpayer.net/budget/katrinaspending/contracts/aslbritt.htm

www.femasbest.com

http:// www.pulitzer.org/year/2006/public-service/works/neworleansps19.html

The Hill / Article

http:// hill16.thehill.com/business—lobby/firm-hired-ex-corps-head-before-winning-deal-200

MSNBC Report

http://www.msnbc.msn.com/id/11995762/from/rss

http://www.buildingline.com/news/viewnews.pl?id=4452

http:// www.hq-usace-army-mil/cepa/releases/katrinacontracts.htm

Blue Roof / Debris

http:// www.zoominfo.com/people/klein.jack.493245203.aspx

http:// www.zoominfo.com./people/kiein_jack_493245203.aspx

http:// www.corpwatch.org/article.ph?id=14014

Tarps / Debris

http:// www.buidingonline.com/news/viewers.pl?id=4452

http:// www.fema.gov/news/newsrelease.fema?=18708

http:// www.ccrpuatch.org/article.php?id=14037

http:// www.washingtonpost.com/wp-dyn/content/article/2006/08/09/Ar2006080901931

http:// www.fema.gov/newsrelease.fema?id18708

http:// www.enr.construction.com/news/finance/archives/060417.asp-49k

http:// www.risingfromruin.msnbc.com/2006/01/fighting.over_t.html

http:// www.denverpost.com/searchc1_4158778

http:// www.pogo.org/p/contracts/katrina/co-katriancontractingb.html

http:// www.seattletimes.nwsource.com/hjml/nationworld/2002530403_canetarps30.html

http:// www.macraesbluebook.com/searching/company.cfm?company

http:// www.corpwatch.org/article.php?id=14029

http:// www.zoominfo.com/people/klien_jack.493245203.aspx

http:// www.hsgac.senate.gov/_files/041006burnette.pdf

http:// www.pogo.org/p/contracts/katrina/co-katrinacontractingb.html

http:// www.Pulitzer.org/year/2006/works/public-service/neworleansps19.html

http:// www.dodig.osd.mil/audit/reports/fyo7/07-038.txt

http:// www.fedspending.org

http:// www.dodig.osd.mil/audit/reports/fyo7/07-38.txt

http:// www.dodig.osd.mil/audit/reorts/fy0/07-38.txt

http:// www.hq.usace.army.mil/cepa/releases/katrinacontracts.htm

Toxic Trailers

http:// www.nbcnews.com/id/14011193/ns/us_news-katrina_the_long_road_back/t/are-fema-trailers-   toxic-tin-cans/#.V0SJ01fnJ0c

Note: found site on trailers above in the internet

Stafford Act

http:// www.en.wikipedia.org/wiki.robert_stafford

http:// www.dem.dcc.state.nc.us/mitigation/library/stafford.pdf

http:// www.pogo.org/p/contracts/katrina/co-katrinacontractingb.html

FEMA Trailers

http:// www.yourlawyer.com/topics/overview/toxic_fema_trailers

http:// www.cache.search.yahoo.ht2.akadns.net/search/cache?ei=utf-8&p=the+acceptable+level

http:// www.oversight.house.gov/story.asp?id=2030

http:// www.oversight.house.gov/story.asp?id=1420

http:www.ucsusa.org/scientfic_integrity/interference/fema-trailers.html

http:// www.arkansasnews.com/archive/2006/03/02/washingtondcbureau/334574.html

Government Accounting Office

Note: report #GAO -08-106

www.femasbest.com

http:// www.gao-gov/mtext/do8106.html

http:// www.fema.gov/media/archives/2007/032807.shtm

http:// www.cnn.com/pollution/article/22814/print

http:// www.msnbc.msn.com/id/14011193

Chad Beckwith Smith was a former veteran FEMA housing inspector. He now spends his time between Canada and the United States and is currently a full-time writer.

www.femasbest.com